ISSUES IN
SECOND LANGUAGE ACQUISITION

ISSUES IN SECOND LANGUAGE ACQUISITION

MULTIPLE PERSPECTIVES

Leslie M. Beebe, *Editor*
Teachers College, Columbia University

NEWBURY HOUSE PUBLISHERS
A division of Harper & Row, Publishers, Inc.
New York, Philadelphia, San Francisco, Washington, D.C.
London, Mexico City, São Paulo, Singapore, Sydney

Sponsoring Editor: Leslie Berriman
Project Coordination: Total Concept Associates
Cover Design: 20/20 Services Inc., Graphic Design
Compositor: Alpha Graphics
Printer and Binder: McNaughton & Gunn

Issues in Second Language Acquisition: Multiple Perspectives

NEWBURY HOUSE PUBLISHERS
A division of Harper & Row, Publishers, Inc.

Language Science
Language Teaching
Language Learning

For information address Harper & Row, Publishers, Inc., 10 East 53d Street, New York, NY 10022.

Library of Congress Cataloging in Publication Data

Issues in second language acquisition.

Bibliography: p.
1. Second language acquisition.   I. Beebe, Leslie M.
P118.2.I87   1988   401'.9   87-23958
ISBN 0-06-632049-6

Printed in the U.S.A.
63-20493

First Printing: 1987
2 4 6 8 10 9 7 5 3 1

FOR BRUCE
w.t.p.b.

Acknowledgments

First and foremost, I want to thank the contributors, who discovered how difficult it is to summarize a whole field of research in a single chapter. I am also indebted to many friends and colleagues for their support during the editing of this anthology. I am especially grateful to Tomoko Takahashi for substantive and editorial comments on the entire book. Jane Zuengler was instrumental in the earliest conception of the book. Robin Uliss-Weltz not only made valuable suggestions for my own chapter, but also read and commented on several others. Special thanks also go to the Newbury House staff, particularly Leslie Berriman, and the three anonymous reviewers who put serious time and effort into their comments on the manuscript. Other friends and associates have helped in their own ways. High among them are Michael and Jeannette. And a final grand tribute goes to Bruce Nussbaum, whose support, patience, and good humor helped me carry this book through to completion.

L.M.B.

Contents

Biographical Statements on the Contributors

Leslie M. Beebe (Ph.D., University of Michigan, 1974) is professor of Linguistics and Education in the TESOL and Applied Linguistics programs at Teachers College, Columbia University. She has been teaching courses in second language acquisition, sociolinguistics, grammar, and ESL methods and materials since 1975. She is currently chair of the Department of Languages and Literature. Her major area of research is sociolinguistics and second language acquisition. She has published in *Language Learning, TESOL Quarterly, International Journal of the Sociology of Language*, and a variety of teacher training books. She is author of a forthcoming book, *The Social Psychological Basis of Second Language Acquisition*, to be published in the Longman Applied Linguistics and Language Series.

Jim Cummins (Ph.D., University of Alberta, 1974) is associate professor in the Modern Language Centre at the Ontario Institute for Studies in Education (OISE) in Toronto. He also directs the National Heritage Language Resource Unit at OISE. He is the recipient (with J. P. Das) of the International Reading Association 1979 Albert J. Harris Award for the best paper on the detection and remediation of reading disability. His publications include *Bilingualism and Special Education: Issues in Assessment and Pedagogy* (Multilingual Matters and College-Hill Press, 1984) and *Bilingualism in Education: Aspects of Theory, Research, and Policy* (Longman, 1986; with Merrill Swain).

Fred Genesee (Ph.D., McGill University, 1974) is associate professor in the Psychology Department, McGill University in Montreal, where he has taught courses on the psychology of language, statistics, research methods, and human intelligence. Professor Genesee has also taught courses on bilingual education, second language testing, and sociolinguistics in ESL in the Department of ESL, University of Hawaii at Manoa. He has published research articles on the effectiveness of alternative forms of second language immersion programs, individual differences in second language learning, bilingual code switching, motivational factors in second language learning, and neuropsychological aspects of second language learning. He has recently completed a book on *Learning through Two Languages: Studies of Immersion and Bilingual Education*, published by Newbury House.

Michael H. Long (Ph.D., University of California, Los Angeles, 1980) is associate professor of ESL at the University of Hawaii at Manoa, where he specializes in second language acquisition, second language classroom research, ESL research methods, and language teaching methodology. He is a member of the editorial advisory boards of *TESOL Quarterly* and *Studies in Second Language Acquisition*, and coeditor of two series, *Issues in Second Language Research* (Newbury House) and *Cambridge Applied Linguistics Series* (Cambridge University Press).

Thomas Scovel (Ph.D., University of Michigan, 1970) is associate professor in the English Department at San Francisco State University. He has taught EFL and Applied Linguistics for many years in Asia—specifically in Thailand and the People's Republic of China—and has taught in summer programs or given lectures in several European nations. His publications and research focus mainly on the application of psycholinguistic insights to foreign language pedagogy, and he is currently working on a book that deals with a long-standing research interest of his—the etiology of foreign accents.

Herbert Seliger (Ed.D., Columbia University, 1969) is professor of Linguistics at Queens College and CUNY Graduate School, New York. Professor Seliger has taught courses in linguistics, second language acquisition, ESL methods, bilingualism, and research methods in applied linguistics. He has published articles on topics related to second language acquisition and is editor with Michael Long of *Classroom Oriented Research in Second Language Acquisition* (Newbury House, 1983). Research interests include natural and classroom second language acquisition and first language attrition in child and adult bilinguals.

Introduction

Leslie M. Beebe, Teachers College, Columbia University

The origin of this book stems from a need I have perceived while teaching second language acquisition (SLA) at Teachers College, Columbia University. For the past ten years I have taught at least one course on second language acquisition, and every year I find myself in need of a single collection of articles on SLA that presents a variety of different interdisciplinary perspectives on the field. Although some scholars have considered SLA to be basically psycholinguistics, I don't see it that way. Rather, I view second language acquisition as the core phenomenon—that is, the linguistic development of the learner in the second language—and I think it can be viewed from multiple interdisciplinary perspectives—psycholinguistic, sociolinguistic, and neurolinguistic.

In addition to these strictly interdisciplinary perspectives, there are other perspectives, such as the classroom-centered research perspective and the bilingual education perspective, that must be addressed in order to achieve a full view of SLA. Most courses in SLA emphasize only certain of these perspectives; yet a true survey of the field would introduce students to all of them. Clearly no individual professor can do justice to all of these approaches, and this leaves the teacher or linguist coming into the field at a loss for a general overview of SLA. Likewise, it is difficult for professors in TESOL, applied linguistics, bilingual education, or foreign language teaching to keep up with the latest developments in all aspects of the field.

Current books on the market are often collections of conference papers on a theme, or single-authored presentations of SLA from limited perspectives.

The courses taught on SLA generally must rely on narrow, unconnected research studies within each perspective, for example, neurolinguistics or psycholinguistics. As examples of research, these are individually valuable, but they do not provide a broad view. It is difficult for professors to tie them together in a lecture, to paint the big picture while doing justice to the details of individual research studies. It is even more difficult for new linguists and teachers in training to read such narrow articles and see the connections.

To remedy this situation, I have called on experts in five different areas of SLA to describe the state of the art from their different perspectives: psycholinguistic, sociolinguistic, neurolinguistic, classroom research, and bilingual education. The collection ends with a chapter in which implications of SLA research are discussed based on the preceding five chapters.

The first chapter, Seliger's "Psycholinguistic Issues in Second Language Acquisition," deals with such a vast area that it is not a state-of-the-art paper in quite the same way as the other chapters. Rather than trying to focus on very recent developments in psycholinguistics, Seliger attempts to give essential background for newcomers to the field that will enable them to read more current articles. Thus, the chapter acts as a broad introduction to SLA from a psycholinguistic perspective. It begins by emphasizing that current work has been influenced by two important historical milestones—what Seliger calls revolutions. First, the Chomskyan revolution, with the development of transformational-generative grammar, led us to abandon the behaviorist view of language as a set of habits and to adopt the notion that language is represented by an abstract set of rules that the speaker has internalized from the language he or she hears. Second, a less well known revolution occurred in applied linguistics when, in 1967, Corder (see individual chapters for references) directed us to study the learner's systematic errors and ignore the random mistakes. This focus became the foundation of error analysis, an area of inquiry that was very popular in the 1970s.

In reviewing both processing and acquisition studies, Seliger focuses on three general issues. First, how does the learner develop his or her language, and what are the processes involved? Seliger introduces the notions of transitional competence, approximative systems, and interlanguage, reviewing Selinker's five central psycholinguistic processes for acquiring a second language. Seliger points out that many of these processes overlap—the categories are not fully distinct. For example, language transfer, transfer of training, and overgeneralization all seem to be types of generalization, but the source material— what gets generalized—is different. Seliger explains that the basic process of SLA is now believed to be hypothesis testing.

Second, Seliger asks: What is the role of previous knowledge, particularly the first language, in second language development? Seliger explains that the classic contrastive analysis viewpoint of the structuralists who were influenced by behaviorist psychology was that differences between the first language (L1) and the second language (L2) would lead to difficulty for the learner, and that similarities would lead to facility. This, however, was simply not always true. Seliger reviews research by Dulay and Burt (1974) and Bailey, Madden, and Krashen (1974) that demonstrates that most errors were not due to L1 influence, but occurred regardless of the learner's L1. Schachter (1974) described an "error in error analysis" when she demonstrated that areas of difficulty could be errors of high (not low) accuracy because learners could avoid structures altogether in free compositions.

Third, Seliger addresses the issue of affective factors that influence SLA. He asks: What psychological characteristics of the learner lead to successful SLA? And are there good and bad learners? In this section of the chapter he reviews Rubin's (1975) notion of the good language learner—someone with a strong drive to communicate who is willing to appear foolish, and can live with vagueness. He notes that Schumann (1975) makes affective factors the central focus of his acculturation model of SLA. Seliger devotes most attention, however, to Krashen's *monitor model*, now developed into his *input hypothesis*. Explaining very briefly some of the basic tenets of Krashen's model, Seliger focuses on an examination of the model and, in particular, on the debate over whether the model lacks factors known to affect SLA or whether it really leads us to understand more fully how and why SLA comes about—or, in the case of fossilization, does not come about.

Seliger's chapter leads us to see psycholinguistic issues in SLA as unresolved. It provides no pat phrases or answers but, rather, seeks to ask questions. Although this could be disturbing for classroom practitioners faced with pressing daily problems that require solutions, Seliger encourages us to accept the immense complexity of the field of psycholinguistics and second language acquisition.

The second chapter, Beebe's "Five Sociolingustic Approaches to Second Language Acquisition," reviews sociolinguistic and social psychological issues in SLA, both subsumed under the term *sociolinguistic*. Although many have advocated that sociolinguists and social psychologists communicate with each other and profit from each other's perspectives, an integration of the two perspectives has been difficult for researchers to achieve because sociolinguists are trained primarily as linguists and social psychologists primarily as psychologists. Interdisciplinary viewpoints are, by nature, complex and, therefore, difficult to achieve. Bringing two interdisciplinary fields together in one review necessarily involves making a very broad overview.

In this review Beebe has dealt with issues from five "sociolinguistic" (i.e., social psychological or sociolinguistic) traditions. Each tradition is viewed as having stemmed from the work of a mentor. The issues discussed have grown out of researchers' attempts to answer five broad questions:

1. Is interlanguage variation systematic or random and, if systematic, according to what social variables does it vary?
2. Does the learner's interlanguage change over time?

3. What is the role of sociolinguistic transfer in L2 development?
4. What is the nature of L2 communicative competence?
5. What is the "cause" of variation in interlanguage?

Beebe devotes the most space to the Labovian *attention to speech paradigm* and its application to SLA research. Tracing the research of L. Dickerson, W. Dickerson, Tarone, and Beebe, she documents the origins and development of the debate over the applicability of Labov's attention to speech paradigm to second language learning situations. As Beebe demonstrates, early research was concerned with whether or not interlanguage was systematic in its variability. Later, once systematicity had been established, a greater concern developed over whether attention to speech was actually the cause of style shifting in learners. Both Beebe and Tarone have worked within the Labovian paradigm and have now come to claim that the paradigm is insufficient to explain L2 style-shifting data.

In opposition to the Labovian paradigm, Beebe describes Bickerton's *dynamic paradigm*, whose major proponents in L2 research are Gatbonton-Segalowitz and Huebner. Gatbonton-Segalowitz proposed the *gradual diffusion model* in which second language development is the product of two phases—first, an acquisition phase wherein a new, correct categorical rule gradually comes to be used simultaneously with an old, incorrect categorical rule in a given set of environments, and, second, a replacement phase, wherein the new, correct rule begins to "win out" and replace the old, incorrect rule successively in that set of environments. Gatbonton-Segalowitz's research was important in that her data supported the gradual diffusion model, which she believes to be preferable to the Labovian approach of writing variable rules based on the statistical probability of occurrence of each variant in each linguistic or social environment. It was also important in that she emphasized the way in which phonetic variation in speech reflected feelings of ethnic group affiliation.

The third approach to sociolinguistics is the description of communicative competence. Hymes may be seen as the mentor of this research, although Searle and Austin initiated the study of speech acts, the subset of research on communicative competence that is discussed in this chapter. Beebe describes research on apologies, invitations, compliments, refusals, requests, complaints, and expressions of gratitude. Perhaps the most extensive work has been done on apologies. Cohen and Olshtain (1981) compared apologies in native Hebrew, native English, and Israeli English as a second language (ESL) and found that some, though not all, patterns in ESL were reflective of sociocultural transfer. Blum-Kulka and Olshtain (1984) have reported on CCSARP, the Cross-Cultural Speech Act Realization Project, an international effort to look at both requests and apologies in various native languages and ESL in Israel, Europe, the United States, Canada, and Australia.

Another body of extensive research is that of Wolfson, who has studied compliments, invitations, greetings, partings, and judgments, with most detail on compliments and invitations. Expressions of gratitude have been studied by Eisenstein and Bodman, and refusals in Japanese, English, and Japanese ESL have been investigated by Beebe, Takahashi, and Uliss-Weltz.

In the last two approaches she outlines, Beebe branches out to include social psychological approaches to SLA. First she examines Giles's *speech accommodation theory*, which attempts to describe and explain speech shifts and to explain speakers' reactions to speech variation. Beebe first explains the descriptive labels *convergence* and *divergence*, used by speech accommodation researchers, and then summarizes the four social psychological theories that Giles and colleagues have brought together to make up speech accommodation theory: similarity attraction theory, social exchange theory, causal attribution theory, and intergroup distinctiveness theory. Through examples illustrating each theory and a review of some seminal studies, Beebe attempts to give the reader a feel for the way speech accommodation theorists analyze speech shifts. Finally, Giles and Byrne's *intergroup approach to second language acquisition* is briefly outlined and explained.

The last sociolinguistic approach to SLA is again a social psychological one. This is the approach of Wallace Lambert, using attitudes and motivations to explain differential success in SLA by different learners. This approach, collaboratively created by many social psychologists, but in particular by Robert Gardner in conjuction with Lambert, has been developed since the 1950s in Canada. It is such a vast body of research that only a few highlights are reviewed in this chapter. At the outset, Beebe attempts to show how this approach differs from the others. It focuses not on an individual's speech variation from one moment to another (style shifting) but, instead, on how one learner or group of learners differs from another in terms of success in acquiring a second language.

Perhaps the most important outcomes of the Gardner and Lambert research have been: (1) the development of the "matched guise" procedure and (2) the elaboration of two motivational orientations—instrumental versus integrative. Through the matched guise procedure, researchers have asked subjects to evaluate voices of bilinguals in their two language guises. Assuming the voices belonged to different people, the subjects rated them differentially in terms of kindness, honesty, trustworthiness, intelligence, attractiveness, and even height. Through this procedure, Lambert and Gardner have been able to determine attitudes toward native speakers of French and English in French Canada. As for the research on motivational orientations, the chapter demonstrates the diversity of research findings. Whereas early studies in Quebec province indicated that an *integrative orientation* (a desire to integrate with the target culture) was most effective in leading to successful SLA, later studies in Maine, Louisiana, Connecticut, and the Philippines showed that under certain circumstances, an *instrumental orientation* (e.g., a need to know the language in order to get a good job) could be more effective, or that both orientations could be useful. It seems that ethnic minority groups in North America and

Filipinos learning English, a language of international prestige, needed both instrumental and integrative orientation to be most successful in learning the second language.

Chapter 3, Genesee's "Neuropsychology and Second Language Acquisition," reviews experimental (and some clinical) neuropsychological research on bilinguals, that is, studies that investigate the relationship between the brain and development of two languages. He organizes the research around the discussion of three major issues: (1) the localization of the L1 and/or the L2 in the left and right hemispheres of the brain; (2) the ways in which languages with different characteristics are represented in the brain (e.g., languages like English with phonetically based scripts versus languages like Chinese with ideographic representations); and (3) the critical period hypothesis for second language acquisition.

In dealing with the first issue, on hemispheric localization, Genesee explains that early views contended that the first language was localized in the left hemisphere, whereas the second language was localized in the right. Current thinking does not concur with this point of view. Rather, it is thought that the manner of processing is different in each hemisphere of the brain, with the left hemisphere specializing in processing information analytically and serially and the right hemisphere having a more holistic and parallel processing mode. This specialization is not thought to be absolute. Genesee discusses the issues surrounding hemispheric localization in terms of three factors: age of SLA, level of L2 proficiency (stage), and manner of SLA. The age hypothesis states that "There will be more right-hemisphere involvement in second language processing the later the second language is learned relative to the first, or conversely, there will be greater left-hemisphere involvement in second language processing the earlier the second language is learned relative to the first" (see Chapter 3, page 86). Reviewing different types of experiments that support and disconfirm the hypothesis, Genesee concludes that the bulk of the evidence favors the hypothesis. The same cannot be said, however, for the stage hypothesis, which deals with level of L2 proficiency. The stage hypothesis states that "right-hemispheric involvement in second language processing will be more evident among nonproficient bilinguals than among proficient bilinguals" (Chapter 3, page 87). Because studies did not support the hypothesis, or could not be replicated, or supported it with interpretations that were questionable, Genesee concludes that this hypothesis as yet has very little reliable empirical support. The third factor that was said to be correlated with hemispheric localization was manner of SLA. The manner hypothesis states that "there may be greater right-hemispheric involvement in processing languages that are learned informally or, conversely, greater left-hemispheric involvement in processing languages that are learned formally" (Chapter 3, page 90). This hypothesis is generally supported by the literature.

Next, Genesee tackles the issue of language-specific effects in bilinguals, particularly as a result of three linguistic characteristics: (1) type of script (i.e., phonetic or ideographic); (2) direction of script (i.e., left to right or right to left); and (3) language mode (i.e., appositional or propositional). Genesee summarizes the experimental evidence as suggesting that propositional languages using analytical, abstract modes of thought like English may be associated with left-hemispheric language processing; so, too, may be phonetically based scripts. On the other hand, appositional languages using holistic, integrated modes of thought, like Navajo and Hopi, may be associated with right-hemispheric processing. This is also thought to be the case with ideographic scripts. As for the research on directionality of the script, Genesee concludes that there is not much empirical support for the hypothesis that it entails differential hemispheric processing.

The final issue with which Genesee grapples is the one best known to researchers on second language acquisition—the issue of the *critical period hypothesis* (CPH). This hypothesis states that "there is a neurophysiologically determined critical period during which second language acquisition occurs easily. After the critical period, second language learning becomes impossible or at best difficult" (Chapter 3, page 97). Genesee traces the evolution of the hypothesis from its origins with Penfield and Roberts (1959), who emphasized the notion of general neurological plasticity before puberty. Then Lenneberg (1967) contributed an emphasis on hemispheric specialization of function, claiming that lateralization was complete by the time of puberty.

Genesee examines the critical period hypothesis on conceptual and empirical grounds. Lenneberg's assertion that the critical period ends when lateralization of language functions in the left hemisphere is complete has not found empirical support. Genesee questions whether localization occurs only between hemispheres, and whether it is sudden. He discusses a "sensitive period" hypothesis, which asserts that certain linguistic skills are acquired more easily at particular times than at others and that some are learned after the critical period. In effect this hypothesis asserts that there are many critical periods. Genesee maintains that the sensitive period hypothesis cannot be used to salvage the critical period hypothesis because we have not defined it and cannot test it. Genesee concludes from his review of the literature that learning, at least in the initial stages, is more efficient and possibly easier for older learners than for younger learners. Second, he concludes that nativelike phonology, syntax, and comprehension can be achieved by learners past puberty. It has been found that prepubertal learners achieve higher, more nativelike L2 proficiency than postpubertal learners, but Genesee points out that this does not constitute unequivocal support for the critical period hypothesis.

Given the lack of conceptual and empirical support for the critical period hypothesis, educational decisions should not be based on it. In fact, Genesee underscores the idea that it is not advisable at this point to use neuropsychological findings as a basis for practical prescriptions in the classroom. Teachers may then wonder what value this research has for their work. It should be understood that the field of neuropsychology contributes a growing understanding of how students may be processing second languages. This field is quite separate from the field of teaching and from issues surrounding sound pedagogy, but it enriches us because it informs us about the very mechanics of second language development, and some day (granted, in the distant future) it may develop so that practical applications can be drawn. The supreme value of Genesee's chapter, then, is the straightforward and thorough way in which he informs teachers and SLA researchers of the current state of the art in a field that is technical and, therefore, difficult for us to comprehend, yet so central to the process of SLA we seek to promote.

The fourth chapter in this book presents a classroom research perspective on second language acquisition. Long's "Instructed Interlanguage Development" first presents early research suggesting that the interlanguage (IL) of instructed (classroom) learners is quite similar to that of naturalistic (uninstructed) learners. Then he discusses methodological prescriptions that emanated from earlier findings. Next he examines some of the research evidence that favors instructed IL development and, finally, returns to extant methodological prescriptions, viewing them with a critical eye.

Evidence that instructed IL development and naturalistic development are similar surfaced in the 1970s and early 1980s. Burt and Dulay (1980, and in earlier publications) were perhaps most influential of all with their suggestion that child learners' morpheme usage was similar regardless of first language background. Krashen, Sferlazza, Feldman, and Fathman (1976) made a tremendous impact with their claim of similarities in grammatical morpheme usage between naturalistic and instructed learners. Felix (1981) and Wode (1981) also found similarities between instructed and naturalistic acquirers. A related development was Krashen's formulation of his now famous prescription for comprehensible input as a necessary provision for second language acquisition to occur.

The major thrust of this chapter is the assessment of evidence that instruction affects IL development. Long reviews research on the effect of instruction on (1) acquisition processes, (2) acquisition sequences, (3) rate of acquisition, and (4) ultimate level of second language attainment. By "acquisition processes," Long means processes such as transfer, (over)generalization, pidginization, or fossilization. A key study by Pica (1983) demonstrated that instructed learners overapplied grammatical morphology more than uninstructed learners did. Also, unlike uninstructed learners, they avoided pidginization strategies (e.g., *two book*). This was true at nearly all proficiency levels. Long suggests that such differences between the two groups may translate into probability of eventual targetlike attainment, with instructed learners being favored because they would be more likely to drop overgeneralization than uninstructed learners would be to start using communicatively redundant features of a language they have not been using over a prolonged period. Research is needed to take us beyond mere speculation about long-term effects of initial differences in acquisition processes.

A number of studies have been done to investigate the effect of instruction on acquisition sequences, but they have been less successful in establishing a correlation. There have been some instances of alteration in acquisition sequence, but studies in general seem to show that whatever changes occur are temporary. Also, although there can be an initial acceleration of learning, there is often the harmful side effect of overuse resulting from instruction. Pienemann (1984) found that instruction could make children progress faster if they were "ready" for it but had no effect if they were not "ready" and could not make them skip a stage in acquisition sequence. In the end, Long concludes that "acquisition sequences may well be immutable."

As for the effect of instruction on rate of acquisition, the findings are somewhat more heartening for teachers. Long cites eight studies that support the notion that instruction speeds up acquisition, whereas he finds two studies ambiguous, and three with minor or no support. As Long points out, Krashen interprets the beneficial effect of instruction as evidence that the classroom is useful as a source of comprehensible input. Long, however, argues that it is not this simple and contends that the findings of studies are contrary to the predictions of Krashen's monitor theory.

Very little research has been done to date on the effect of instruction on the level of ultimate second language attainment, but the existing evidence suggests that there is an effect. In Long's view, Pavesi (1984) demonstrated that instructed learners did better than naturalistic learners in a relativization task; her data show the powerful influence of universals and/or the failure of instruction to match readiness to learn and receive teaching. Pavesi interprets the superiority of the instructed learners' performance as deriving from a difference in the input to which the two groups of learners were exposed, the instructed learners being exposed to "planned discourse"—more elaborated and more complex linguistic input. Long argues that grammatical features in the elaborated discourse would not be perceptually salient for learners, whereas instruction, which often focuses on form, does make it likely that items acquired were attended to by learners. As support, Long cites Schmidt and Frota's diary study (1986), which contends that Schmidt (the L2 learner) noticed forms outside class after they had been taught in class. Long also cites Swain (1985), who demonstrated that immersion students, although they made tremendous progress, failed to acquire unmarked morphology and syntax even after seven years in the program. In addition, Long cites three studies reported by Zobl (1985) that demonstrate the positive effects of exposure to marked elements in the language (i.e., not the basic, typical, or canonical form, but the less basic or more exceptional one). Long argues that the probable focus on marked forms in second language instruction is a possible explanation for why instructed learners have a higher level of ultimate second language attainment than naturalistic learners.

To summarize, Long concludes that second language instruction has a beneficial effect on the processes, rate, and ultimate level of second language attainment, but that the sequence in which forms are acquired remains unaltered, or changed only in temporary or trivial ways. He also warns that theorists are premature and probably wrong in telling teachers that formal instruction in a second language has a very limited use.

In Chapter 5, "Second Language Acquisition within Bilingual Education Programs," Cummins introduces us to the bilingual education policy debate and offers a review of theory and research that enables us to sort through the claims and counterclaims in a principled way. Cummins points out a common misconception—that the Canadian research results and the U.S. research results on bilingual education are contradictory. He attempts to reconcile apparent differences and to show that basic principles of second language acquisition underlie both.

The bilingual education policy debate is traced from its U.S. origins in the late 1960s, when proponents argued that bilingual education was necessary to promote a healthy self-concept in minority children and to ensure that they did not lag in academic development. The imposition of bilingual education programs after the *Lau* v. *Nichols* decision in 1974 triggered hot debate. Cummins describes three main challenges to the rationale for bilingual education. First, he discusses Noel Epstein's 1977 monograph challenging the belief that children could not learn in a language they did not already understand, and citing as evidence the Canadian immersion results. The AIR study (1978) by the American Institute for Research posed a second major challenge, reporting teacher judgments and claiming that Title VII students were not ahead of other minority students who were not receiving bilingual education. Third, Baker and de Kanter (1981) claimed there was no reliable empirical evidence for transitional bilingual education, and this too fed the fire of debate.

Cummins enlightens us particularly by showing that part of the controversy stems from different meanings attached to the word *immersion*. He points out, rightly, that so-called U.S. immersion programs are really often *submersion* programs, with exclusive use of the L2 and no accommodation made for the L2 learner in a class with native speakers of the language. Cummins gives us a useful guide to characteristics of so-called immersion programs that we must assess before making judgments and comparisons: (1) whether the L1 or the L2 is emphasized at first, (2) whether the teacher and the program are bilingual or monolingual, and (3) whether the participants are majority or minority students. Comparisons are justified only when these characteristics are considered. Nevertheless, in the United States, four different types of bilingual programs have been called "immersion" programs. No wonder there is confusion.

Cummins systematically reviews the research findings from evaluations of several bilingual programs from California to Canada and from South Africa to Australia. There is no need to repeat the details of these studies here, but it may be useful to show that careful review leads to refutation of arguments commonly voiced by proponents and opponents of bilingual education.

Proponents like to make the "linguistic mismatch" argument—that minority students will suffer academically if required to study in their weaker language, their L2. Yet, as Cummins points out, the Canadian research refutes this claim. English-speaking students in French immersion programs caught up or surpassed others in English language skills by grade 5 or 6. Opponents of bilingual education cling to the "maximum exposure" argument—that a maximum of exposure to English is needed if minority students are to learn English adequately. Cummins refutes this argument as well. Both minority and majority students who spend less time learning in English do at least as well as, and sometimes even better than, those who learn in English only. Thus, Cummins effectively dispels popular myths held by those favoring as well as opposing bilingual education.

Cummins invokes two theoretical principles in trying to explain what works in bilingual education programs. First, he discusses his own *common underlying proficiency generalization*, which shows us that L1 and L2 academic skills are interdependent. Basically, Cummins asserts that cognitive/academic skills developed in the L1 will transfer to the L2 because they involve development of a common underlying proficiency on which the student can draw. Cummins explains that transfer from the minority language to the majority language is the more likely because conditions of exposure and motivation are more favorable in this direction than in the reverse. As a result of this transfer, we can happily promote learning in a minority native language and be assured that development in the academic skills of the second language will not suffer.

The second principle used to explain the success of bilingual education programs is the *sufficient comprehensible input generalization*. Krashen (1982) asserts that sufficient, comprehensible, interesting/relevant, and not grammatically sequenced input is necessary for second language acquisition to occur. Long (1983) would add that input is made comprehensible by being focused on the here and now and by having its interactional structure modified—that is, by containing repetitions, confirmation and comprehension checks, and clarification requests. What Cummins argues is that bilingual or immersion programs are more successful than traditional second language programs and that this success is due in part to the provision of sufficient comprehensible input when the L2 is used as a medium of instruction. He also attributes success to the transfer of skills that occurs because all knowledge acquired via L1 will help to make input in L2 more comprehensible. Thus, the two theoretical principles Cummins cites are interrelated.

Cummins identifies three crucial distinguishing characteristics of programs that, once assessed, tell us how much comprehensible input the program is providing. These three are: (1) whether the teacher is bilingual, (2) whether the input is modified, and (3) whether L1 literacy is promoted. In his summary table, Cummins demonstrates why he believes that the truly *bilingual* immersion programs are the most successful. They have a bilingual teacher, they provide modified L2 input, and they promote L1 literacy (which transfers to the L2). Thus, they provide high levels of comprehensible input and deliver the best results.

The value of this chapter lies partly in its impressive survey of viewpoints, programs, and research findings. It is perhaps most valuable, however, in its provision of clear definitions of types of programs, along with a theoretical framework for analyzing the results of these programs. By doing this, Cummins allows us to reconcile seemingly contradictory findings and to see that there are generalizations to be made about the success of various bilingual and monolingual programs.

In Chapter 6, "Multiple Perspectives Make Singular Teaching," Scovel reviews the preceding five state-of-the art papers, picking implications of the research discussed for language teachers. To give us an appreciation of how theory influences practice, Scovel draws an analogy between the applied fields of high jumping and language teaching. High jumpers have steadily increased their ability to jump higher over the last decades by benefiting from insights gained from the theoretical discipline of physics. Language teaching has benefited from theoretical insights in linguistics and psychology. The lessons Scovel draws are important ones. First, we must build teaching methods on theoretical foundations. Second, we must keep building on knowledge gained from the past. Third, just as it is the coach who needs to understand physics and the high jumper who needs to practice jumping, so it is the second language teacher who needs to study linguistics and the second language learner who needs to practice speaking the target language.

Scovel discusses selected implications of each chapter in turn. From Seliger's psycholinguistic perspective, he examines the two "revolutions." Regarding the Chomskyan revolution, he cautions the teacher to watch out for sentences that appear the same or similar in surface structure but are very different in deep structure. He also shows us that four sentences of very different surface structure can have a common underlying deep structure; here, it is the fact that the four sentences are paraphrases that is important for ESL/EFL students to know. From the Corder "revolution," he reminds us that errors are usually a reflection of intelligent attempts to master a language. A teacher should not criticize them but, rather, should attempt to paraphase the learner's statements in correct English. Paraphrase surfaces again as a useful tool for the teacher in Scovel's discussion of avoidance. We are reminded that we can deal with students' avoidance of difficult structures by showing them a range of ways to communicate the same idea.

Looking at Beebe's sociolinguistic perspective on second language acquisition, Scovel underscores several important pedagogical implications. First and foremost, he emphasizes the systematic nature of interlanguage. Interlanguage is regular and rule governed, even when it contains errors. From the discussion of the Labovian paradigm and, in particular, of the finding that high attention to speech may lead to low accuracy, Scovel sees another parallel with the high jump. The high jumper must focus on form and detail before the jump; during it, however, there is no time or place for such activity. A unified effort is needed. Similarly, the language teacher may encourage students to focus on linguistic form in class, but during natural communication such monitoring may lead to hesitancy or error. Scovel believes that high attention to linguistic form is most appropriate for learners with a low knowledge of form.

Turning to Genesee's neuropsychological perspective, Scovel underscores Genesee's own prescription. The prescription is, in fact, for no prescription. That is, we should not attempt to apply neuropsychological research to the field of classroom methodology. It is too early even to consider this, and attempts to do so can lead us to ludicrous and even harmful activities.

Unlike the neuropsychological perspective, the classroom research perspective is rich with pedagogical implications. Scovel extrapolates from Long's chapter that formal instruction does make a difference. For example, in Pica (1983) instructed learners outscored others with less or no instruction in using certain morphemes, suggesting that the focus on form present in most classrooms promotes eventual accuracy.

Scovel is obviously a proponent of having teachers use their own common sense. He clearly endorses having teachers profit from the richness of their everyday observations. Discussing Pienemann's (1984) learnability and teachability hypotheses, Scovel advocates that teachers carefully make use of information they glean on the gap between what they teach and what the students learn. He advocates, in essence, that the teacher simultaneously act as researcher. But Scovel also notes the value of the teacher stepping back. In particular, he notes that classroom research supports the efficacy of group work.

In reviewing Cummins's bilingual educational perspective, Scovel focuses on three reasons Cummins gives for why bilingual policymakers have ignored research findings in bilingual education. In applying this information, however, Scovel turns these reasons into three pieces of advice for language teachers:

1. Don't ask preordained and unanswerable questions.
2. Don't cling to conventional wisdoms if they are not well founded.
3. Do try to put facts and data into a coherent theory.

Bilingual policymakers would be of much better service to the community if they could follow this advice. And if we could learn these three things from Cummins, we would be much the better teachers.

These are important lessons. The greatest value of Scovel's chapter, however, is perhaps the model he sets for critical reexamination of old ideas and creative application of new ones. His parting thought is a crucial one: Teachers must find a way to integrate experiential information with experimental knowledge. If there is any one activity that this book is primarily intended to stimulate, this is certainly it!

If you are a teacher, relatively new to the field of SLA, it is suggested that you read each of these chapters as background and then choose a selection of the Suggested Readings to go through afterward. If you read the chapters one at a time in conjunction with primary sources, they should help you integrate otherwise isolated articles and see them in a theoretical context. It would also help to read a general text on second language acquisition in conjunction with this book. If you are a professor or an advanced graduate student, you may have already read many of the Suggested Readings, but you will also find the book useful as an overview of current theory in a variety of disciplines too disparate for anyone to have mastered, and the bibliographies may serve as a guide for your future reading. The book is very flexible; it can be used as assigned reading in courses on second language acquisition and bilingualism. Each chapter attempts to present the state of the art in second language acquisition from one of many perspectives on the field. The very unity of the book lies in its diversity.

one

PSYCHOLINGUISTIC PERSPECTIVE

Psycholinguistic Issues in Second Language Acquisition

Herbert Seliger, Queens College

HISTORICAL PERSPECTIVES

No survey of psycholinguistic issues in second language acquisition (SLA) can ignore the significance of certain historical milestones in the literature of this field. These milestones have marked changes in the direction and focus of research and have left their imprint on the unconscious thought processes of anyone who thinks about SLA. That is, the very way in which we think about SLA is affected by fundamental scientific revolutions that have occurred in the way we view language and the process by which language is acquired. These changes have in turn affected the basic paradigms and methodologies used to research SLA.

One obvious influence on the field of SLA was the publication of Chomsky's *Syntactic Structures* (1957) and the subsequent development of transformational-generative (TG) grammar. No other theory has so deeply affected our views of how language, first or second, is processed and acquired.

A second revolution, albeit a less noticed one, took place in 1967 with the publication of S. P. Corder's article "The Significance of Learners' Errors." Though related philosophically to the Chomskyan revolution, this article changed the way researchers in SLA viewed learners and the language they produced. Although there may be some debate about the relative importance of Chomsky's and Corder's milestones, there is no denying their impact on our thinking up to now and probably into the foreseeable future.

One basic change in perspective resulting from transformational-generative theory has been the shift from viewing language acquisition as habit (Fries, 1945) to viewing it in terms of a set of abstract rules that are internalized and unconscious. That is, SLA research accepts the important distinction between external behavior, which is infinite in variety (*performance*), and the internal finite set of rules residing in our unconscious, which we know but cannot explicitly describe (*competence*). The distinction between competence and performance has been generally accepted as useful. This will become more evident later in this chapter when we discuss such issues as the role of the first language in SLA, the role of formal language teaching, the role of practice in SLA, and how one decides what may be considered relevant data for the study of the psycholinguistic aspects of SLA. (For a fuller discussion of the applicability of competence theory to second language acquisition, see Newmeyer, 1982).

Corder's contribution to our understanding of the factors involved in second language acquisition has primarily dealt with what to look at and what to ignore in the data from the learner. The essential question addressed by Corder (1967) is: What should one examine in order to discover what is involved in the process of second language acquisition? Should we look at all the utterances of the learner? Should we look at some aspects of production but not at others? Building on Chomsky's distinction between competence and performance, Corder proposed that only some of what a learner actually produces can be examined for evidence of acquisition. Other aspects of production may be classified as random performance mistakes that are not rule governed and may not lead to generalizations about the processes of acquisition.

To capture this distinction, Corder proposed that we examine only the *systematic errors* produced by learners of a language, not their random mistakes, which could conceivably be infinitely variable. He was, of course, taking his cue from studies that had begun to appear in the mid-1960s by Roger Brown and Ursula Bellugi (1964) with regard to first language acquisition by children, and from work done by George Miller (1966) in psycholinguistics.

The impact of Corder's work gave rise to a new field called *error analysis* because the emphasis was now on examining systematic errors in order to arrive at some description of the underlying rules that governed the learner's evolving interim grammars. The field of error analysis included within it the contrastive analysis of the structuralist grammarians, along with new insights derived from the Chomskyan perspective. In addition, this new view looked at other possible sources of learner deviation from the target grammar that might have nothing to do with the learner's first language. The role of the first language was now questioned; it could no longer be assumed to be the sole cause or reference point for errors. Studies done with both children and adults claimed to show that most of the errors were in fact derived from sources other than the first language. More on this issue will be examined next.

THE PSYCHOLINGUISTIC STUDY OF
SECOND LANGUAGE ACQUISITION

So far the discussion has been concerned with the historical impact of work by Chomsky and Corder on the study of psycholinguistic aspects of SLA. Today, the field has progressed far beyond those starting points, and studies are concerned with more than just acquisition per se. Psycholinguistic studies of SLA may be divided into two general complementary areas:

1. *Processing studies* concerned with describing the underlying psychological mechanism that allows the learner to comprehend second language utterances and to produce utterances emanating from his or her particular grammatical system.
2. *Acquisition studies* concerned with describing how the second language user acquires the interlanguage system in the first place.

Although these two areas, processing and acquisition, are distinct, there is naturally some overlap. It may be assumed that no acquisition can take place without the ability to process the language material being acquired. On the other hand, all instances of language processing are not instances of processing for the purposes of acquisition. The language processing ability of nonnative speakers may be studied with the assumption that such studies are necessarily related to acquisition. For example, we can study the strategies used by second language learners to make themselves understood by others. These "communication strategies" are interesting to study for their own sake but do not necessarily reflect processing for the sake of acquisition.

PSYCHOLINGUISTIC ISSUES IN
SECOND LANGUAGE STUDIES

It is apparent to anyone who has contact with second language learners or first language learners that they do not acquire control over the target language system all at once. Rather, one observes that learners acquire bits and pieces of the system they wish to acquire. Even the untrained researcher can see the difference between adults and children in the extent and ease of acquisition of a second language. Although Wong Fillmore (1979) demonstrates that there are individual differences and that many problems exist with children acquiring a second language, it has been observed that children, for the most part, are at least capable of acquiring another language completely when given adequate exposure and motivation. On the other hand, the adult who completely acquires another language and can pass as a native speaker of that language is the exception. (The biological reasons for this difference are discussed in Genesee's chapter, Chapter 3 of this book.)

For our purposes, however, the difference between children and adults in extent of acquisition raises several questions that have been and continue to be studied from a psycholinguistic point of view. Given the scope of this chapter, however, we will touch on only some of the major aspects of such questions:

1. How does the learner develop his or her second language system? What are thought to be the processes involved?
2. What role does previous knowledge, such as the first language, play in second language acquisition?
3. What psychological characteristics contribute to successful second language acquisition? Are there good learners and bad learners?

How does the learner develop his or her second language system?

The variety of the target language that the second language learner develops has been referred to as "transitional competence" (Corder, 1967), "approximative systems" (Nemser, 1971) and "interlanguage" (Selinker, 1972). Each of these terms captures a slightly different aspect of the system that the learner evolves. Corder's term, "transitional competence," expresses the idea that the second language (L2) knowledge system being developed by the learner is a dynamic one in a state of flux, constantly changing as new knowledge of the second language is added. Each new acquisition necessitates adjustments in the competence already acquired. This problem has been noted by later researchers because the very transitional nature of the learner's competence makes it difficult to study. How does one know, given a set of utterances by a learner, whether we are dealing with rules permanently fixed in the grammar of the learner like the stabilized rules in the grammar of a native speaker?

Nemser's term, "approximative systems," captures the characteristic incompleteness of the learner's second language. In the sense implied by this metaphor, the learner may be viewed as progressing along a continuum from zero knowledge of L2 to a level closely resembling the linguistic competence of the native speaker of the target language (see Figure 1.1). This concept states nothing about the length of time it takes for the learner to progress from zero knowledge to almost complete knowledge, nor does it explain how the learner moves along this continuum.

Given the idea of transitional competence, or approximative systems, we can see that it would be possible to describe the learner's knowledge of the second language in a number of ways. It would be possible to collect a sample of the learner's L2 production at point a, b, or c. Data at any of these points could be described in terms of the system of rules possessed by the learner at

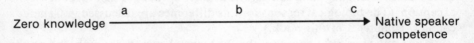

Zero knowledge ——————————————————————▶ Native speaker competence

Figure 1.1 Approximative system continuum (see Nemser, 1971)

that point and as the learner's transitional competence. Following Corder (1967), an analysis of the errors produced by the learner at any of the points on the approximative system continuum should also allow us to extrapolate the underlying psycholinguistic processes involved in producing these errors. This aspect of L2 acquisition will be discussed further later on.

Notice also that in addition to describing the transitional competencies or transitional grammars at point a, b, or c, the comparison of grammars of individual learners sampled over time will provide descriptions of possible developmental stages through which learners are progressing. In other words, if one sampled the language production for an individual learner *longitudinally* over a period of several months or even several years, a pattern of linguistic change within the individual's grammatical rules would be observed. Based on these longitudinal comparisons, additional extrapolations may be made with regard to the individual psychological strategies that the learner is following, the possible sources of his or her hypotheses about the second language, and a natural definition of what is difficult and what is simple in the target language based on the order of what is acquired first and what next in the target language.

Corder's work in 1967 and Nemser's 1971 paper were followed closely by Selinker's (1972) article titled "Interlanguage." Although the term, "interlanguage," is closely related to "transitional competence" and "approximative systems," it is unique in attempting to demonstrate that the system the learner develops is neither based entirely on his or her first language (L1) nor based completely on the target language. Selinker claimed that the interlanguage system was a unique grammar that did not belong to either the source language or the target language and that contained rules found only in systems resulting from a second language learning context.

In this article, Selinker also attempted to describe what he considered to be the five central *processes* responsible for the creation of interlanguage systems, as follows:

1. Language transfer, that is, the transference of rules from the learner's first language (L1) and used to produce utterances in the second language (L2)
2. Transfer of training that resulted from the learner's being overdrilled in a particular form in the second language class
3. Strategies of second language learning
4. Strategies of second language communication
5. Overgeneralization of target language linguistic material

Selinker proposed that these five processes exist in a *latent psychological structure* that could be activated for the purposes of learning another language after the close of the critical period for language acquisition around the onset of puberty. Selinker also suggested the term *fossilization* for linguistic structures that are deviant from the structure of the target langauge but remain in that deviant form no matter how much exposure or correction the learner receives.

It is clear that Selinker's (1972) proposals fit into the Chomskyan tradition of attempting to build a description of the possible psychological structures used by the language learner, whether of a first or a second language, based on the observable data produced by the learner. These proposals also conform to Corder's concept of transitional competence and extend this idea further by attempting to suggest how transitional competencies within the approximative system are created by the learner and why some forms seem to be permanently fixed no matter how much correction and feedback are provided.

Selinker's proposals did, however, raise some serious questions for second language research that are still being debated today. What types of psychological processes are involved in acquiring a second language? Are all such processes equally important? Are all the "processes" described by Selinker really processes? Do all processes contribute to acquisition, or are some concerned with the encoding and decoding of language material and others more relevant to acquisition? What is the real psychological status of fossilization?

Not all the processes proposed by Selinker are equally important, nor should all be considered processes. For example, native language transfer, transfer of training, and overgeneralization can all be categorized as types of some generic form of generalization, differing only with respect to the source material on which the generalization is based. This generic form of generalization can itself be considered a form of hypothesis testing. Selinker's process, called "strategies for second language communication," may or may not be concerned with actual acquisition and may represent rather specialized behaviors for functioning in second language contexts. Selinker's "second language learning strategies" could be fit into the basic categories of hypothesis testing and generalization.

As a result of the work of Corder (1967) and the development of learning theories in cognitive psychology, it is generally agreed that the central learning process for acquiring a language is hypothesis testing. This process consists of five steps:

1. Identifying the characteristics of a particular target concept or observing a relationship between a new form and one already learned
2. Forming a hypothesis based on that identification or observation
3. Testing the hypothesis by producing an utterance or listening for a similar example
4. Receiving feedback on the hypothesis
5. Deciding whether to continue accepting this hypothesis or to reject it on the basis of the feedback

Feedback for the language learner can be in the form of correction, comprehension by the interlocutor, or some other indicator that leads the learner either to keep his or her hypothesis or to reject it and form a new one. (See Levine, 1975, for a full discussion of hypothesis testing within a cognitive theory of learning.)

Since human beings of all ages learn second languages in all kinds of learning contexts, it is reasonable to assume that the acquisition of a second language must fit within the scope of the general learning capabilities of human beings. Although language learning is certainly different from learning to drive a car, play tennis, or identify nonpoisonous mushrooms, it must share at some level a set of general learning procedures used to acquire all forms of new knowledge. This was described earlier as hypothesis testing.

Within the general area of learning, we can distinguish between learning that requires meaningful use of the learned material and learning that requires little more than the automatic use of the learned material, with minimal analysis at the conscious or unconscious level. Typing could be described as the automatic use of a learned skill. The use of language, however, may be said to require a higher level of decision making, which, though unconscious, is meaningful in terms of ideas expressed and of matching the appropriateness of linguistic form to the context in which the language is being used.

Ausubel (1968) proposed a schema to handle such meaningful learning. His schema can include some of the issues raised by Selinker and others. Ausubel claims that all meaningful learning requires the relating of new material to knowledge already acquired. Bruner, Goodnow, and Austin (1956), in their now classic study of concept development, arrived at the same conclusion. The problem in learning new material, however, lies not just in relating it to what is already stored in a system of knowledge in order to help retention. The question addressed by Ausubel is what happens to this newly acquired knowledge once it becomes attached to already existing knowledge. Does it retain its uniqueness? Does it become recoded as similar to what the learner already knows? Does it become a subset or an extension of already existing knowledge?

The reader can already see the application of these general learning theory questions to the issues of second language acquisition, language transfer, and other related problems. Ausubel proposed that once hypotheses are tested, the resultant confirmed hypotheses become subsumed under already existing conceptual schema. The manner of subsumption will determine whether the newly learned material can be retrieved in its original form or will be erased or lost in the process of grouping new material under already existing rules or concepts. For example, in learning a second language, learners will attempt to relate the new concepts of the second language to what they already know about language. The most salient set of facts they possess about language are those of their first language. In the process of attempting to relate the new language to the language they know, they will hypothesize about the similarity (or difference) between the target and the source language. In so doing, they will attempt to subsume this new knowledge under categories already existing in their first language competence. An unconscious internal monologue describing this process might be as follows: "I see that the second language has a way of expressing questions embedded in a sentence. My language also has embedded questions. I assume that I can use the rules from my first language to create embedded questions in the second language—*I don't know how do you change a tire.*"

The internal monologue is, of course, imaginary, but the actual produced sentence is not. It is, in fact, a common error found in the production of learners of English as a second language (ESL). Sometimes these errors can be traced back to the first language, sometimes not. More will be said about this problem later. The error does illustrate, however, what Ausubel intends by the term *obliterative subsumption.* The second language form has been categorized as being essentially the same as the first language with regard to word order and embedding rules. The learner does not see that in English we must reinvert the word order of the embedded question. The act of subsuming the second language form under the first language rule obliterates the features in the second language form that distinguish it from the first language.

Note that Ausubel's concept does explain how the process of transfer works. In addition, the concept of subsumption can be used to explain the fifth process in Selinker's five processes for the creation of interlanguages: the overgeneralization of rules within the second language itself. In this case, the process consists of the learner acquiring a grammatical rule in the second language that may not be comparable to any rule already acquired in the first language. Having acquired a new second language rule, the learner then overextends this rule to apply to inappropriate cases.

An example of overgeneralization would be as follows: The simple present verb system in English is ususual and troublesome for ESL learners because it is uninflected except for the third person singular form, which requires the suffix -*s*. Learners of English as a second language almost universally have problems remembering to add the third person suffix. The explanation usually given for this error is that the learners have acquired the general rule that the verb in the simple present is not inflected, and overgeneralize the rule to the third person. In Ausubel's sense, the third person singular is subsumed under the general rule for noninflection and thus is not inflected because the learner has developed the wrong hypothesis.

What role does previous knowledge, such as the first language, play in second language acquisition?

What does the knowledge of a language, first or second, consist of? This has been a central question both in the study of language acquisition and in the teaching of a second language. It is apparent that the way we define language knowledge will affect the way we describe the process of acquiring that knowledge.

The study of second language acquisition has been very much affected by changes and trends found not only in linguistics but also in the field of psychology. In the past, linguistics has been affected by theories of learning from psychology and has in turn effected changes in how psychologists view language knowledge and language acquisition. For example, earlier in this century, the dominant school in American psychology was behaviorism. Behaviorists believed that only externally observable behavior was psychologically relevant for study and that internal mechanisms responsible for that behavior could not be investigated scientifically. A basic unit of behavior for this school was the habit, which was the result of externally determined conditions.

The behaviorists influenced proponents of the American linguistic school of structuralism in the way these linguists viewed language (see Bloomfield, 1933). These linguists believed that language itself consisted of externally conditioned habits. The knowledge of a language, then, consisted of that set of habits demonstrated by the language user. According to this approach, learning a second language consisted of the acquisition of a new set of habits (Fries, 1945). The mechanism for acquiring them was the habit formation paradigm of response conditioned to a particular stimulus and then generalized to other similar stimuli.

Since, however, according to the structuralist school, language knowledge was synonymous with a set of habits, learning a second language might mean displacing one set of habits with another. Learning a second language, therefore, meant overcoming a habit formed when the first language was acquired and replacing it, or at least overcoming its influence, when learning the second language. The set of habits that made up the first language was seen as interfering with the acquisition of a new set.

Contrastive analysis is based on this school of thought. The classic statement of this hypothesis may be found in Lado (1957) and in more recent versions in James (1980). Vowel sounds, lexical items, or sentence types are compared across languages; then, a list of what is similar and what is different for the two languages is drawn up. It is the assumption of the classical contrastive analysis approach that differences between two languages inevitably mean learning difficulty due to contrast between two different habits, whereas similarities mean learning facility due to transfer of similar structures from the L1 to the L2. Unfortunately, such predictions do not always hold true in practice. For example, although the order of adjective and head noun is different for Spanish and English, native speakers of English and of Spanish almost never have any problem with the difference in the other language. On the other hand, differences in the phonological system almost always cause problems for learners. It has also been found that near similarity is sometimes more difficult to overcome than clear difference. This, of course, might be predicted on the basis of Ausubel's concept of subsumption, discussed earlier.

Although all researchers admit that the first language of the second language learner must play some role in the acquisition process, there has been some debate about the importance of this role. In the 1970s, because of the declining importance of the structuralist school and its displacement by the cognitively oriented theory of transformational-generative grammar, the specific role of first language influence and the general validity of contrastive analysis was called into question.

In a series of studies with children acquiring a second language, Dulay and Burt (1974) claimed that children from different language backgrounds did not use their first language as the source for developing hypotheses about the second language but, rather, used universal, developmentally determined processes to learn a second language. In their study, they examined the acquisition of English as a second language by Chinese- and Spanish-speaking children, ages 6 to 8. Their methodology consisted of taking a speech sample of English language production and comparing the relative amount of error found for all subjects for use with 11 different grammatical functors such as present progressive (-*ing*), plural (-*s*), irregular past, possessive, and so on. They chose this set of grammatical markers because there had been previous work done by developmental psycholinguists such as Roger Brown (1973) on the order of acquisition of grammatical functors for children acquiring English as a first language. (See McLaughlin, 1978a, for a review of these and similar studies.)

In addition to examining the role of the first language in second language acquisition, these studies introduced a research methodology hitherto unique in second language studies and research in first language acquisition. Dulay and Burt extrapolated longitudinal patterns of second language acquisition— that is, the order that would be followed by individual learners over time— from the collective performance of many learners on a set of grammatical morphemes at one point in time. This research claimed that with a single sample of performance for particular linguistic structures of a group of learners from different language backgrounds, the picture that would emerge from such cross-sectional sampling would be the same statistically as that which would emerge from the longitudinal study of single learners over time. The findings of these cross-sectional studies and their methodology have been controversial and have raised a number of questions related to the interpretation of findings.

Following Dulay and Burt (1974), Bailey, Madden, and Krashen (1974) used the same research methodology on adult learners of English as a second language, with similar results. That is, regardless of native language, the subjects displayed the same order of acquisition of the grammatical morphemes.

The cumulative conclusion of these studies was that the learning of a second language did not involve transference of structures from the first language, but, rather, involved what was called *creative construction* (Dulay & Burt, 1974). This meant that the process of acquiring a second language was controlled primarily by universal cognitive principles that determined how the learner would approach the language regardless of previous knowledge. The evidence for this, according to these studies, was both the apparent universality of the order of acquisition for speakers of different first languages and for learners of different ages, and the consistent qualitative nature of the errors themselves.

The results of the research, however, are far from conclusive if such factors as learning contexts and experimental design are taken into consideration. Would we find a different effect for first language transfer in contexts where learners have little or no exposure to the second language outside the classroom and where all the other learners speak the same first language? That is, is an additional variable affecting the use of transfer as a language acquisition strategy?

What is the effect of the experimental condition itself on the nature of the language data elicited and on the response of the subjects in the research? Sociolinguists have shown that the external conditions under which data are elicited will affect style along a formality continuum ranging from vernacular under informal conditions to superordinate under formal or experimental conditions (Tarone, 1982). Since qualitatively different kinds of language are elicited under different conditions, first language transfer might appear under one set of conditions but not under another. These are just a few of the questions that remain to be investigated before conclusions can be reached about the role of the first language.

An interesting possibility related to the role of the first language in second language acquisition was raised by Schachter (1974). Most research in second language acquisition is concerned with examining the production of learners to see what the errors found in their interlanguage will reveal about the underlying processes involved. We might refer to these errors as errors of *commission*. That is, in order to study the learner's processing of second language material, we must study the errors that he or she commits. Suppose, however, that a learner, sensing a contrastive difference between his or her first language and the target language, decides that such a difference will cause him or her to make mistakes. One possible choice open to the learner is to avoid situations that will require the troublesome form. Another choice, assuming the meaning of the form must be expressed, is to find a possible paraphrase for that form in the second language that the learner feels he or she can control.

For example, suppose a learner was not certain about the rules pertaining to combining two simple sentences into a more complex sentence, as in:

1a. Tom Brown is an American.
1b. Tom Brown is a linguist.

These two sentences might be combined in English in a number of ways, such as:

2. Tom Brown, who is an American, is a linguist.
3. Tom Brown, who is a linguist, is an American.
4. Tom Brown is an American, and he is a linguist.
5. Tom Brown is an American and a linguist.

There are, of course, other possibilities, but these will suffice to demonstrate Schachter's findings.

After carrying out a contrastive analysis of Arabic, Persian, Chinese, Japanese, and English, Schachter concluded that Arabic and Persian had rules similar to English for combining simple sentences into relative clause sentences like numbers 2 and 3. Japanese and Chinese, on the other hand, contained rules for creating relative clause sentences that were quite different from those of English. She therefore predicted that Japanese speakers would produce far more errors when attempting relative clause sentences than would speakers of Arabic and Persian.

Schachter collected data from the compositions of adult learners who were studying English as a second language in an American university. To her surprise, when she examined the compositions and counted the number of relative clause errors for speakers of the languages listed, she found that Japanese and Chinese speakers had made proportionately fewer relative clause errors than had speakers of Arabic and Persian.

Schachter then reexamined the compositions of the subjects in her study for the number of relative clause sentences that they had attempted. The results of the second analysis revealed that Arabic and Persian speakers did in fact make many more errors than the Japanese and Chinese subjects but, more important, the Japanese and Chinese subjects had attempted far fewer relative clauses to begin with.

Schachter concluded that the Japanese and Chinese speakers had avoided relative clauses, which were troublesome for them because of salient differences between their L1 and English. They stuck to sentence types with which they felt secure and, for this reason, tended to combine sentences according to the pattern of sentences 4 and 5 above or to state potentially combinable sentences as two simple sentences. Schachter claimed that this type of "avoidance strategy" was an error of omission resulting from influence of the first language. Avoidance must be considered when evaluating the role of the first language in second language acquisition.

Kleinmann (1977) also investigated avoidance as a possible strategy used by the second language learner. He also concluded that the use of avoidance strategies cannot always be attributed to lack of knowledge of the second language structure, but may also be due to other factors, such as anxiety, attitude, and influence from the first language. Like Schachter, he concluded that there has been an overemphasis on error analysis to the exclusion of the possible contribution of contrastive analysis in predicting the areas where second language learners will experience problems.

One of the most interesting and potentially powerful developments in SLA research has been the return in recent years to an interest in cross-linguistic influence as a source of explanation for second language development. This renewed interest, however, has not been simply a recapitulation of previous contrastive analysis but, rather, an investigation stimulated by changes taking place in linguistic theory itself. Even more interesting, these recent developments in linguistic theory, previously considered inaccessible or inapplicable by many second language researchers, have provided SLA research with an important research tool.

Chomsky's theory of government and binding (Chomsky, 1981) allows an important role for both a universal grammar and the first and second languages. It is still not clear just how these different grammar systems interact, and it would be far beyond the scope of this chapter to present an adequate treatment of such a theory. Briefly, however, the new theory, referring to *first language acquisition*, claims that all humans (and thus all human languages) are constrained or limited in what they can do because of biological traits that are native to our species. In terms of language, this would translate into capabilities for language with which all human babies are born. Within this given capacity for language, there are some capabilities that are shared by all languages and some that are not. Those capabilities or "rules" that are shared by all languages are called the *universal grammar* (UG). The UG may be said to consist of a set of limitations or *parameters* for language. Different languages set their parameters differently, thereby creating the characteristic grammar for that language.

In first language acquisition, the child's task is to discover where the universal grammar differs from the language the child is trying to acquire. Where the first language conforms to the universal grammar, the child's task is supposedly simplified because the rules or descriptions are already within the child's language "organ," as Chomsky metaphorically calls it. The problem for the child arises where a specific language differs in selecting out of all the possible constraints of the universal grammar those that apply to the specific language the child is trying to acquire. In terms of this new theory, the child is said to be setting the *parameters* for the new language, that is, discovering where the target language sets the limits or constraints of the universal grammar.

One can immediately see the potential of this new theory for investigating the psycholinguistic processes of second language acquisition. For SLA, the problem would be to see to what extent already identified universal constraints or parameters are true for second language acquisition situations as well and to what degree they differ from those identified for first language acquistion. (An example of an investigation of this type would be White [1985].) That is, how does the second language learner go about setting or resetting the parameters of the grammar? Of course, the acquisition of a second language is complicated by the fact that *two* languages are now confounding the picture, and it may be difficult to identify clearly the influence of first language, second language, and UG constraints.

Another interesting implication of this new direction of second language research is related to the hypothesis-testing model previously discussed. The new theory rejects unlimited hypothesis testing because learners are thought to lack the necessary "negative input" with which to reject incorrect hypotheses. If this is true, how do learners discover what is acceptable and what is not? From the UG point of view, learners cannot help themselves from applying universal constraints and are thus severely limited in how and where they may apply their hypotheses. This does not mean, of course, that hypothesis testing is not a viable explanation. Rather, the problem now becomes one of understanding where it is useful and where it is not in explaining second language acquisition.

Examples of research in this direction are found in two collections, Eckman, Bell, and Nelson (1984) and Gass and Selinker (1983) and in recent articles by Cook (1985), van Buren and Sharwood Smith (1985), and Flynn and Espinal (1985).

What psychological characteristics contribute to successful second language acquisition? Are there good learners and bad learners?

Up to this point we have been considering linguistic factors that impinge on the process of second language acquisition. We have seen that in order to acquire the abstract knowledge necessary to use a language, the learner must develop hypotheses about the new language and then test them. It has also been shown that these hypotheses either may be based on the learner's already existing knowledge of the first language or may be developed from knowledge already acquired from the second language. The learner draws on a number of knowledge sources in order to develop the grammar of the second language, and these knowledge sources may be linguistic only in the broadest sense. For example, knowing what register to use—formal or informal—is related to language form as well as to language function in social settings.

Since language is used in social exchanges, the feelings, attitudes, and motivations of learners in relation to the target language itself, to the speakers of the language, and to the culture will affect how learners respond to the input to which they are exposed. In other words, these affective variables will determine the rate and degree of second language learning. Personal characteristics of learners will affect how they approach the language data. For example, how much are they willing to gamble before they construct a hypothesis about the second language? What personal traits will determine whether they will be willing to risk the embarrassment of a mistake in order to try out a new language form? How do factors such as strength of motivation and attitude toward the other language group, language learning peers, and teachers affect learning? The catalogue of learner characteristics that may facilitate or hinder second language acquisition is extensive. According to Figure 1.2, the language input (i.e., data to which learners are exposed) on which they will base their hypotheses interacts with the learners' affective and social characteristics. In a sense, it is these factors that determine how much of the *input*—that is, language to which the learner is exposed—will become *intake*—language that will be used to develop the L2 system (see Corder, 1967).

A number of studies have been conducted to discover what makes a good language learner as opposed to a poor one. It is immediately clear to any teacher that, in a given class, some learners seem to make quick progress, whereas others seem to make slow, often imperceptible progress. Why? If we assume that all learners must use hypothesis testing as the basic learning strategy (Seliger, 1983), then why do some seem more adept than others at learning a second language?

Unfortunately, although there is a growing literature about the affective characteristics that lead to successful second language learning, there are few empirical studies showing that possessing a particular characteristic or constellation of characteristics will lead to successful language learning. The first problem, of course, is to define *successful language learning*. Is success measured by achievement on a language proficiency test? Is it measured by the learner's ability to function within specific contexts for language use? Is it measured on the subjective basis of how comfortable the learner feels about him- or herself as a member of the society that speaks the target language? For example, it is clear that learners who are good at meeting the goals established for classroom language learning may nevertheless be quite poor at using the language outside the classroom with native speakers. Many readers of this chapter have received high grades in foreign language study within a school context, but realize that the grades themselves are no measure of one's willingness to risk using that language knowledge in situations where the goal is communication rather than passing an exam.

LANGUAGE INPUT: The language to which the learner is exposed	CHARACTERISTICS OF THE SOCIAL SETTING PERSONAL CHARACTERISTICS OF LEARNER (COGNITIVE AND LEARNING STYLE)	LANGUAGE INTAKE: The language that the learner actually uses to build hypotheses and that determines degree and rate of acquisition

Figure 1.2   The relationship between social-affective variables and second language acquisition

Rubin (1975, 1981), Naiman, Fröhlich, and Stern (1975), and others point to a number of activities or strategies that good language learners carry out during second language acquisition. Implicit in all this work is the assumption that if we learn the characteristics of the good language learner, perhaps, through external manipulation (e.g., modification of materials and method), we can somehow convert poor language learners into good ones. This, of course, is an issue in the psycholinguistics of second language acquisition that is yet to be resolved. Note, however, from the discussion of learner characteristics to come, that some traits are related to personality variables. The implication, therefore, is that external manipulation or intervention can somehow change these personality variables in order to produce a better language learner.

What are some of the characteristics associated with the good language learner? Rubin (1975) states that the good language learner has a strong drive to communicate. The good language learner is "willing to appear foolish . . . to make mistakes . . . [and] to live with a certain amount of vagueness" (Rubin, 1975, p. 47). Beebe (1983) has expanded on this feature of the good language learner by exploring the personality characteristic of risk taking. Logically, a learner who is willing to guess with a lower probability of success, that is, to take chances, is more of a risk taker than is a learner who needs to be confident that his or her grammer is correct before attempting a sentence in the second language. Beebe's review of the social psychological literature concludes that moderate risk takers have the highest probability of success in terms of the accuracy of their guesses. She hypothesizes, however, that high risk taking may favorably affect overall language learning in the long run.

It may be that high risk takers will also chance more encounters with the language and thereby develop other areas of language ability not necessarily related to linguistic accuracy but more related to skills of social interaction and communication. Seliger (1983) found that high input generators or high-level interactors in the classroom were more willing to develop contacts with native speakers of the second language, were more willing to volunteer information and to initiate language interactions, but were not necessarily more grammatical in their speech than peers who interacted at lower levels. That is, they still made errors, but their errors were based more in L2 overgeneralizations and less in transfer from L1. Seliger concludes that this indicates a higher level of development than that of the lower level interactor whose hypotheses are still based primarily on his or her native language.

Schumann (1975) considers factors in the affective domain to be so important in second language acquisition that he sees them as the initiator and controller of the process itself. In his arguments for the centrality of affective variables, Schumann reviews research that indicates that attitude, motivation, type of motivation, and the personality trait of empathy are the primary initiating factors.

Probably the most ambitious attempt to embed affective variables into a comprehensive theory of second language acquisition has been Krashen's *monitor theory* (1978, 1981, 1982). This theory has caught the attention of many in the field of second language acquisition research and in the field of language teaching, but perhaps for the wrong reasons. The theory, which will be discussed next, is impressive for its scope; unfortunately, however, this is its very weakness because it must necessarily include as well a number of inconsistencies. Although it is not within the scope of this chapter to present an exhaustive examination of the theory, there have been several critical analyses of various aspects of the theory (McLaughlin, 1978b; Seliger, 1979; and, most recently, Gregg, 1984, 1986).

The monitor theory has developed into a complex of interrelated parts but takes its name from Krashen's attempt to deal with several paradoxes that seem to exist in the acquisition of a second language either in a formal or classroom context or in natural circumstances. One paradox is that learners in a language class often exhibit a range of capabilities such that under one set of conditions, second language performance might be better than under another set of conditions. For example, a learner's performance might be better when that learner is writing a composition than when he or she is speaking extemporaneously. Similarly, the learner's performance might be better on some kinds of language tests than on others.

To explain this paradox, Krashen postulates the monitor model and the distinction between *learning* and *acquisition*. What is learned formally, he claims, is a different kind of learning from what is acquired naturally. The difference in learners' performance on different kinds of tasks is the result of their using either the "acquired" grammar or the "learned" grammar. According to this distinction, the two types of grammar are stored separately in the learner's mind.

The learned grammar can be accessed only when three conditions are met:

1. The learner must have time to think about the grammar rule that is stored in the monitor device (i.e., learned grammar).
2. The learner must be focused on form. Here, Krashen means by "form" assumedly formal as opposed to substantive or content aspects of the language, especially those formal aspects of the language that might be taught as "grammar" in a language class.
3. The learner must know the rule.

When all of these conditions are met, the learner still may or may not use the monitor to edit his or her output of the second language.

The model shown in Figure 1.3 is from Krashen (1978) but is not substantially different from later versions of the model. Even with the description of this model, a number of problems remain to be resolved. For example, suppose all three conditions are met, but the learner still produces errors. Krashen attempts to explain variation in the effectiveness of the monitor by claiming that there are three types of monitor users: overusers, optimal users, and underusers. Those learners whose performance exhibits hesitation and hypercorrection are apparently too dependent on the monitor, whereas those who produce lots of errors even though they can demonstrate knowledge of formal grammar rules as taught in a language lesson are thought to be underusing their knowledge.

A serious problem for any theory that postulates a distinction between knowledge acquired subconsciously under natural conditions and knowledge acquired consciously in a formal environment is the assumption that the two forms of knowledge are indeed different versions of the same thing. That is, can it be claimed, for example, that the knowledge of a pedagogical rule for the formation of the passive is equivalent to the underlying knowledge of forming and using the passive? If I can verbalize a rule for forming the passive that I learned in a language class or from a language textbook, can that rule actually function as a device for producing real passive sentences outside of a language drill in a language class? One problem with this approach is that it ascribes too much validity to the rules taught in language classes. Although pedagogical rules may be useful for many purposes, it is questionable whether these same rules can in fact be said to represent what a native speaker knows when he or she uses passivized sentences in everyday speech.

In recent writings, Krashen (1982) has developed further ideas related to the type of input that would be necessary for a learner to develop the grammar of the second language. This part of the monitor theory, which has become known as the *input hypothesis*, basically states that we move from stages of our grammar that are known into new stages of development by being exposed to input that goes a little beyond what we already know. In addition, according to Krashen, the input hypothesis refers only to the acquisition grammar, not to what he calls "learning."

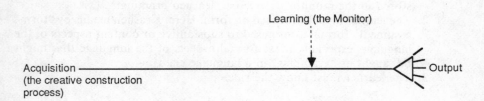

Figure 1.3 The Monitor Model for adult second language performance (*Source*: Reprinted by permission of Academic Press from "Individual Variation in the Use of the Monitor" by S. D. Krashen, in W. C. Ritchie, Ed., *Second Language Acquisition Research*, New York: Academic Press, 1978, p. 176.)

There are several problems with this hypothesis. Since acquisition is more important than learning—and, in fact, Krashen feels that only acquisition can be involved in getting a language—it is not clear why some of us are better at this than others when we are all exposed to the same input. There can be no under- or overusers of the acquisition grammar, in the explanation offered for the difference in performance while learners were supposedly engaging the monitor. The second problem with the input hypothesis is how it explains the process of acquisition or the getting of knowledge itself. I shall relate only to these two questions. The reader is referred to the excellent analysis by Gregg (1984, 1986) for further views on the input hypothesis.

If all language learners are exposed to the same input in a given situation such as a language classroom, and if it all more or less conforms to what Krashen would call comprehensible input, how then do we explain differences in learner performance? Here we return to the factor of affective variables discussed earlier. One of the claims of the monitor theory is that all adults from the Piagetian formal operations stage and beyond develop an affective filter, the composition of which determines how much of the language will reach the acquisition device. According to this view, all input passes through the filter, so only that input which passes can become grist for the mill of acquisition.

That affective variables influence language acquisition is not a new idea, and it is not clear why this component must necessarily be part of the total monitor model, since the monitor itself does not play a role in acquisition. Nor is it clear what role attitude, motivation, and other personality character-istics play in preventing input from reaching that part of the mind responsible for the acquisition of new language knowledge. We have known for some time that learners with a poor attitude toward the target language or toward speakers of that language will not progress as well as those with a positive attitude and high motivation. But how does labeling this phenomenon *affective filter* and embedding it into the monitor model bring us any closer to understanding the way these affective factors work to hinder or facilitate language acquisition? If learners with a high affective filter are exposed to input, how do they filter out input that may cause their grammar to improve? How is it that learners with no formal instruction speak with a grammar that contains a great many fossilized errors and yet seem to comprehend fully native speakers with whom they deal on a daily basis in business or other social settings? In other words, it is not the fact of the existence of affective factors that is debatable but, rather, how they work for the improvement or detriment of second language acquisition.

The second problem raised by the input hypothesis is how new language knowledge reaches the developing grammar and is embedded in it. Although it is logical to surmise that input must be available to a language learner in order for language to be learned, we know very little about the nature of that input. The input hypothesis states that ideal input is a little beyond the learner's capability (in Krashen's terms, "$i + 1$"). This causes the learner to "stretch" his or her grammatical ability and call on contextual cues in order to comprehend the new input.

It is reasonable to surmise that when we are in states of noncomprehension, we guess at the possible meanings in the messages we are receiving. This usually means, however, that we are trying to comprehend the content of the message rather than a particular grammatical structure that may be unfamiliar to us. In fact, many learners learn to function quite well with little attention to the grammatical subtleties of the language they are acquiring or have stopped acquiring. It would seem that any hypothesis that builds on the reasonable assumption that more than grammatical systems are involved in the acquisition of the grammar itself would have to develop a theory of how the grammatical and pragmatic systems interact to cause concomitant or mutual changes in each other.

Another problem that exists for understanding how input is used to build a new grammar is that of explaining how learners acquire those parts of the grammar that carry little or no meaning. For example, it is difficult to imagine at this stage in our knowledge of language acquisition how one acquires the rules for allophones or allomorphs of a language. Think what is involved in the rules for the plural or past tense morphemes in English, or what is involved in learning allophonic variation related to syllable structure such as vowel reduction. Although it is clear that these bits of knowledge can only come from exposure to appropriate input—and no one has ever argued against this—it is not at all clear how this happens. To say that comprehensible input is necessary for language acquisition to take place doesn't really move us any closer to understanding the process itself.

In relation to the foregoing discussion of the monitor theory, it is interesting to return for a moment to the previous discussion on the good language learner. Rubin (1981) describes the good language learner as someone with a strong motivation to communicate. It is possible that having the ability to monitor or edit one's output may be unrelated to this high motivation to communicate or, for that matter, to the ability to communicate. Some learners may be so concerned with communication that grammatical correctness plays a minor role. These learners know the correct form but are not concerned with editing simply because they have "decided" that grammaticality is secondary as long as they are able to communicate fluently and as long as the frequency and degree of deviance of their errors does not go beyond some subjectively determined point of acceptability. This degree of tolerance for error may be in a sense unconsciously negotiated between the learner and his or her interlocutor. The more the native speaker interlocutor seems to tolerate grammatical deviance, the less attention the learner pays to the grammatical formulation of his or her utterances.

This kind of relaxation of self-editing is found quite commonly among bilinguals who will speak a code-switched or code-mixed dialect consisting of a melded grammer of L1 and L2, but only fellow bilinguals who, they sense, possess the same grammatical repertoire. They are usually able to speak an unmixed version of L1 or L2 if they sense that the interlocutor is not a bilingual. Language learners who pay more attention to content than to form are doing more or less the same thing. In a sense, the learner seems to be saying, "I know that I have produced an error, and I may know the correct form, but I'd rather not bother editing my output because I know that it will not interfere with what I have to say."

CONCLUSION

The psycholinguistic study of second language acquisition and processing is concerned with issues such as how knowledge is acquired, what role previous knowledge plays in the acquisition process, and how affective factors influence the way we perceive and process second language data. These issues are not specific to the investigation of second language acquisition but apply to learning in general. It is hoped that potential teachers of a second or foreign language will realize that understanding these issues and being aware of what learners bring with them to the language classroom are crucial to effective teaching.

It should be clear from the discussion in this chapter that we are still a long way from understanding the processes involved in second language acquisition. Much of the research reviewed here has contributed further to our understanding, but none of it has provided more than insights into this very complex process. It is appropriate to all scientific endeavors that findings or claims made for various studies be tested if at all possible to see whether the hypotheses or theories proposed do indeed stand up to logical and experimental analysis. At the same time, it is important that the consumers of scientific research realize that no one study or theory will provide answers to all the questions concerning second language acquisition.

A single chapter on the psycholinguistic issues in second language acquisition that includes both studies in acquisition and studies in processing cannot begin to cover all of the many important and significant articles in the area. This chapter has touched on only some of the research considered to be important background for dealing with the issues. It is hoped that the reader will have been stimulated by the issues and questions raised and will pursue these further.

REFERENCES

Ausubel, D. *Educational psychology: A cognitive approach.* New York: Holt, Rinehart & Winston, 1968.

Bailey, N., Madden, C., & Krashen, S. D. Is there a natural sequence in adult second language acquisition? *Language Learning,* 1974, *24*, 235–243.

Beebe, L. Risk-taking and the language learner. In H. W. Seliger & M. H. Long (Eds.), *Classroom oriented research in second language acquisition*. Rowley, MA: Newbury House, 1983.

Bloomfield, L. *Language*. New York: McGraw-Hill, 1933.

Brown, R. *A first language*. Cambridge, MA: Harvard University Press, 1973.

Brown, R., & Bellugi, U. Three processes in the child's acquisition of syntax. *Harvard Educational Review*, 1964, *34*, 133-151.

Bruner, J., Goodnow, J. J., & Austin, G. A. *A study of thinking*. New York: Wiley, 1956.

Chomsky, N. *Syntactic structures*. The Hague: Mouton, 1957.

Chomsky, N. *Lectures on government and binding*. Dordrecht: Foris, 1981.

Cook. V. J. Chomsky's universal grammar and second language learning. *Applied Linguistics*, 1985, *6*(1), 2-18.

Corder, S. P. The significance of learners' errors. *International Review of Applied Linguistics (IRAL)*, 1967, *5*(4), 161-170.

Dulay, H. C. & Burt, M. K. Natural sequences in child second language acquisition. *Language Learning*, 1974, *24*, 37-53.

Eckman, F. R., Bell, L. H., & Nelson, D. *Universals of second language acquisition*. Rowley, MA: Newbury House, 1984.

Flynn, S., & Espinal, I. Head-initial/head-final parameter in adult Chinese L2 acquisition of English. *Second Language Research*, 1985 *1*(2), 93-117.

Fries, C. C. *Teaching and learning English as a second language*. Ann Arbor: University of Michigan Press, 1945.

Gass, S., & Selinker, L. (Eds.). *Language transfer in language learning*. Rowley, MA: Newbury House, 1983.

Gregg, K. R. Krashen's monitor and Occam's razor. *Applied Linguistics*, 1984, *5*, 79-100.

Gregg, K. R. Review of *The input hypothesis: Issues and implications* by Stephen D. Krashen. *TESOL Quarterly*, 1986, *20*(1), 116-122.

James, C. *Contrastive analysis*. London: Longman, 1980.

Kleinmann, H. Avoidance behavior in adult second language acquisition. *Language Learning*, 1977, *27*, 93-108.

Krashen, S. D. Individual variation in the use of the monitor. In W. C. Ritchie (Ed.), *Second language acquisition research*. New York: Academic Press, 1978.

Krashen, S. D. *Second language acquisition and second language learning*. London: Pergamon Press, 1981.

Krashen, S. D. *Principles and practice in second language acquisition*. London: Pergamon Press, 1982.

Lado, R. *Linguistics across cultures*. Ann Arbor: University of Michigan Press, 1957.

Levine, M. *A cognitive theory of learning*. Hillsdale, NJ: Lawrence Erlbaum Associates, 1975.

McLaughlin, B. *Second language acquisition in childhood*. Hillsdale, NJ: Lawrence Erlbaum Associates, 1978a.

McLaughlin, B. The monitor model: Some methodological considerations. *Language Learning*, 1978b, *28*, 309-332.

Miller, G. A. Language and psychology. In E. Lenneberg (Ed.), *New directions in the study of language*. Cambridge, MA: MIT Press, 1966.

Naiman, N., Fröhlich, M., & Stern, H. H. *The good language learner.* Toronto: Modern Language Center, Ontario Institute for Studies in Education, 1975.

Nemser, W. Approximative systems of foreign language learners. *IRAL,* 1971, *9*(2), 115–123.

Newmeyer, F. J. On the applicability of transformational generative grammar. *Applied Linguistics,* 1982, *3*(2), 89–120.

Rubin, J. What the "good language learner" can teach us. *TESOL Quarterly,* 1975, *9*, 41–51.

Rubin, J. The study of cognitive processes in second language learning. *Applied Linguistics,* 1981, *2*(2), 117–131.

Schachter, J. An error in error analysis. *Language Learning,* 1974, *24*, 205–214.

Schumann, J. Affective variables and the problem of age in second language acquisition. *Language Learning,* 1975, *25*, 209–235.

Seliger, H. W. On the nature and function of language rules in language teaching. *TESOL Quarterly,* 1979, *13*, 359–369.

Seliger, H. W. Learner interaction in the classroom and its effect on language acquisition. In H. W. Seliger & M. H. Long (Eds.), *Classroom oriented research in second language acquisition.* Rowley, MA: Newbury House, 1983.

Selinker, L. Interlanguage. *IRAL,* 1972, *10*(3), 209–231.

Tarone, E. Systematicity and attention in interlanguage. *Language Learning,* 1982, *32*, 69–84.

van Buren, P., & Sharwood Smith, M. The acquisition of preposition stranding by second language learners and parametric variation. *Second Language Research,* 1985, *1*(1), 18–46.

White, L. The acquisition of parameterized grammars: Subjacency in second language acquisition. *Second Language Research,* 1985, *1*(1), 1–17.

Wong Fillmore, L. Individual differences in second language acquisition. In C. J. Fillmore, D. Kempler, & W. S.-Y. Wang (Eds.), *Individual differences in language ability and language behavior.* New York: Academic Press, 1979.

SUGGESTED READINGS

Adjemian, C. On the nature of interlanguage systems. *Language Learning,* 1976, *26*, 297–320.

Eckman, F. R., Bell, L. H., & Nelson, D. *Universals in second language acquisition.* Rowley, MA: Newbury House, 1984.

Gass, S. Language transfer and universal grammatical relations. *Language Learning,* 1979, *29*, 327–344.

Gass, S., & Selinker, L. (Eds.). *Language transfer in language learning.* Rowley, MA: Newbury House, 1983.

Hatch, E. *Psycholinguistics: A second language perspective.* Rowley, MA: Newbury House, 1983.

Hecht, B., & Mulford, R. The acquisition of a second language phonology: Interaction of transfer and developmental factors. *Applied Psycholinguistics,* 1983, *3*, 313–327.

McLaughlin, B., Rossman, T., & McLeod, B. Second language learning: An information processing perspective. *Language Learning,* 1983, *33*, 135–158.

Richards, J. C. Social factors, interlanguage and language learning. In J. C. Richards (Ed.), *Error analysis*. London: Longman, 1972.

Rutherford, W. Markedness in second language acquisition. *Language Learning*, 1982, *32*, 85–108.

Schmidt, R. W., & Richards, J. C. Speech acts and second language learning. *Applied Linguistics*, 1980, *1*, 129–157.

Schumann, J. *The pidginization process: A model for second language acquisition*. Rowley, MA: Newbury House, 1978.

Seliger, H. W. The language learner as linguist. *Applied Linguistics*, 1983, *4*, 179–191.

two

SOCIOLINGUISTIC PERSPECTIVE

Five Sociolinguistic Approaches to Second Language Acquisition

Leslie M. Beebe, Teachers College, Columbia University

The relationship between linguistic variation and social characteristics of speakers, such as age, class, and sex, has intrigued laypeople for centuries, but it is only recently that social scientists have made a commitment to the systematic study of this intuitively captivating subject matter. It is fruitless, if not impossible, to try to pinpoint the birthdate of modern sociolinguistics. What is clear is that pioneering work done since the 1950s by sociolinguists (e.g., Gumperz, Fischer, Labov, Hymes, and Fishman) has irrevocably changed the face of linguistic science. An awareness of the complex and systematic influence of social factors on linguistic performance has been imprinted on our consciousness by the force of so much convincing data. As a result, the formerly common footnote acknowledging the possible influence of social factors is no longer acceptable as analysis. We have graduated to a new level of inquiry where we look not only at the perfect (or "ideal") realization of what people intend to say, but also at the myriad ways in which they actually do say what they want to communicate. We also look at the ways in which their modes of expression vary from one setting to another, from one instance to another, and from one person or group to another.

The author gratefully acknowledges the substantive and editorial suggestions of Tomoko Takahashi, Robin Uliss-Weltz, and Diana Berkowitz.

For a book-length account of sociolinguistics and social psycholinguistics in SLA, the reader is referred to Leslie M. Beebe, *The Social Psychological Basis of Second Language Acquisition*, Longman, Inc., forthcoming.

The recent fascination with social factors that make language performance vary systematically will certainly be a positive force for foreign language teachers and researchers interested in the study of second language acquisition. After all, development in a second language involves a long, slow process of repeated trials in different settings with different interlocutors. It has always been a difficult task for the teacher to differentiate variation that is purely a reflex of the developmental stages of learning from variation that is a natural reflex of the desire for sociolinguistic appropriateness. Research on developmental variation (i.e., interlanguage analysis) combined with research on socially conditioned variation (sociolinguistic analysis) in learner speech can help teachers and researchers sort out the learners' individual grammars and assess both their form-related linguistic competence and their sociocultural competence in the second language. Thus, sociolinguistic research has contributed to second language research in important ways. It has provided a description of systematic, socially conditioned variation in English so that we understand better the target language we are teaching, and has given us scientific methods of inquiry (e.g., Labov, Hymes, Bickerton) that can be applied to interlanguage analysis.

For all its contributions to second language acquisition (SLA), however, there are limitations in the usefulness of first language (L1) sociolinguistics as currently practiced. For one thing, second language performance is qualitatively different from first language performance in at least one important respect: SLA is developmentally incomplete. Second language (L2) performance involves using a repertoire that is both limited and in a state of flux. Native speakers (adults) have a complete command of their mother tongue; any changes in their system are minor in comparison to the changes made by active learners of a second language. So there would be a problem if we were to accept without question the principles of L1 variable language performance. Such principles were discovered through data collection, and that discovery process cannot be circumvented in second language research.

A second objection to the blind adoption of L1 sociolinguistic principles is that sociolinguistics is, at times, narrowly defined to exclude work on the social psychology of language. Social psychologists like Howard Giles express dissatisfaction with current sociolinguistics, claiming that first, it is more descriptive than explanatory, and, second, it places such an overimportance on the connections between linguistic variables and objective social variables (e.g., sex, age, socioeconomic status) that it unfelicitously downgrades the extreme importance of speakers' subjective feelings, values, and motives, which also play a crucial role in determining linguistic behavior (see Beebe & Giles, 1984). This insistence on emphasizing the *why*, not just the *what*, of speech variation, as well as the persistent interest in subjective attitudes, perceptions, and inclinations, is an important area for second language teachers and researchers to consider. After all, SLA usually involves an intergroup, interethnic encounter where a member of one nation and culture interacts with a member of another. And extensive evidence exists to suggest that learners actively choose to adopt (i.e., learn) only those target language varieties that appeal to them on affective grounds and to reject others to which they are sufficiently exposed. (For a review of this literature, see Beebe, 1985; Dulay, Burt, & Krashen, 1982).

Since both the objective social characteristics and the subjective feelings of the participants in a speech event are crucial to the understanding of linguistic variation, literature discussing either or both is reviewed here. Thus, although this chapter purports to discuss "sociolinguistic issues in SLA," the term *sociolinguistic* is henceforth to be broadly construed as covering social psychological concerns as well as strictly sociolinguistic issues. Within sociolinguistics, microsociolinguistic issues (i.e., forces affecting style shifting) will be addressed. Macrosociolinguistics (e.g., the study of language choice, language maintenance, language shift, or governmental language policy) is not, however, within the scope of this review.

This chapter will attempt to meet two goals. First, it will give a very brief overview of five approaches, or traditions, in sociolinguistics. Second, it will review the major issues pertaining to sociolinguistics and second language acquisition that have been discussed in the context of each tradition.

FIVE APPROACHES

Whereas it is simplistic to lump sociolinguistics (broadly defined) into five (and only five) traditions, it is equally misleading to treat every researcher as a totally independent voice. Yet it is also impossible to cover everything and everyone in the field. Thus, a strategy is adopted here of discussing five sociolinguistic traditions headed by a "mentor"—that is, a leader who initiated the tradition and profoundly shaped the paradigm as it unfolded. I am aware that this approach involves oversimplification and some unfairness to the many researchers who have participated in shaping each school of thought. But I hope that readers will accept this as a necessary and useful didactic strategy for achieving breadth, clarity, and organization in summarizing L1 sociolinguistic work in a very small amount of space.

The first approach to sociolinguistics is the Labovian tradition, which recognizes William Labov as its mentor. Labov (1963, 1966, 1972b) has arguably been more influential than any other researcher in establishing the notion that language varies systematically in accordance with social characteristics of the speaker. Other sociolinguists share the same general perspective (e.g., Sankoff, Trudgill, Shuy, Wolfram, Fasold) but Labov's work in particular has influenced linguists to pay heed to systematically patterned variation. Second language researchers who have worked with the Labovian paradigm include L. Dickerson (1974, 1975), W. Dickerson (1976), Dickerson and Dickerson (1977), Schmidt (1977), Tarone (1979, 1982, 1983, 1985a, 1985b), and Beebe (1977a, 1977b, 1980).

The dynamic paradigm is the second approach to sociolinguistics that has influenced second language research. This paradigm recognized Derek Bickerton as its mentor, although, again, other first language researchers worked within the model, and Charles-James N. Bailey (1971, 1973), in particular, helped to shape it. Sociolinguistic researchers who have used the dynamic paradigm to explain change over time in second language acquisition include Gatbonton-Segalowitz (1975), Gatbonton (1978), and Huebner (1979, 1983).

The third great tradition in sociolinguistics is the description of "communicative competence"—the speakers' knowledge of how to use the language in sociolinguistically appropriate ways and to fulfill proper social functions. This approach can be traced to Dell Hymes as a mentor, although complete attribution is certainly more complex than this. Hymes's call (1972) constituted a major influence on the field. Nevertheless, it is simplistic to name Hymes the mentor of all descriptive sociolinguistic studies of communicative competence. First of all, Hymes's influence on L2 research came not from his own data collection but from his programmatic statements—his calls for others to do descriptive research. Second, Hymes specifically advocated ethnographic research, that is, observation of completely natural, unelicited first and second language use. Many have followed the call to describe communicative competence, but they have not found it practical to use Hymes's prescribed ethnographic method. It is also simplistic to view Hymes as the sole mentor because others have had a profound influence as well. Second language researchers' descriptions of communicative competence have focused on speech arts (e.g., compliments, requests, apologies). Thus, they were influenced at the outset by the language philosophers Austin (1963) and Searle (1969, 1976), who discussed speech acts—language as it was used to fulfill social functions. The ethnographic approach in SLA research today has been further honed by Nessa Wolfson. Her work on the "rules of speaking" (compliments, invitations, greetings, partings) has focused primarily on describing native speech, but it has been presented in terms of its usefulness for teachers of English as a second language (ESL) as a description of the way native speakers really talk.

Fourth, there is the research tradition based on speech accommodation theory (SAT)—a social psychological approach shaped by many, but unquestionably headed by Howard Giles. From broad reading in the field of social psychology, Giles and colleagues (Giles, 1980; Giles, Bourhis & Taylor, 1977; Giles & Powesland, 1975; Giles & Smith, 1979) have synthesized four theories to provide an explanation for variation in speech. Giles's main criticism of sociolinguistics is that it has long been too descriptive and not explanatory enough (Beebe & Giles, 1984). The best statement of the application of speech accommodation theory to second language acquisition is found in Giles and Byrne (1982). Although there are many studies of language choice in bilingual settings (e.g., Giles, et al., 1977; Scotton, 1980), there are only a limited number of studies to date that actually analyze variable performance in L2 at one point in time from the SAT perspective (see Beebe, 1982; Beebe & Zuengler, 1983; Zuengler, 1982, 1985) and just as few that look at variable success in acquisition over time (see Hildebrand & Giles, 1980; Platt & Weber, 1984). Speech accommodation theory has been advocated by Beebe (1982) as an alternative explanation for variable data, and models for second language acquisition have been proposed (Beebe & Giles, 1984; Giles & Byrne, 1982), but research in this area is not always well known to SLA researchers, who tend to be linguists by training and who therefore know traditional sociolinguistic approaches better than they do approaches deriving from research on language in the field of social psychology.

There is, however, a notable exception to the generalization that SLA researchers are not, as linguists, particularly familiar with the literature on language done by psychologists. A fifth tradition, the work inspired by Wallace Lambert, is well known to most SLA researchers. Again, to recognize one person as mentor is to oversimplify. Gardner has collaborated with Lambert (Gardner & Lambert, 1972a) and profoundly influenced the field of SLA research with his own model of second language acquisition (Gardner, 1979, 1985). These two researchers with many notable colleagues (e.g., Tucker, Genesee) have created a school of research focusing on attitudes and motivations and their effects on the ultimate success learners will have in mastering a second language. It is not a variation model, however, in the traditional sense of looking at variable performance at one point in time in one learner's use of language. Lambert's approach is only concerned with sociolinguistic variation in the sense that individual learners vary in the level of success they achieve.

SOCIOLINGUISTIC QUESTIONS IN SLA

Although the sociolinguistically oriented studies that exist are widely divergent, there are several questions that run like a loose thread through the literature.

1. Is interlanguage variation systematic or is it random? If it is systematic, does it vary systematically according to social variables? In other words, is there any social significance or social patterning to the variation?
2. Does the learner's interlanguage change over time? If it does, is that change systematic? At what point in a learner's development does the ability develop to vary language systematically according to social variables like setting or interlocutor? Is this skill a characteristic of higher proficiency levels, or is it transferred early on from the first language?
3. What similarities in L2 sociolinguistic patterning exist among speakers of the same native language? In other words, what is the role and extent of sociolinguistic transfer in L2 development?
4. What is the nature of L2 communicative competence? How does it differ from (or resemble) L1 communicative competence? How does it develop? Do linguistic competence and communicative competence develop sequentially or concurrently?
5. What is the "cause" of variation in interlanguage? Why does style shifting occur? Is it due to changes in attention to speech? Is it a matter of speech accommodation?

Despite the existence of issues specific to SLA, it is perhaps not unrealistic to view the union of sociolinguistics and SLA as an emerging field, still strongly influenced by L1 research. For this reason, it may be useful, in cases where this is true, to examine the research issues in light of the L1 sociolinguistic paradigms they seek to apply, test, or evaluate. In the next section, we shall explore five sociolinguistic paradigms and their extension to SLA research.

THE LABOVIAN PARADIGM AND ITS APPLICATION TO SLA RESEARCH

The first person to publish on the applicability of the *Labovian paradigm* to SLA was Lonna Dickerson, whose dissertation (1974) was precisely directed toward discovering whether Labov's model of sound change for native speakers was applicable to second language phonological development. Dickerson studied ten native speakers of Japanese, ages 23–30, who were learning English as a second language at the University of Illinois. She measured their phonological development in terms of their performance on five phonological variables, $/z/$, $/s/$, $/ð/$, $/r/$, ,and $/l/$, as tape recorded at three different times (over a nine-month period) and in three different "styles." The styles were defined sociolinguistically, following Labov, in terms of the task that elicited them: (1) "free" speech, (2) reading dialogues, and (3) reading a list of words in isolation.

Being the SLA pioneer for the Labovian paradigm, Dickerson had extremely basic questions in mind when she began her dissertation research. In a subsequent coauthored article, Dickerson and Dickerson (1977) list succinctly the three general questions behind the early research and later discussion of the findings:

1. Is the learner's pronunciation systematic (or random)?
2. Does it change over time in a systematic patterned fashion?
3. Is there a pattern attributable to subjects' having a common native language?

These correspond quite closely to questions 1, 2, and 3 in the earlier section of this chapter on sociolinguistic questions in SLA.

Presenting only the data on $/r/$, the Dickersons demonstrate that the answer to all the preceding questions is yes. They describe an impressive level of systematicity in the variability. That is, the $/r/$ varied for every subject within one point in time and from one time to another. But this variation was systematically patterned. All ten Japanese subjects used the same five phonetic variants of $/r/$. The order of appearance and the order of difficulty were the same for the whole group. Subjects were also sensitive to the same phonetic environments—that is, whether the $/r/$ preceded a high, mid, or low vowel. And they progressively achieved correct English pronunciation in the environments in the same order. The environments that were easiest for one learner were easiest for all learners, and those that were most difficult for the individual were also most difficult for the whole group. Throughout the three testing periods, subjects maintained a relatively higher correctness, for example, when /r/ preceded a mid vowel than when it preceded a high vowel. Besides this systematicity in the set of variants, the order of appearance, the order of difficulty, and the conditioning environments, there was systematicity in the influence of style. All subjects displayed their highest accuracy in word listing and their lowest accuracy on use of American [ɹ] in free speech.

The Dickersons' research (L. Dickerson, 1974, 1975; Dickerson & Dickerson, 1977; W. Dickerson, 1976) was a landmark effort in demonstrating the systematicity within L2 phonological variability. It was also useful to teachers. L. Dickerson (1975) argued convincingly that knowledge of systematic variability was crucial to understanding speech shifts and accuracy both inside and out of the classroom. Style shifting accounts neatly for the phenomenon informally observed (and often lamented) by teachers—namely, that students will pronounce a word correctly in isolation (cf. Dickerson's listing task) and then mispronounce it in context (cf. connected reading or free speech). This style shifting, common to native and nonnative speakers alike, is something the teacher must accept, understand, and work with slowly, not impatiently try to stamp out, for it is a natural characteristic of human language. It is simply more noticeable in second language speech because the shift is often between a native and a nonnative variant rather than between two native ones.

The Dickersons' research presents a great deal of detailed information on the pronunciation of the five phonological variables in Japanese interlanguage (see L. Dickerson, 1974). Discussion of all the particulars is beyond the scope of this chapter. What should be noted is that they confirmed their hypotheses about the basic systematicity of learner interlanguage and demonstrated effectively that learners, like native speakers, display internal patterning (sensitivity to phonetic environment) as well as external patterning (sensitivity to the nonlinguistic variable of task, which defines style). In addition, L. Dickerson (1974) put forth other important claims about the applicability of the Labovian paradigm. First, she argued on a more theoretical level that her findings demonstrated the applicability to L2 of Labov's model of sound change—ordered decomposition. Ordered decomposition is ordered change toward a target sound—ordered in the set of conditioning environments, ordered in the set of intermediate phonetic stages used, and ordered in the way the sound change proceeds through the community (e.g., from one social group or age group to another). (Two footnotes should be added: first, that W. Dickerson [1976] calls ordered decomposition the "wave mechanism" and, second, that the researchers did not discuss social class or age in any detail, so their work is "sociolinguistic" primarily in its interest in variability and in its sensitivity to task, which is the factor Labov used to define style.)

L. Dickerson's second important claim about the applicability of the Labovian paradigm is also related to style shifting. She claimed that there are no single-style speakers in L2, just as Labov claimed there were none in L1. Third, Dickerson claimed that Labov's "attention to speech" paradigm operated in nonnative as well as native speech. Like native speakers, Japanese learners of English applied more attention to speech in the listing style and therefore displayed higher accuracy. In the free speech style, where attention was at its lowest, accuracy was also at its lowest. Finally, Dickerson affirmed the applicability of the Labovian paradigm and profoundly influenced later SLA research when she drew an analogy between L1 standardness and L2 accuracy. By affirming that attention to speech underlies style shifting in L2 as well as L1, she drew a parallel between accuracy in L2 and standardness in L1. She claimed that attention paid to speech leads to the higher *accuracy of a nonnative* in a formal listing style where high attention is paid to speech, just as it leads to high use of prestige variants, that is, *standardness by native speakers*. Native speakers cannot be said to be accurate or inaccurate, but only standard or less standard, in that their variants are all native and, therefore, "correct" in a linguistic sense.

Ironically, the Dickersons not only initiated the research applying the Labovian paradigm to SLA, but also kicked off the debate questioning its use. Their claims about attention to speech and its effect on L2 ultimately generated the biggest controversy, but initially the Dickersons' claim about the applicability of the Labovian paradigm was what set off discussion. In 1979, Tarone described the learner's interlanguage as a chameleon, changing with context and setting. She argued, "If we assume with Adjemian (1976) that interlanguage is a natural language, then we must assume that it behaves essentially like all other languages in this respect" (p. 181). She reviewed the existing literature to see whether Labov's five methodological axioms and his *observer's paradox* applied to second language performance.

Labov's five axioms are as follows:

1. *Style shifting*: "There are no single-style speakers." All human beings adjust style according to the social situation and the topic of discussion (Labov, 1970, p. 46).
2. *Attention*: "Styles can be measured by speaker along a single dimension, the amount of attention paid to speech" (Labov, 1970, p. 46).
3. *The vernacular*: "In the 'vernacular' style, where the minimum amount of attention is given to speech, the most regular and systematic phonological and grammatical patterns are evidenced. Other styles tend to show more variability" (as rephrased in Tarone, 1979, p. 193).
4. *Formality*: "Any systematic observation of a speaker defines a formal context in which more than the minimum attention is paid to speech" (Labov, 1970, p. 46).
5. *Good data*: "No matter what other methods may be used to obtain samples of speech (group sessions, anonymous observation), the only

way to obtain sufficient good data on the speech of any one person is through an individual, tape-recorded interview: i.e., through the most obvious kind of systematic observation" (Labov, 1970, p. 46).

Labov's main point was expressed by his observer's paradox: "The aim of linguistic research in the community must be to find out how people talk when they are not being systematically observed; yet we can only obtain this data by systematic observation" (Labov, 1970, p. 47).

Having reviewed the L2 literature to see whether Labov's axioms and observer's paradox did in fact apply to interlanguage, Tarone concluded "yes" on all counts. Interlanguage acts like a natural language.

On the other hand, we cannot claim that second language learners are constantly style-shifting on all variables, or that they shift under all the conditions that we predict will lead them to shift, or even that they shift in the direction we expect (see Dowd, 1984; Tarone, 1985a; Zuengler, 1985). What we do know is that second language learners have style-shifting capability and are sensitive to such things as topic, listener, and task. Beebe (1977a) showed that ethnic Chinese-Thai children style-shifted significantly on five out of six vowel variables when speaking to an ethnic Chinese listener instead of an ethnic Thai listener in their second language, Thai. Beebe (1977b) showed that ethnic Chinese-Thai adults made similar style shifts on three consonant variables under the same conditions. And, in some additional data on the Chinese-Thai children, Beebe showed that the children were sensitive to the "Chineseness" of the topic being discussed. That is, they sounded significantly more Chinese (i.e., they displayed more Chinese language influence) when they discussed Chinese holidays with a Chinese listener than when they discussed Thai holidays with a Chinese.

Larsen-Freeman (1976) showed that few statistically significant correlations existed among morpheme orders on five different tasks (speaking, listening, reading, writing, and elicited imitation), thereby demonstrating that task is a significant factor influencing style shifting. Thus, we know that second language learners shift, and we know that shifts according to topic and task can be both systematic and statistically significant, but we do not yet know whether the same level of sensitivity to subtleties exists among L2 learners as among native speakers. This is a matter of research needed more than a topic of heated discussion in the present literature. We simply do not have sufficient data.

What really has become controversial, however, is the axiom of attention as it has been applied to interlanguage by L. Dickerson (1974) and Tarone (1982, 1983, 1985a, 1985b). Labov admits that there are numerous styles and stylistic dimensions. Yet he claims that styles can be ranged along a single dimension, measured by the amount of attention paid to speech (Labov, 1970). Labov (1981) adds that he is not discussing a naturalistic analysis of style, which might require a large number of dimensions. Still, he is claiming that styles can be ordered along the single dimension of attention to speech, and his followers are applying the paradigm to varied situations far beyond the Labovian interview. Beebe (1982) contends that many style shifts are *not* the result of increased or decreased attention to speech—even shifts that could be elicited by Labov's own methodology.

Labov's methodology is based on manipulating the situation to elicit shifts in speech style. For example, he manipulates verbal task, topic, interlocutor, setting, or participant roles. He claims that these affect attention to speech and that a shift in attention brings about a style shift. Verbal task is Labov's primary tool. He uses face-to-face interview conversation to elicit "careful" speech, the reading of passages to get his "reading" style, and the reading of words in citation form to generate his "listing" style. Sometimes Labov's "casual" speech is obtained outside the interview in, say, an unanticipated telephone call from a close friend or relative. At other times, Labov uses the planned interview setting to deliberately ask questions that cause the subject to become quite emotional. Strong emotions are evoked by his famous "danger of death" question: "Have you ever been in a situation where you were in serious danger of being killed?" Labov's question not only evokes strong emotion; it challenges the speaker to justify feeling this emotion. The question "ropes the subject in," making him or her feel that "this answer better be good." The resulting speech is in the vernacular—the casual but systematic style where Labov claims the least amount of attention is paid to speech.

Labov's methodology was used in numerous studies in the 1960s and 1970s, first in his own research and then in replications elsewhere (e.g., Shuy, Wolfram, & Riley, 1967), and finally in studies of L2 learners (L. Dickerson, 1974; Beebe, 1980). L. Dickerson (1974) extends Labov's claims for L1 to the L2 situation, contending:

1. "There are no single style speakers" (pp. 201–202).
2. "The dimension of attention operates whether the language is native or nonnative" (p. 202).
3. The style where there is the least amount of attention to speech is the vernacular. When attention is focused on speech, we get the superordinate style. The vernacular is the most regular and systematic style, the superordinate the least regular and systematic.

In three recent papers, Tarone (1979, 1982, 1983) has supported these contentions. Dickerson makes a fourth claim, however, that Tarone does not totally support. Dickerson makes a crucial analogy between "standard" or "prestige" variants in L1 and "correct" variants in L2. She claims:

4. The superordinate (formal) style has more correct, targetlike variants than does the vernacular (casual) style.

Tarone (1982) cites evidence to show that this is *not always* true. The formal style can display more native language interference and therefore *lower* correctness.

Gatbonton-Segalowitz (1975) studied phonological variables in the English of French Canadians and found a lower level of correctness in casual speech than in formal speech or reading aloud. However, Felix (1977) found, on the contrary, that structures used in spontaneous interactions in the home displayed a higher level of correctness than did those used in formal experimental settings. Beebe (1980) argued that there is no categorical predilection for more or less correct speech in formal situations. Studying the /r/ of nine Thai ESL learners, Beebe showed that their level of correctness in formal listing of words aloud in the target language depended on the social meaning of the variable in the native language. The initial /r/ variable in Thai has a strong social significance, with trilled [r̃] being recognized, since a decree of Rama II (the present king is Rama IX), as the most formal and "correct" and /l/ as the most informal and incorrect. Beebe showed that in a formal listing style Thais shifted significantly toward higher correctness with final /r/, which is not socially marked and not even a sound in Thai, but shifted significantly toward lower accuracy on initial /r/, which is a socially marked sound. The decrease in accuracy with initial /r/ in English resulted from the Thais transferring the trilled [r̃] sound from Thai into English under formal conditions (word listing) where this sound is socially preferred in Thai. Tarone (1979) argued, following Labov, that interlanguage, like native languages, would be more permeable to the superordinate rule system of the target language under formal conditions, but she also questioned what the superordinate rule system would be for interlanguage. Would it be the native language (NL) or the target language (TL)? Beebe (1980) demonstrated it could be either, depending on circumstances.

In 1982 Beebe extended her argument, based on her Thai data and many other social psychological studies on accommodation. Not only did she question whether formal style is always the most correct (i.e., Dickerson's fourth claim), but she also questioned the entire applicability of the attention to speech paradigm (see also Bell, 1984; Rampton, 1985). Beebe argued that attention to speech was not the "cause" of style shifting, as Tarone (1982, 1983) has argued, or even the single dimension underlying all style shifts, as both Tarone (1982, 1983, 1984, but not 1985a, 1985b; Parrish & Tarone, 1986) and L. Dickerson were apparently claiming in their extension of the Labovian paradigm to L2. Beebe further questioned the parallel that L. Dickerson (1974) makes between L1 standardness or prestige variants and L2 correctness. Tarone (1985a, 1985b; Parrish & Tarone, 1986) presented arguments and data to show that attention to speech may not be, as she originally claimed, the single dimension underlying style shifting.

Many questions have been raised over the years about Labov's theory (e.g., Bell, 1984; Coupland, 1981; Gal, 1979; Rampton, 1985; Wolfson, 1976). Having used and supported the use of the Labovian paradigm in interlanguage research, Beebe (1982) somewhat ironically ended up arguing some of its shortcomings. She formulated three general reservations about Labov's claim that attention to speech is positively correlated in L1 with increased standardness; L. Dickerson's (1974) extention of the claim for L2, that it is positively correlated with increased correctness; and Tarone's (1982, 1983) view that it is the cause of style shifting in interlanguage. The three reservations are:

1. Attention to speech is sometimes negatively correlated with standardness or correctness (see Beebe, 1980; Burmeister & Ufert, 1980; Tarone, 1985b).

2. Style can be manifested in linguistic shifts that do not fall along the standardness or correctness dimensions. Shifts have been found in amount of talk, degree of elaboration, speech rate, duration, vocal intensity, pause and utterance length, stress, pitch, intonation, content expressed, and even complete code switches (see Ledvinka, 1971; Lieberman, 1967; Natalé, 1975; Webb, 1970).

3. Attention to speech is inadequate as an explanation for style shifting in most situations. It can be causally unrelated to style shifting in experimental or naturalistic situations. Social psychological variables such as feelings of ethnic identity, solidarity, topic expertise, and relative status of participants seem to provide explanations for style shifts (see Beebe, 1977a; Bourhis & Giles, 1977; Bourhis, Giles, Leyens, & Tajfel, 1979; Ervin-Tripp, 1968; Goldstein & Mooney, 1978; Thakerar, Giles, & Cheshire, 1982).

One problem with the extension of the Labovian paradigm to interlanguage is that interlanguage is influenced by at least two distinct systems—NL and TL—and even this is an oversimplification since neither system is homogeneous. Another problem is that attention to speech must be assumed; it cannot be measured. A third big problem is that Labov's methodology does not involve what he would describe as a "naturalistic analysis of style." To be fair, many of the criticisms of the Labovian paradigm and its extension to L2 data are a function of this restriction in its applicability. Labov gives absolutely no guidelines for extending his paradigm to include a naturalistic analysis, but second language researchers seeking to serve second language teachers are interested in tasks beyond the interview speech, reading, and listing that Labov used. Thus, we have *style* defined in terms of task, yet no real guidelines for deciding where the classroom tasks that teachers typically employ should be placed on the attention continuum. Moreover, we have absolutely no guidelines for deciding whether these tasks are "naturalistic" in Labov's sense or whether they are comparable to Labov's experimental tasks.

In the interest of studying style shifting in morphology and syntax, of pursuing overriding questions about style shifting, and of addressing another well-known theory of language performance, Krashen's monitor theory, Tarone (1985a, 1985b) decided not to deal with the problems inherent in defining style in terms of task. She notes that more is known about phonological style shifting than about shifts in interlanguage (IL) morphology or syntax. Thus, Tarone (1985b) investigated variable performance on six IL structures—three morphemes (the third person singular -*s*, the article, and the noun plural -*s*) and three grammatical structures (feminine gender on pronouns, third person direct object pronouns, and third person subject pronouns) in the speech of 20 ESL speakers—10 speakers of Arabic and 10 of Japanese. Tarone hypothesized that:

1. There would be systematic variability in the morphological and grammatical structures.
2. The subjects' performance on a grammaticality judgment task would differ from oral performance.
3. More than two styles (monitored and unmonitored in Krashen's terms) would be evidenced.
4. Styles defined by task could be ranged along a single continuous dimension defined by amount of attention to linguistic form.
5. Each style would contain some variable and some categorical regularities.
6. The vernacular style (defined as the one where the least attention is paid to speech) would show the least influence from the target language, whereas the careful style would display the greatest influence.

Support (though not always unqualified) was found for the first five hypotheses, but the sixth hypothesis was not confirmed. Only one of the six structures showed evidence that the vernacular was the least influenced by the target language. Tarone (1985b) writes:

> Some (like plural morphemes) did not shift at all as tasks required greater or lesser degrees of attention to language form. Some (like third person singular) improved with attention to form. And the accuracy rates of some (like articles and direct object pronouns) decreased on tasks which required greater attention to form. (Reprinted with permission of *Language Learning* from "Variability in Interlanguage Use: A Study of Style-Shifting in Morphology and Syntax" by E. Tarone, *Language Learning*, *35*, no. 3 (1985), p. 385.)

Tarone concludes that where there is task-related variability in interlanguage, the variability is related to more than just attention to form (1985a, 1985b). She notes that the type of discourse elicited by the task and, in particular, the level of cohesiveness required by that discourse may affect accuracy. Tarone's data are consistent with the position maintained by Beebe (1980, 1982) that high attention to speech is not consistently correlated with higher accuracy rates. They are counter to the position maintained by L. Dickerson (1974).

Sociolinguistic Transfer   The interest in systematic variability and the role of attention to speech (found in the work of the Dickersons, Tarone, and Beebe) is not the only vein of L2 research inspired by the Labovian paradigm. Schmidt (1977) asked another basic question: (cf. question 3 on page 47 of this chapter). "Does a sociolinguistic pattern in a native language transfer into the interlanguage of a nonnative speaker of English?"

In a previous study, Schmidt (1974) had demonstrated that the TH variable, as in the English word *three*, is a marker of socioeconomic class that has three variants in Egyptian Arabic: (1) a stop frequently used in speaking (but not reading), (2) a sibilant occurring often in reading but less frequently in speaking, and (3) interdental fricatives most commonly used in reading listed words. This statistically significant pattern in Arabic was found to appear at a statistically significant level in the English reading and listing of 34 male native speakers of Egyptian Arabic in a subsequent study (Schmidt, 1977). The English study was not designed to study socioeconomic variables, but later analysis of the data showed that there were significant differences between terminal and nonterminal secondary students. Thus, the study provided evidence that: (1) the TH marker of Egyptian Arabic was transferred into English along similar (though not identical) patterns of stylistic stratification, and (2) variation in English as well as the variation in Arabic reflected social stratification among speakers.

Beebe (1980) provided a second example of sociolinguistic rule transfer where a marker was transferred. Beebe (1974) demonstrated that Thais use [ɭ] for the Thai R variable an average of 95 percent of the time, even in interview conversation. They shifted to trilled [r̃] increasingly when moving from informal speech to reading passages aloud to reading word lists. In the study of nine Thai ESL learners referred to earlier, Beebe (1980) provided evidence that the Thais transferred the socially conditioned trilled Thai [r̃], which represents formality, into formal English listing. The Thais increased their use of trilled [r̃] to a statistically significant level in formal English listing style over interview conversation style.

Beebe (1983, in press) argues that these two examples represent only a small portion of the sociolinguistic transfer that occurs in second language performance. Presenting a taxonomy of sociolinguistic transfer, she contends that there are three main types: (1) sociolinguistic rule transfer, (2) transfer of sociocultural competence, and (3) socially motivated transfer. The first involves transfer of an L1 variable rule, as in Schmidt (1977) or Beebe (1980). The study of this type of transfer has been inspired by the Labovian paradigm and investigated using its method. The second type of transfer is also known as pragmatic transfer—transfer of sociocultural norms at the discourse level in writing or conversation. The third type of transfer in taxonomy focuses not on *what* is transferred but, rather, on *why* it is transferred. Socially motivated transfer possibly involves a categorical rule that is transferred to fulfill a social psychological purpose such as accommodating to one's interlocutor. These last two types of transfer, though sociolinguistic, are not inspired by the Labovian paradigm. Pragmatic transfer owes more to the work of Hymes, Searle, and Austin, whereas socially motivated transfer is more inspired by work on speech accommodation theory by Howard Giles and colleagues.

THE DYNAMIC PARADIGM

The *dynamic paradigm*, founded by Derek Bickerton and others, was pitted against the Labovian paradigm in the early 1970s, and second language researchers, like first language researchers, had to choose which paradigm to work under. The dynamic paradigm has fewer proponents in second language research circles, but some contend that it is better suited to SLA research than the Labovian paradigm.

The major proponent of using the dynamic paradigm for L2 research is Elizabeth Gatbonton-Segalowitz (1975; Gatbonton, 1978). Like Lonna Dickerson, she also wrote a dissertation attempting to show that interlanguage phonology varied systematically, but rather than focusing on task as a means of identifying styles, she emphasized variation as it reflected feelings of ethnic group affiliation. Thus, Gatbonton-Segalowitz's research was much more social psychological than was Dickerson's, reflecting influence from the social psychologists of language at McGill University, not simply the influence of Derek Bickerton. Gatbonton-Segalowitz contrasts the Labovian paradigm (which she and others refer to as the *quantitative paradigm*) and the dynamic paradigm. She summarizes that the Labovian paradigm involves determining linguistic environments where different variants occur, calculating frequency of occurrence, and then statistically estimating the probability of occurrence of each variant in each relevant linguistic (or social) environment. The result of this computation was a variable rule. Although proponents of the dynamic paradigm share the interest in variability, they do not view it as a function of a variable rule. Rather, they see it as a function of two competing categorical rules in similar linguistic environments. Taking the side of the dynamic paradigm, Gatbonton (1978) views second language phonological development as the product of two phases: *acquisition* and *replacement* (see Table 2.1).

Gatbonton-Segalowitz (1975) studied three phonological variables (/ð/, /θ/, and /h/) in the English as a second language of French Canadian subjects in Quebec. She was interested in more than verifying systematic variation; she wanted to test the applicability of the dynamic paradigm. Thus, she asked specifically whether the occurrence of correct and incorrect variants in the speech of the subjects was predictable and whether the systematicity or randomness of the data was related to the acquisition and replacement of correct and incorrect variants. Of 21 observed speech patterns, all but 6 conformed to Gatbonton-Segalowitz's *gradual diffusion* model to a statistically significant

Table 2.1   GRADUAL DIFFUSION MODEL

Stages	EC1	EC2	EC3
	Acquisition phase		
a	1	1	1
b	1,2	1	1
c	1,2	1,2	1
d	1,2	1,2	1,2
	Replacement phase		
e	2	1,2	1,2
f	2	2	1,2
g	2	2	2

Source: Reprinted with permission of the *Canadian Modern Language Review* from "Patterned Phonetic Variability in Second-Language Speech: A Gradual Diffusion Model" by Elizabeth Gatbonton, *Canadian Modern Language Review, 34*, no. 3 (1978), p. 337.

Notes: EC = environment category; 1 = incorrect variant; 2 = correct variant.

degree ($p < .001$) for voiced /ð/. Twenty-two out of 27 matched the model to a significant degree for /θ/, and 24 out of 27 did for /h/ in the reading data. This, Gatbonton-Segalowitz argued, showed that the gradual diffusion model was appropriate and predictive in describing second language phonological development. It is, in fact, an appealing model in that it recognizes implicational relationships among variants to be acquired (i.e., acquisition of one may presume previous acquisition of another). It also makes clear claims about developmental stages, which the Labovian paradigm does not, and which teachers or researchers can test empirically with longitudinal data on second language learners. Thus, although less work has been done using this paradigm, there is some reason to favor its use for SLA research. In fact, Huebner (1979, 1983) has done exactly such a longitudinal study as the model invites. His study of Ge, a native speaker of Hmong and a fluent speaker of Lao, documents this Hmong immigrant's progress in English, starting less than one month after his arrival in Hawaii.

DESCRIPTIVE RESEARCH ON COMMUNICATIVE COMPETENCE

Research on *communicative competence* is a broad area, which can be classified into five categories:

1. Speech acts
2. Tone or emotion
3. Conversational features
4. Conversational management
5. Topic selection

The majority of the research on communicative competence focuses on speech act realization, and this chapter will deal exclusively with this category. Well-known research exists on apologies, invitations, compliments, refusals, requests, complaints, and expressions of gratitude.

Influenced by an early version of Fraser (1980), Cohen and Olshtain (1981) analyzed the apologies of 44 college students in Israel—32 native speakers of Hebrew learning intermediate-level ESL and 12 native English speakers. They compared native English, native Hebrew, and Israeli ESL apologies, delineating five semantic formulas that speakers use to realize an apology:

1. Direct apology (e.g., "I apologize" or "I'm sorry")
2. Explanation of why we did what we did
3. Acceptance of responsibility (e.g., "It's all my fault")
4. Offer of repair (e.g., "Let me pay for it")
5. Promise of forbearance (e.g., "It'll never happen again")

In written role-played responses, Cohen and Olshtain found that Israeli ESL students were less likely to offer repair, were less likely to acknowledge responsibility, and expressed less intensity of regret than did American native speakers of English. Cohen and Olshtain argue that their patterns often (though not always) reflect sociocultural transfer of native Hebrew patterns.

Olshtain (1983) reported on a related study of apologies in Israel where the target language was Hebrew, rather than English. She collected data from 63 subjects—36 subjects (12 each) using native English, Russian, or Hebrew, and 27 from L1 English or Russian backgrounds using Hebrew as a second language. She found that the five semantic formulas were "universal" (i.e., present in all three languages studied). The average frequency of appearance for each formula, however, was not consistent across languages. English had the highest rate of apology on all semantic formulas, and Hebrew had the lowest on all except the offer of repair. Thus, the general pattern was:

English > Russian > Hebrew

(In the offer of repair, native Hebrew apologies outnumbered Russian.)

Olshtain (1983) argues that apologies are influenced by a host of different factors, including NL transfer, perception of language specificity versus universality, situation, perceived seriousness of the offense, status or distance of the apologizee. A great deal of other work is being done or has been done on apologies, as well as on requests (Blum-Kulka, 1982), particularly by researchers working on CCSARP—the Cross-Cultural Speech Act Realization Project—an international effort to look at requests and apologies in various native languages and in ESL in Israel, Europe, the United States, Canada, and Australia (Blum-Kulka & Olshtain, 1984). A considerable amount of work has also been done on complaints (Giddens, 1981; Olshtain & Weinbach, 1986; Rader, 1977).

Wolfson has studied compliments, invitations, greetings, partings, and judgments, with most detail on compliments and invitations as spoken natively in English (Manes & Wolfson, 1981; Wolfson, 1981, 1983a, 1983b; Wolfson, D'Amico-Reisner & Huber, 1983; Wolfson & Manes, 1980). Based on a corpus of 686 compliments, she discovered that three syntactic patterns accounted for 85 percent of the data and that nine patterns accounted for 97.2 percent of the data. The largest category included compliments like "Your dress is beautiful," using five common adjectives. Clearly the repetitive and formulaic nature of compliments, combined with their important function in establishing rapport, makes them a fine candidate for explicit teaching early on in ESL classes.

Invitations, on the other hand, were not so short, formulaic, or obvious. In fact, Wolfson notes that many foreign students' complaints about the "insincerity" of Americans arise from misunderstandings about invitations. A request to come to dinner at a specific time and place (e.g., "Would you like to come to dinner tomorrow night?") is a real invitation in English, whereas "We must get together some time" is not a real invitation. It's merely what Wolfson calls a "statement of good intention," unless, of course, subsequent negotiation turns it into a full-fledged invitation. Invitations, because they are a long, negotiated sequence and not a short formula, like compliments, are much subtler and harder for ESL students to grasp. They do not lend themselves to drill, and the entire social interaction of invitation and acceptance or refusal may not be appropriate for the lowest language learning levels.

Expressions of gratitude are another speech act that have come under recent scrutiny. Eisenstein and Bodman (1986) looked at both native and nonnative thank-you's on questionnaires asking subjects to write what they thought they would say when they received a gift, favor, reward, or service. The researchers found all kinds of difficulties, ranging from grammatical or lexical problems (e.g., "I very appreciate") to other sources of error. Most interestingly, some students did not yet have the sociocultural competence in English to know when to express gratitude. In a situation where thanks were required, one Asian student told the researchers, "I would be so grateful, I wouldn't say anything at all." Sociocultural competence involves following the social norms that govern a verbal interaction—including knowing when to speak and when to say nothing at all.

Beebe, Takahashi, and Uliss-Weltz (in press) investigated the speech act of refusals, finding considerable evidence for sociocultural transfer in the order, frequency, and content of semantic formulas used. Using the written role-play method of Cohen and Olshtain (1981), the researchers compared 20 Japanese speaking Japanese, 20 Japanese speaking English, and 20 Americans speaking English. There were many differences in the ordering of semantic formulas. As an example, excuses were used in most role-play situations by most of the subjects in each group. Japanese speakers of English, however, resembled Japanese native speakers in making their excuses earlier. Americans tend to start out by refusing a request with a statement of positive feeling—for example, "I'd love to help you out." Then they express regret ("but I'm sorry"), and finally they make their excuse ("I have to go to a funeral that day"). Japanese start out with the statement of regret and go next to the excuse, skipping the statement of positive feeling with a lower status interlocutor. With a higher status interlocutor, they use it or substitute an expression of empathy (e.g., "I understand your situation") which Americans are much less prone to doing. Thus, Japanese speaking English show transfer from native Japanese in the order in which they use semantic formulas. They also show transfer in the frequency of usage of various formulas. For example, a lower status Japanese more frequently expresses apology or regret when asked by the boss to stay late at the office. Also, Japanese express empathy 60 percent of the time to an employee when refusing in Japanese a request for a raise. In English, they do so 20 percent of the time. Americans, however, never did so. Clearly, the patterns are different across cultures, and the ESL pattern lies between the native Japanese and the native American patterns. And not just the countable features are different. Japanese speakers of English often resemble their native Japanese counterparts in the content of their refusals. They make excuses, as Americans do, but the excuses are not very specific by American standards. In refusing the boss's invitation to a party, the Japanese might say without explanation "Sunday will be inconvenient" or "I have some things to take care of at home." This is not the type of airtight excuse Americans expect and prefer.

SPEECH ACCOMMODATION THEORY

Although *speech accommodation theory* has been developed by a large number of scholars, the founder and moving force behind its development has been Howard Giles, a British social psychologist. Giles has built the theory by integrating four established social psychological theories and applying them to the study of variation in language use and acquisition. In addition to integrating the four social psychological theories, Giles has developed speech accommodation theory by working with a very broad network of social psychologists and linguists, including Bourhis, St. Clair, Smith, Powesland, St. Jacques, Cheshire, Scherer, Taylor, Ryan, Byrne, Hildebrand, Lambert, Genesee, Beebe, and many others—too many to name.

Speech accommodation theory has addressed three major questions:

1. How can we describe speech variation?
2. How can we explain speech variation?
3. How can we explain other speakers' reactions to and interpretations of speech variation?

Research on speech accommodation has relied on a set of descriptive linguistic labels to deal with the first question, but first and foremost in its priorities is looking at the *why* of speech variation more than the *what*. The theory is particularly directed at explaining the interaction between speakers in terms of their feelings, values, and motives.

First, let us look at the descriptive labels that speech accommodation theorists use to describe different types of speech variation. To put it succinctly, speech accommodation refers to adjustments in one's speech. Speakers can adjust their speech to become more similar to the speech of their interlocutor. In this case, their adjustment is known as *convergence*. An example of this would be the case of American speakers who, when talking to a speaker of British English, drop postvocalic /r/ as in the word *aren't*, say they were "in hospital" instead of "in the hospital" or refer to the "lorry" transporting fruits and vegetables to the supermarket. Speakers can also adjust their speech to become *less* similar to the speech of their interlocutor, an adjustment known as *divergence*. Instead of imitating the style of the interlocutor, the speaker diverges from the listener, for example when a French Canadian shopkeeper who is bilingual in French and English responds in French to an English Canadian customer who addresses him in English. Of course, there is always the possibility that a speaker does not change his or her speech. This phenomenon is known as *speech maintenance*. Since Giles views speech maintenance as a failure or refusal to converge toward the interlocutor (the norm in most situations), it is seen as a subtype of divergence. Speech accommodation of all types is a psychological phenomenon, but it has, of course, a linguistic reflex. Thus, Giles and colleagues may speak of *psychological convergence*, a situation where the speaker intends to converge (i.e., on the psychological level) but in reality diverges (i.e., on the linguistic level). Very often the speaker converges toward a stereotype or expected norm. An example of this occurs when a lower-middle-class speaker hypercorrects when speaking to an upper-middle-class interlocutor, saying "a person like I." The intention is to sound more upper class, but the reality shows that the speaker is not in command of the prescriptive, prestige rule that the upper-middle-class interlocutor probably uses without thinking.

As seen from the preceding examples, speech accommodation can involve shifts in all linguistic domains (phonology, lexicon, content, speech rate, etc.) and can involve shifts in style within one language as well as code switches or shifts from using one language to using another. Most frequently, speech accommodation theorists speak of "speech shifts," but many speech shifts are the same as the "style shifts" referred to by proponents of the Labovian paradigm. Speech shifts seems to be the more general category, however, because it includes virtually any variation, whether within form per se (e.g., phonology/grammar) or outside it (e.g., in rate of speech), whether within a single language or across languages.

Before we turn to the explanations for shifts and evaluations of these shifts, it is important to discuss a couple of other descriptive labels used by speech accommodation theorists. Both convergence and divergence, it should be noted, can be seen as upward or downward. Upward convergence would occur in the situation of a job interview, where the applicant converges toward the boss, the person with the higher status. If the boss converged toward the employee, this would be labeled downward convergence. Similarly, divergence can be upward or downward. When speakers of a nonstandard dialect emphasize the nonstandard features of their speech to interlocutors who speak standard dialect, this could be viewed as downward divergence. When the speaker of standard dialect emphasizes his or her standardness, this could be viewed as upward divergence.

Behind the various manifestations of accommodation (e.g., convergence, divergence) lie the explanations for these different types of speech shifts and the reactions speakers have to them when they are used by others. As previously mentioned, speech accommodation theory is an umbrella theory covering four social psychological theories established to explain nonlinguistic phenomena. First, and perhaps foremost, there is *similarity attraction theory* (Bishop, 1979; Byrne, 1969), which claims that we are most attracted to people whose beliefs, values, and attitudes are similar to our own. Giles and Smith (1979) use similarity attraction theory to explain most linguistic convergence. They also explain that not only does convergence result in approval from others, but that the greater one's need for approval, the greater will be the tendency to converge.

A second theory subsumed under the speech accommodation umbrella is *social exchange theory* (Homans, 1961). According to this theory, there are trade-offs involved in converging or diverging. Social exchange theory says that we weigh the costs and the rewards and then tend to choose the alternative that will maximize the rewards and minimize the costs. Most frequently, convergence is a strategy that will lead to social approval, simply on the basis of similarity attraction. In a situation of unequal status, such as a job interview, we might expect the job applicant to converge toward the speech of the job interviewer. Failure to converge or outright divergence might be perceived as hostile; thus, convergence, which usually brings with it approval, is the expected behavior. There are times, however, when convergent acts do not entail a positive outcome. Adolescents frequently fail to converge toward the more standard language of their parents and teachers, especially in the presence of their peers. Thus, a black teenager in class may use nonstandard Black English and incur the disapproval of the teacher simply because this cost is outweighed by the reward of gaining approval from other students in the room who prefer to use Black English. Similarly, second language learners may never attain nativelike proficiency to the best of their ability because they may find that the reward of being fluent in the target language is not worth the cost in lost identification and solidarity with their own native language group.

The third theory comprised by speech accommodation theory is *causal attribution* (Jones & Davis, 1965; Kelly, 1967). According to causal attribution theory, people do not take the behavior of others at face value. Rather, they evaluate their motives and intentions first and then attribute the cause of their behavior. Thus, if a male employee devotes a huge amount of time to helping female employees in the same corporation, we do not automatically assume that he is generous, hard-working, or devoted to the good of the company. If a wealthy tycoon donates a huge sum to charity, we do not automatically assume that he is altruistic—we suspect the need for a tax deduction. If a young lawyer stays late at the office night after night, we do not automatically credit him or her with being industrious. Rather, we first look for a motive and then decide that the lawyer is unhappily married, or wants to be a partner. Just as there is a constant process of causal attribution going on in nonlinguistic behavior, there is also causal attribution going on whenever we interact linguistically with others. Thus, when someone converges toward your speech style, you are likely to search for the motive or intention before automatically giving your approval. Causal attribution is a complex process. For instance, if a black person uses Black English with another black, the process may be very favorably received, whereas if a white person does the very same thing, the black interlocutor is likely to suspect some motive he or she finds annoying. The black interlocutor may not expect or accept such a show of solidarity from a nonblack but, rather, may suspect that the nonblack is trying to get something.

Convergence between native and nonnative is just as tricky as convergence across ethnic or racial boundaries. If, for example, a native speaker of English, say a teacher, simplifies his or her English to help a nonnative speaker understand what is being said, this may be very favorably evaluated because the process of causal attribution may lead the nonnative to conclude that the speech shift is done with altruistic intentions. But not all speech shifts to nonnatives get such a warm reception. Sometimes, when well-meaning native speakers oversimplify the speech they direct to nonnatives, the nonnatives find them condescending. They may feel that the native speaker is implying they are stupid or slow or simply not very fluent. The same type of negative evaluation occurs when native speakers misguidedly speak loudly to nonnatives, who complain that they are not deaf. In sum, although convergence most frequently results in a favorable reaction, it can be a two-edged sword; it is the process of causal attribution that determines whether or not convergence will be appreciated.

Intergroup distinctiveness (Tajfel, 1974, 1978) is a fourth theory subsumed under the rubric of accommodation theory. This theory states that members of different social groups make comparisons across groups on valued social dimensions. They look to see what ethnic characteristics exist, which group has more possessions, or who has more social prestige. They compare themselves across groups and, rather than try to reduce differences, they may try to accentuate differences, looking for ways to assert their intergroup distinctiveness and an alleged superiority over the other group. If, for example, we look at black and white Americans, we find that there are distinctive patterns in dress, hairstyle, body language, and very strikingly their use of English. These 6differences are not just an automatic distinctiveness related to different lifestyles and social circumstances, they are differences that are continually reinforced. Black English and standard English are said to be moving farther and farther apart. This seems to be a matter of intergroup distinctiveness. The members of both groups look for ways to make themselves psychologically distinct in a favorable way according to their own values. Thus both groups strongly value their distinctive way of speaking English. This fact is often obscured by the prestige attached to standard English in predominantly white institutions—radio and TV stations, schools, big corporations, and the like. But it is obviously not a universal prestige. Black adolescents have repeatedly been shown to favor Black English (see Labov, 1972a). And as one black student of mine said to a white classmate who suggested that he use standard English all the time, "No one's goin' to tell me how to talk to my mama!" Black English is a symbol of intimacy and solidarity among black people in America and, as such, is valued by the black community as an important feature of intergroup distinctiveness from the white community.

As mentioned earlier, speech accommodation research focuses on explaining both what people actually do when they vary their speech and the way they evaluate others who vary their speech. There are a huge number of empirical studies done on these topics, making a complete review impossible. A few studies are mentioned here to highlight some of the issues that have been addressed. First, looking at what people actually said, Natalé (1975) found that there was more convergence in volume and pause length toward an interlocutor's speech among speakers with a high need for approval than among speakers with a low need for approval. Bourhis and Giles (1977) had ethnically Welsh native speakers of English respond in English to an RP-accented Englishman and found that the type of motivation the subject had was related to his or her level of convergence. Instrumentally motivated subjects were more likely to converge, whereas integratively motivated subjects were more likely to diverge by increasing their Welsh accent in English. This divergence tended to occur when intergroup differences were emphasized, and particularly when ethnic Welsh identity was being threatened by negative statements being addressed to the subject. Bourhis, Giles, Leyens, and Tajfel (1979) conducted a similar study in Belgium. Flemish subjects were asked to respond to a francophone speaker in English. When intergroup distinctions were not specifically mentioned, subjects did not diverge into Flemish when speaking to the francophone. When intergroup distinctions were made explicit, however, 50 percent of the subjects diverged from English into Flemish.

Another type of study was done by Thakerar, Giles, and Cheshire (1982) who tape recorded conversations between British nurses of unequal rank in their occupational status. They looked at how their speech was rated by judges in terms of convergence and also actually tabulated the use of /ʔ/ versus /t/ in their speech. Both analyses turned up the same result. Higher status nurses were judged to decrease their speech rate and become less standard, whereas lower status nurses were judged to increase their speech rate and their standardness. Higher status nurses were also found to use a higher proportion of the nonstandard /ʔ/, and lower status nurses were found to use a higher proportion of the standard /t/. The authors use these findings to document the phenomenon of psychological convergence and to demonstrate that even when speakers wish to converge on the psychological level, they may end up diverging on the descriptive linguistic level. The study shows that speakers may be converging toward a stereotype of their interlocutor's speech, not toward the actual pattern being used in the interaction.

Several examples of research on speakers' evaluations of their interlocutors give us a small taste of the vast amount of research that has been carried out on reactions to speech. In general, it has been found that speakers with high-prestige accents are positively valued on many dimensions (Giles & Powesland, 1975; Giles & Smith, 1979). Giles (1979) found that high-prestige RP-accented British speakers were seen as more intelligent, self-confident, industrious, and determined than speakers who had regional British accents. Looking at female instead of male subjects, Elyan, Smith, Giles, and Bourhis (1978) found that RP-accented women were viewed as more competent, independent, adventurous, and feminine, but as less weak. Upward convergence seemed to have more rewards for females than for males. Bourhis, Giles, and Lambert (1975) looked at reactions to upward and downward convergence and divergence. They found that upward convergence was the most successfully perceived strategy, and the upward converger was rated higher in intelligence. Bourhis and Genesee (1980) looked at evaluations of a recorded conversation between a French Canadian salesman and an English Canadian customer. By making different versions of the tape in which the two interlocutors used different languages with each other, they were able to investigate how convergence in terms of the language used (not merely the accent) was valued. Failure to converge (i.e., maintenance of French) by the French Canadian salesman was devalued, not surprisingly, but convergence by the English Canadian customer using French to the salesman did not result in higher ratings. Thus, convergence is not always positively valued. In this situation, perhaps, the use of English by the English Canadian customer was considered to be a proper norm despite the fact that it represented divergence.

Thus far, it has appeared that speech accommodation research has been aimed at the explanation of speech performance, not at the process of acquisition. This, however, is misleading. In fact, there exist two models of second language acquisition that are framed in terms of speech accommodation theory (see Ball & Giles's model as revised in Beebe & Giles, 1984; Giles & Byrne, 1982). Furthermore, Trudgill (1981) proposed that we view accommodation as consisting of two types: *short-term accommodation*, which accounts for speech shifts in performance at one point in time, and *long-term accommodation*, which accounts for shifts that occur in language over time. The latter can be used as a way of analyzing shifts in native dialects over time or can be used equally well to explain shifts among nonnative speakers toward or away from their target second language. It is, therefore, long-term accommodation that is of most interest to the researcher on second language acquisition.

Although Giles and Byrne (1982) do not explicitly label their intergroup approach to second language acquisition as a process of long-term accommodation, it is specifically this process that they are attempting to explain when they extend intergroup theory to the second language learning context. The intergroup approach to SLA is quite complex but can be summarized for the instrumentally motivated group as follows:

. . . we propose that subordinate group members will most likely acquire nativelike proficiency in the dominant group's language when:

(1a) ingroup identification is weak and/or L1 is not a salient dimension of ethnic group membership;

(2a) quiescent inter-ethnic comparisons exist (e.g., no awareness of cognitive alternatives to inferiority);

(3a) perceived ingroup vitality is low;

(4a) perceived ingroup boundaries are soft and open;

(5a) strong identification exists with many other social categories, each of which provides adequate group identities and a satisfactory intragroup status. (Reprinted with permission of the *Journal of Multicultural and Multilingual Development* from "An Intergroup Approach to Second Language Acquisition" by H. Giles and J. L. Byrne, *Journal of Multicultural and Multilingual Development, 3* (1982), pp. 34–35.)

Giles and Byrne make the opposite prediction, namely, that subordinate group members will probably not achieve nativelike competence if conditions (1b) to (5b), the opposites of (1a) to (5a), are operant. In the first scenario, Giles and Byrne anticipate that the five conditions provide an integrative orientation (i.e., where acquisition is for personal enrichment and cultural assimilation) and create a situation where language acquisition is *additive* (i.e., where the first language will not be lost). In the second scenario, the group members identify strongly with each other and will not acquire the second language well, despite economic or political advantages, because they will perceive the social cost to their group to be high. There will be fear of assimilation—fear of a *subtractive* bilingualism situation where learning the second language ultimately leads to loss of the first language by the group.

These examples of research on language performance at one point in time and on language acquisition over a period of time are only the tip of the iceberg. Speech accommodation theory is very powerful and provides a rich framework for understanding the variations that occur in speech in terms of the feelings, values, and motives behind them. Despite the strength of this approach, it should be noted, however, that not all variation in speech is a matter of accommodation. Other motivations for variation exist, such as conforming to norms; negotiation of one's identity; and the drive for positive, competent self-presentation (see Beebe & Giles, 1984).

ATTITUDES AND MOTIVATION IN SLA

In the 1950s a group of researchers at McGill University in Montreal, Quebec, started a line of inquiry that continues today and that has had a profound effect on our understanding of second language acquisition. This research has been carried out by social psychologists of language and focuses primarily on the attitudes and motivations that affect SLA. The work generated by this group is quite vast and will be dealt with somewhat summarily here, partly because it would be impossible to cover it in any detail. It is being discussed very briefly also because the research does not quite fit the mold of research that is being covered in this chapter. The other approaches to second language acquisition focus on variation—how speech performance differs from one moment to another or from one situation to another. Giles's speech accommodation theory has now begun to look at variation in proficiency attained, and this has been discussed briefly. The research done in French Canada focuses exclusively on different outcomes under different social psychological conditions. It does not deal at all with performance variation, which has been the major theme of this chapter, nor has it been focused on second language acquisition as it is narrowly defined. Rather, it has been framed in terms of bilingualism—that is, second language acquisition that occurs in a bilingual environment. Nevertheless, it would not seem proper to write about social factors in SLA while ignoring the very large and impressive body of research done in and around Montreal on achievement.

Lambert and his former student, Gardner, have worked so closely together since the late 1950s that it seems a bit unfair to name Lambert as the sole mentor for research in this area. They have worked collaboratively as a team and in conjunction with many other researchers (e.g., Smythe, Clément, Genesee, Tucker, Fillenbaum, Hodgson, Anisfeld, Peal). Their work has been extensive (Gardner, 1985; Gardner & Lambert, 1972a), but we might summarize by saying that it has centered around answering three questions:

1. What are people's attitudes toward language—that is, how do they evaluate speakers on the basis of language use?
2. How can we measure and describe motivational orientations?
3. What conditions—aptitude, intelligence, and particularly social psychological conditions related to attitudes and motivations—facilitate (or impede) second language development?

In order to answer the first question—how people evaluate other speakers based on their use of language—Lambert and Gardner, with others, developed the *matched guise* procedure in the late 1950s (Lambert, Hodgson, Gardner, & Fillenbaum, 1960; W. E. Lambert, 1967). Matched guise involved making two tape recordings—one of a French Canadian voice and one of an English Canadian voice. Sometimes a French French voice was also used. Although subjects in the research thought they were listening to a different person, they were actually hearing a bilingual using two languages—one and the same person being heard in different "guises." The subjects evaluated the speakers on a range of different characteristics. English Canadians were found to have a relatively pejorative perception of French Canadians; they rated the bilingual as less intelligent, less trustworthy, shorter, and less attractive in his French language guise than in his English language guise. Interestingly, however, French Canadians did not reciprocate by downgrading the opposite group. Instead, they downgraded members of their own group in relation to English Canadians, except when they rated them for kindness, and they were even harsher in their negative perceptions of French Canadians than English Canadians were (W. E. Lambert, 1979). S. M. Lambert (1973) also found that they downgraded themselves relative to French French. Teachers and students held the same views about the English Canadian, French Canadian, and French French speakers. As W. E. Lambert (1979) has pointed out, both teachers and parents can unconsciously help perpetuate negative images held by the minority group. Canadian French parents do so when they choose to send their children to English language schools.

Turning now to the second major question of the research done in the Lambert-Gardner tradition, let us ask how motivational orientations that affect second language learning can be measured and described. Gardner and Lambert (1972a) have described two motivational orientations: integrative and instrumental. A questionnaire was used to measure the extent to which subjects were integrative or instrumental in their orientation. *Integrative orientation* for English speakers is indicated by those who say that learning French will help them understand French people and the French way of life, make good friends among French-speaking people, think and behave as French people do, or meet and converse with more and varied people. Those who endorse one of the following reasons for learning French were judged to have an *instrumental orientation*: using French to get a job, needing to know a foreign language for social recognition, feeling that knowledge of French is a sign of being an educated person, or needing French to finish high school. Although Lambert and Gardner are most famous for their research on motivational orientations, it is important to note that, when they did their research in the American setting, they also asked questions trying to assess students' feelings of anomie, authoritarianism, ethnocentrism, preference for America over France, and desire to learn French.

This leads us to the final and most important question on which the Canadian research is centered: What social psychological conditions facilitate second language acquisition, and to what extent are aptitude and intelligence predictors of successful achievement? Gardner and Lambert (1972b) tested English-speaking Montreal high school students studying French as a second language for linguistic aptitude, verbal intelligence, and a range of attitudinal and motivational variables. They found that "maximum prediction of success in second-language acquisition was obtained from tests of: verbal intelligence, intensity of motivation to learn the other language, students' purposes in studying that language, and one index of linguistic aptitude" (p. 197). Gardner (in Gardner & Lambert, 1972a, based on doctoral research, 1960) studied 83 English-speaking high school students in Montreal and found, in short, that an integrative motivation was important for successful second language acquisition. He also found that an integrative orientation reflected the same orientation on the part of the student's parents and that it was fostered by favorable attitudes held by the parents about the target language community.

In addition to the large number of studies conducted in French Canada, Gardner and Lambert went to three areas of the United States to investigate the importance of attitudes and motivation among English-speaking and minority French-speaking learners of French, comparing the French-speaking learners in their English. They studied subjects in Maine, Connecticut, and Louisiana. Then they went out to test their findings in a very different type of setting, the Philippines, where English is the second national language and is the medium of instruction in the schools, not to mention the vehicle for economic success. Instrumental motivation was very important for French Americans learning English. This was not the case for the Anglo-Americans learning French, who, like the English Canadians learning French, needed an integrative motivation for success (see p. 130). In the Philippines, English has enormous instrumental value, and instrumental orientation is very important. Gardner and Lambert (1972a) write:

> . . . Filipino students who approach the study of English with instrumental orientation and who receive parental support for this outlook were clearly successful in developing proficiency in the language. Thus, it seems that in settings where there is an urgency about mastering a second language—as there is in the Philippines and in North America for members of linguistic minority groups—the instrumental approach to language study is extremely effective. (Reprinted with permission of Robert Gardner from *Attitudes and Motivation in Second-Language Learning* by R. C. Gardner and W. E. Lambert, Rowley, MA: Newbury House, 1972, p. 141.)

They point out that for a particular subgroup of Filipinos, integrative motivation was nevertheless important. Summarizing their position, they write:

> . . . the typical student of *foreign* languages in North America will profit more if he is helped to develop an integrative outlook toward the group

whose language is being offered. For him, an instrumental approach has little significance and little motive force. However, for members of ethnic minority groups in North America as for those living in nations that have imported prestigious world languages and made them important national languages, the picture changes. Learning a *second* language of national or worldwide significance is then indispensable, and both instrumental and integrative orientations towards the learning task must be developed. (Reprinted with permission of Robert Gardner from *Attitudes and Motivation in Second-Language Learning* by R. C. Gardner and W. E. Lambert, Rowley, MA: Newbury House, 1972, p. 142; emphasis in original.)

CONCLUSION

This chapter has described five major approaches to the disciplines of sociolinguistics and the social psychology of language as they relate to the study of second language acquisition. It is clear that this interdisciplinary field has made tremendous strides and that there is a depth and variety to the existing research. The five approaches that I have chosen to discuss do not do justice to the scope of the work being done. For example, reactions to speech, particularly dialect sensitivity (see Eisenstein, 1982, 1983) constitute an important area of study. Also, the study of pragmatic ability in a second language is much larger and richer than simply the discussion of speech act realization (see Rintell, 1981, on deference; Scarcella, 1979, on politeness; and Thomas, 1983, on types of cross-cultural pragmatic failure). Although this chapter is by no means all-inclusive, it is hoped that its organization will provide a guideline to the themes and issues currently being discussed in sociolinguistics and second language acquisition.

REFERENCES

Adjemian, C. On the nature of interlanguage systems. *Language Learning*, 1976, *26*(2), 297–320.

Austin, J. L. *How to do things with words.* Cambridge, MA, and Oxford: Harvard University Press and Oxford University Press, 1962.

Bailey, C.-J. N. Trying to talk in the new paradigm. *Papers in Linguistics*, 1971 *4*(2), 312–338.

Bailey, C.-J. N. *Variation and linguistic theory.* Arlington, VA: Center for Applied Linguistics, 1973.

Beebe, L. M. Socially conditioned variation in Bangkok Thai. Unpublished doctoral dissertation, University of Michigan, 1974.

Beebe, L. M. Dialect code-switching of bilingual children in their second language. *CUNY Forum*, 1977a, *3*, 141–158.

Beebe, L. M. The influence of the listener on code-switching. *Language Learning*, 1977b, *27*(2), 331–340.

Beebe, L. M. Sociolinguistic variation and style shifting in second language acquisition. *Language Learning*, 1980, *30*(2), 433–448.

Beebe, L. M. Reservations about the Labovian paradigm of style shifting and its extension to the study of interlanguage. Paper presented at the Third Annual TESOL and Sociolinguistics Colloquium, TESOL Convention, Honolulu, 1982. Expanded version, The social psychological basis of style shifting. Plenary session paper presented at Second Language Research Forum, University of California at Los Angeles, 1982.

Beebe, L. M. Examining transfer from a sociolinguistic perspective. Paper presented at Los Angeles Second Language Research Forum, November 12, 1983.

Beebe, L. M. Input: Choosing the right stuff. In S. M. Gass & C. G. Madden (Eds.), *Input in second language acquisition*. Rowley, MA: Newbury House, 1985.

Beebe, L. M. Sociolinguistic transfer: Chapter 1. *The social psychological basis of second language acquisition*. London: Longman, in press.

Beebe, L. M., & Giles, H. Speech accommodation theories: A discussion in terms of second-language acquisition. *International Journal of the Sociology of Language*, 1984, *46*, 5-32.

Beebe, L. M., Takahashi, T., & Uliss-Weltz, R. Pragmatic transfer in ESL refusals. In R. C. Scarcella, E. Andersen, & S. D. Krashen (Eds.), *On the development of communicative competence in a second language*. Rowley, MA: Newbury House, in press.

Beebe, L. M., & Zuengler, J. Accommodation theory: An explanation for style shifting in second language dialects. In N. Wolfson & E. Judd (Eds.), *Sociolinguistics and language acquisition*. Rowley, MA: Newbury House, 1983.

Bell, A. Language style as audience design. *Language in Society*, 1984, *13*, 145-204.

Bishop, G. D. Perceived similarity in interracial attitudes and behaviors: The effects of belief and dialect style. *Journal of Applied Social Psychology*, 1979, *9*(5), 446-465.

Blum-Kulka, S. Learning to say what you mean in a second language: A study of the speech act performance of learners of Hebrew as a second language. *Applied Linguistics*, 1982, *3*(1), 29-59.

Blum-Kulka, S., & Olshtain, E. Requests and apologies: A cross-cultural study of speech act realization patterns. *Applied Linguistics*, 1984, *5*(3), 196-213.

Bourhis, R. Y., & Genesee, F. Evaluative reactions to code-switching strategies in Montreal. In H. Giles, W. P. Robinson, & P. Smith (Eds.), *Language: Social psychological perspectives*. Oxford: Pergamon Press, 1980.

Bourhis, R. Y., & Giles, H. The language of intergroup distinctiveness. In H. Giles (Ed.), *Language, ethnicity and intergroup relations*. New York: Academic Press, 1977.

Bourhis, R. Y., Giles, H., & Lambert, W. Some consequences of accommodating one's style of speech: A cross-national investigation. *International Journal of the Sociology of Language*, 1975, *6*, 55-72.

Bourhis, R. Y., Giles, H., Leyens, J. P., & Tajfel, H. Psycholinguistic distinctiveness: Language divergence in Belgium. In H. Giles and R. N. St. Clair (Eds.), *Language and social psychology*. Baltimore: University Park Press, 1979.

Burmeister, H., & Ufert, D. Strategy switching. In S. W. Felix (Ed.), *Second language development: Trends and issues*. Tübingen: Gunter Narr Verlag, 1980.

Byrne, D. Attitudes and attention. *Advances in Experimental Social Psychology*, 1969, *4*, 35-89.

Cohen, A., & Olshtain, E. Developing a measure of sociocultural competence: The case of apology. *Language Learning*, 1981, *31*(1), 113-134.

Coupland, N. J. R. Social differentiation of functional language use: A sociolinguistic investigation of travel agency talk. Unpublished doctoral dissertation, UWIST, 1981.

Dickerson, L. Internal and external patterning of phonological variability in the speech of Japanese learners of English. Unpublished doctoral dissertation, University of Illinois, Urbana, 1974.

Dickerson, L. The learner's interlanguage as a system of variable rules. *TESOL Quarterly*, 1975, *9*(4), 401-407.

Dickerson, L., & Dickerson, W. Interlanguage phonology: Current research and future directions. In S. P. Corder and E. Roulet (Eds.), *The notions of simplification, interlanguages and pidgins and their relation to second language pedagogy*. Neuchâtel: Faculté des Lettres, 1977.

Dickerson, W. The psycholinguistic unity of language learning and language change. *Language Learning*, 1976, *26*(2), 215-231.

Dowd, J. Phonological variation in L2 speech: The effects of emotional questions and field-dependence/field-independence on second language performance. Unpublished doctoral dissertation, Teachers College, Columbia University, 1984.

Dulay, H., Burt, M., & Krashen, S. D. *Language two*. Oxford: Oxford University Press, 1982.

Eisenstein, M. A study of social variation in adult second language acquisition. *Language Learning*, 1982, *32*(2), 367-391.

Eisenstein, M. Native reactions to non-native speech: A review of empirical research. *Studies in Second Language Acquisition*, 1983, *5*(2), 160-176.

Eisenstein, M., & Bodman, J. "I very appreciate": Expressions of gratitude by native and non-native speakers of American English. *Applied Linguistics*, 1986, *7*(2), 167-185.

Elyan, O., Smith, P., Giles, H., & Bourhis, R. Y. RP-accented female speech: The voice of androgyny? In P. Trudgill (Ed.), *Sociolinguistic patterns in British English*. London: Arnold, 1978.

Ervin-Tripp, S. An analysis of the interaction of language, topic, and listener. In J. A. Fishman (Ed.), *Readings in the sociology of language*. The Hague: Mouton, 1968.

Felix, S. How reliable are experimental data? Paper presented at the Eleventh TESOL Convention, April 1977.

Fraser, B. On apologizing. In F. Coulmas (Ed.), *Conversational routine*. The Hague: Mouton, 1980.

Gal, S. *Language shift*. New York: Academic Press, 1979.

Gardner, R. C. Motivational variables in second-language acquisition. Reading number two, Appendix C. In R. C. Gardner & W. E. Lambert, *Attitudes and motivation in second-language learning*. Rowley, MA: Newbury House, 1972a.

Gardner, R. C. Social psychological aspects of second language acquisition. In H. Giles & R. St. Clair (Eds.), *Language and social psychology*. Oxford: Basil Blackwell, 1979.

Gardner, R. C. *Social psychology and second language teaching: The role of attitudes and motivation*. London: Edward Arnold, 1985.

Gardner, R. C., & Lambert, W. E. *Attitudes and motivation in second-language learning.* Rowley, MA: Newbury House, 1972a.

Gardner, R. C., & Lambert, W. E. Motivational variables in second-language acquisition. Reading number one, Appendix C. In R. C. Gardner & W. E. Lambert, *Attitudes and motivation in second-language learning.* Rowley, MA: Newbury House, 1972b.

Gatbonton-Segalowitz, E. Systematic variations in second language speech: A sociolinguistic study. Unpublished doctoral dissertation, McGill University, 1975.

Gatbonton, E. Patterned phonetic variability in second-language speech: A gradual diffusion model. *Canadian Modern Language Review*, 1978, *34*(3), 335–347.

Giddens, D. An analysis of the discourse and syntax of oral complaints. Unpublished MA-TESL thesis, University of California at Los Angeles, 1981.

Giles, H. Patterns of evaluation in reactions to RP, South Welsh and Somerset accented speech. *British Journal of Social and Clinical Psychology*, 1971, *10*, 280–281.

Giles, H. Accommodation theory: Some new directions. In S. de Silva (Ed.), *Aspects of linguistic behavior.* York, England: York University Press, 1980.

Giles, H., & Powesland, P. F. *Speech style and social evaluation.* London: Academic Press, 1975.

Giles, H., Bourhis, R. Y., & Taylor, D. M. Towards a theory of language in ethnic group relations. In H. Giles (Ed.), *Language, ethnicity and intergroup relations.* London: Academic Press, 1977.

Giles, H., & Byrne, J. L. An intergroup approach to second language acquisition. *Journal of Multicultural and Multilingual Development*, 1982, *3*, 17–40.

Giles, H., & Smith, P. M. Accommodation theory: Optimal levels of convergence. In H. Giles & R. St. Clair (Eds.), *Language and social psychology.* Oxford: Basil Blackwell, 1979.

Goldstein, L., & Mooney, W. The use of in-tandem and mirror-image prototypes and code-switching for female Black English speakers. Unpublished manuscript, Teachers College, Columbia University, 1978.

Hildebrand, H., & Giles, H. The English language in Japan: A social psychological perspective. *JALT Journal*, 1980, *2*, 63–82.

Homans, G. C. *Social behavior: Its elementary forms.* New York: Harcourt, Brace and World, 1961.

Huebner, T. Order-of-acquisition vs. dynamic paradigm: A comparison of method in interlanguage research, *TESOL Quarterly*, 1979, *13*(1), 21–28.

Huebner, T. *A longitudinal analysis of the acquisition of English.* Ann Arbor, MI: Karoma Publishers, 1983.

Hymes, D. On communicative competence. In J. B. Pride and J. Holmes (Eds.), *Sociolinguistics.* Harmondsworth, England: Penguin Books, 1972.

Jones, E. E., & Davis K. E. From acts to dispositions: The attribution process in perception. In L. Berkowitz (Ed.), *Advances in social psychology* (Vol. II). New York and London: Academic Press, 1965.

Kelly, H. H. Attribution theory in social psychology. *Nebraska Symposium on Motivation*, 1967, *14*, 192–241.

Labov, W. The social motivation of a sound change. *Word*, 1963, *19*, 273–309.

Labov, W. *The social stratification of English in New York City.* Washington, DC: Center for Applied Linguistics, 1966.

Labov, W. The study of language in its social context. *Studium Generale*, 1970, *23*, 30–87.

Labov, W. *Language in the inner city: Studies in the Black English vernacular.* Philadelphia: University of Pennsylvania Press, 1972a.

Labov, W. *Sociolinguistic patterns.* Philadelphia: University of Pennsylvania Press, 1972b.

Labov, W. Field methods of the project on linguistic change and variation. *Sociolinguistic Working Paper*, 1981, *81*, 1–37.

Lambert, S. M. The role of speech in forming evaluations: A study of children and teachers. Unpublished master's thesis, Tufts University, 1973.

Lambert, W. E. The social psychology of bilingualism. *Journal of Social Issues*, 1967, *23*, 91–109.

Lambert, W. E. Language as a factor in intergroup relations. In H. Giles & R. St. Clair (Eds.), *Language and social psychology.* Baltimore: University Park Press, 1979.

Lambert, W. E., Hodgson, R. C., Gardner, R. C., & Fillenbaum, S. Evaluational reactions to spoken language. *Journal of Abnormal and Social Psychology*, 1960, *60*, 44–51.

Larsen-Freeman, D. An explanation for the morpheme acquisition order of second language learners. *Language Learning*, 1976, *26*, 125–134.

Ledvinka, J. Race of interviewer and the language elaboration of Black interviewers. *Journal of Social Issues*, 1971, *27*(4), 185–187.

Lieberman, P. *Intonation, perception and language.* Cambridge, MA: MIT Press, 1967.

Manes, J., & Wolfson, N. The compliment formula. In F. Coulmas (Ed.), *Conversational routine.* The Hague: Mouton, 1981.

Natalé, M. Convergence of mean vocal intensity in dyadic communication as a function of social desirability. *Journal of Personality and Social Psychology*, 1975, *32*(5), 780–804.

Olshtain, E. Sociocultural competence and language transfer: The case of apology. In S. Gass & L. Selinker (Eds.), *Language transfer in language learning.* Rowley, MA: Newbury House, 1983.

Olshtain, E., & Weinbach, L. Complaints—A study of speech act behavior among native and nonnative speakers of Hebrew. Unpublished manuscript, Tel Aviv University, 1986.

Parrish, B. & Tarone, E. Article use in interlanguage: A study in task-related variability. Paper presented at the TESOL Conference, Anaheim, California, 1986.

Platt, J., & Weber, H. Speech convergence miscarried: An investigation into inappropriate accommodation strategies. *International Journal of the Sociology of Language*, 1984, *46*, 131–146.

Rader, M. Complaint letters: When *is* conflicts with *ought.* Unpublished manuscript, University of California, Berkeley, 1977.

Rampton, M. B. H. Stylistic variability and not speaking "normal" English: Post-Labovian approaches and their implications for the study of interlanguage. Paper presented at the BAAL Seminar on Contextual Variability and Second Language Acquisition, Ealing, 1985.

Rintell, E. Sociolinguistic variation and pragmatic ability: A look at learners. *International Journal of the Sociology of Language*, 1981, *27*, 11–34.

Scarcella, R. On speaking politely in a second language. In C. Yorio, K. Perkins & J. Schachter (Eds.), *On TESOL '79*. Washington, DC: TESOL, 1979.

Schmidt, R. W. Sociostylistic variation on spoken Egyptian Arabic: A re-examination of the concept of diglossia. Unpublished doctoral dissertation, Brown University, 1974.

Schmidt, R. W. Sociolinguistic variation and language transfer in phonology. *Working Papers on Bilingualism*, 1977, *12*, 79–95.

Scotton, C. M. Explaining linguistic choices as identity negotiations. In H. Giles, P. Robinson, & P. Smith (Eds.), *Language: Social psychological perspectives*. Oxford: Pergamon Press, 1980.

Searle, J. R. *Speech acts: An essay in the philosophy of language*. Cambridge: Cambridge University Press, 1969.

Searle, J. R. The classification of illocutionary acts. *Language in Society*, 1976, *5*(1), 1–14.

Shuy, R., Wolfram, W., & Riley, W. K. A study of social dialects in Detroit. Report on Project 6-1347. Washington, DC: Office of Education, 1967.

Tajfel, H. Social identity and intergroup behavior. *Social Science Information*, 1974, *13*, 65–93.

Tajfel, H. (Ed.). *Differentiation between social groups: Studies in intergroup behavior*. London: Academic Press, 1978.

Tarone, E. Interlanguage as chameleon. *Language Learning*, 1979, *29*(1), 181–191.

Tarone, E. Systematicity and attention in interlanguage. *Language Learning*, 1982, *32*(1), 69–84.

Tarone, E. On the variability of interlanguage systems. *Applied Linguistics*, 1983, *4*(2), 142–163.

Tarone, E. On the variability of interlanguage systems. In F. Eckman, L. Bell, and D. Nelson (Eds.), *Universals of second language acquisition*. Rowley, MA: Newbury House, 1984.

Tarone, E. On chameleons and monitors. Plenary session paper presented at Second Language Research Forum, Los Angeles, 1985a.

Tarone, E. Variability in interlanguage use: A study of style-shifting in morphology and syntax. *Language Learning*, 1985b, *35*(3), 373–403.

Thakerar, J. N., Giles, H., & Cheshire, J. Psychological and linguistic parameters of speech accommodation theory. In C. Fraser & K. R. Scherer (Eds.), *Advances in the social psychology of language*. Cambridge: Cambridge University Press, 1982.

Thomas, J. A. Cross-cultural pragmatic failure. *Applied Linguistics*, 1983, *4*(2), 91–112.

Trudgill, P. Linguistic accommodation: Sociolinguistic observations on a sociopsychological theory. In *Papers from the parasession on language and behavior*, Chicago Linguistic Society. Chicago: University of Chicago Press, 1981.

Webb, J. T. Interview synchrony: An investigation of two speech rate measures in an automated standardized interview. In A. W. Siegman & B. Pope (Eds.), *Studies in dyadic communication*. Oxford: Pergamon, 1970.

Wolfson, N. Speech event and natural speech: Some implications for sociolinguistic methodology. *Language in Society*, 1976, *5*, 189–209.

Wolfson, N. Invitations, compliments and the competence of the native speaker. *International Journal of Psycholinguistics*, 1981, *24*.

Wolfson, N. An empirically based analysis of complimenting in American English. In N. Wolfson & E. Judd (Eds.), *Sociolinguistics and language acquisition.* Rowley, MA: Newbury House, 1983a.

Wolfson, N. Rules of speaking. In J. C. Richards and R. W. Schmidt (Eds.), *Language and communication.* London: Longman, 1983b.

Wolfson, N., D'Amico-Reisner, L., & Huber, L. How to arrange for social commitments in American English: The invitation. In N. Wolfson & E. Judd (Eds.), *Sociolinguistics and language acquisition.* Rowley, MA: Newbury House, 1983.

Wolfson, N., & Manes, J. The compliment as a social strategy. *International Journal of Human Communication,* 1980, *13,* 391–410.

Zuengler, J. Applying accommodation theory to variable performance data in L2. *Studies in Second Language Acquisition,* 1982, *4*(2), 181–192.

Zuengler, J. The effect of induced expertise on the language performance of native and nonnative speakers. Unpublished doctoral dissertation, Teachers College, Columbia University, 1985.

SUGGESTED READINGS

Beebe, L. M. Reservations about the Labovian paradigm of style shifting and its extension to the study of interlanguage. Paper presented at the Third Annual TESOL and Sociolinguistics Colloquium, TESOL Convention, Honolulu, 1982.

Cohen, A., & Olshtain, E. Developing a measure of sociocultural competence: The case of apology. *Language Learning,* 1981, *31*(1), 113–134.

Dickerson, L. The learner's interlanguage as a system of variable rules. *TESOL Quarterly,* 1975, *9*(4), 401–407.

Gardner, R. C., & Lambert, W. E. *Attitudes and motivation in second-language learning.* Rowley, MA: Newbury House, 1972.

Giles, H. & Smith, P. M. Accommodation theory: Optimal levels of convergence. In H. Giles & R. St. Clair (Eds.), *Language and social psychology.* Oxford: Basil Blackwell, 1979.

Labov, W. *Sociolinguistic patterns.* Philadelphia: University of Pennsylvania Press, 1972.

Tarone, E. C. Interlanguage as chameleon. *Language Learning,* 1979, *29*(1), 181–191.

Wolfson, N. Rules of speaking. In J. Richards & R. Schmidt (Eds.), *Language and communication.* London: Longman, 1983.

three

NEUROLINGUISTIC PERSPECTIVE

Neuropsychology and Second Language Acquisition

Fred Genesee, McGill University

Neuropsychological research on bilinguals seeks to establish relationships between the brain and phenomena associated with acquiring, knowing, and using two or more languages. There has been a long-standing interest in the relationship between language functions and the brain in monolinguals. One of the earliest and primary interests among researchers working with monolinguals has been the localization in the brain of distinct language functions, for example, speech production versus comprehension. This type of research not only serves to identify particular areas of the brain that are responsible for specific language subskills, but also helps to identify these different subskills of language.

Phrenologists, popularly known for their speculations regarding mental functions through an examination of the bumps and depressions in the human skull, were among the first to suggest that specific behaviors, including language, are localized in different areas of the brain. This work dates from the early nineteenth century. Scientific investigations of brain functions soon followed. Early scientific research in the field was based on clinical examinations of aphasics, that is, individuals suffering language impairment as a result of brain damage or disease. The method of investigation involved discovering what specific types of language impairment were associated with damage to different areas of the brain.

In 1836 Dax (see discussion in Kolb & Whishaw, 1980) described a series of aphasic cases who exhibited language difficulties following injury to their left hemispheres but not their right hemispheres (see Figure 3.1 for a schematic representation of the brain and its major parts). It was the work of Dax that first established the now widely accepted notion of left-hemisphere "dominance" for language. Subsequent research with aphasic individuals found an association between the frontal regions of the left hemisphere and speech production (see discussion of Broca in Kolb & Whishaw, 1980) and between the posterior temporal regions of the left hemisphere and language comprehension (see discussion of Wernicke in Kolb & Whishaw, 1980). Language impairments resulting from damage to these areas of the brain have come to be known as Broca's aphasia and Wernicke's aphasia, respectively, in recognition of these early investigators.

Reports on bilingual or polyglot aphasia started to appear around the same time as Broca's and Wernicke's reports on monolingual aphasia. In contrast to studies of monolingual aphasics, which were concerned primarily with the localization of specific language functions (e.g., speech production versus comprehension), studies of bilingual aphasics were distinguished by their interest in the relationship of the bilingual's languages. In particular, they were concerned with whether the bilingual's languages were processed in the same ways and in the same areas of the brain (see Albert & Obler, 1978, and Paradis, 1977, for reviews of this research).

Until recently, the investigation of the relationship between language and the brain was limited to individuals suffering language impairment following

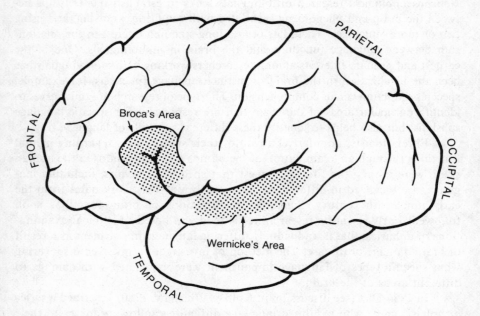

Figure 3.1 Lateral view of the left hemisphere

brain damage or disease. Such individuals served as natural experiments for researchers. Recently, neuropsychological and electrophysiological techniques have been developed that allow researchers to examine these relationships in normal individuals without brain damage. Although originally developed in conjunction with the study of monolinguals, these "experimental" techniques have been used increasingly with bilinguals. Indeed, Vaid and Genesee (1980) point out that almost half of all the experimental studies related to neuropsychological aspects of bilingualism that were available in 1980 had been carried out since 1977.

In the remainder of this chapter, we will examine three different neuropsychological issues pertaining to second language acquisition:

1. The localization of first and second languages in the left and right hemispheres of the brain
2. Differences in the way that languages with different linguistic characteristics are represented in the brain (e.g., phonetic languages, such as English, versus ideographic languages, such as Chinese)
3. A critical neuropsychological period for second language learning

The emphasis in this chapter will be on experimental studies of these issues; evidence from clinical research on aphasics will be included where appropriate. The implications of some of the research findings for second language teaching and learning will also be examined.

HEMISPHERIC DIFFERENCES IN LOCALIZATION OF FIRST AND SECOND LANGUAGES

The first evidence that bilinguals' or polyglots' languages might not be localized in the same area of the brain came from case studies of individual bilinguals who exhibited different patterns of impairment in their languages following brain damage or disease. In some cases, it was reported that one language was more impaired than the other immediately after the injury, and in other cases it was reported that the languages did not recover from the injury to the same extent or at the same rate (see Paradis, 1977). Different hypotheses have been put forward to explain such differential patterns of impairment and recovery. Perhaps the best known early hypotheses were those of Ribot and Pitres (see Paradis, 1977). According to Ribot, languages that are learned in infancy are more deeply encoded in memory and, therefore, are more resistant to the effects of brain damage than are languages that are learned later on; this is known as the primacy effect. According to this hypothesis, one would expect first-learned languages to be less severely affected by brain damage or disease and/or to recover more completely from such damage than would second or subsequently learned languages. In contention with Ribot, Pitres hypothesized that it was the language that was most familiar to the patient prior to injury that would be less impaired by injury and/or would recover more completely, irrespective of its orders of acquisition. There are weaknesses in both of these hypotheses. It is often difficult to identify the most familiar language as distinct from the first-learned language, because the first-learned language is often the most familiar. In the case of polyglots, it may be difficult to tell exactly which language was learned first or which one was most familiar prior to injury. There is, in fact, little empirical support in the aphasiological literature for either Ribot's or Pitres's hypotheses (Albert & Obler, 1978; Galloway & Krashen, 1980).

As noted earlier, the finding that the languages of a bilingual aphasic do not always react to brain injury in the same way also suggests that they may not be located in the same part of the brain but, rather, in different parts. This would certainly explain why one language might be less impaired than another following damage to a specific area of the brain. A number of investigators have suggested, more specifically, that whereas the left hemisphere is specialized for first language acquisition, the right hemisphere is specialized for second language acquisition (Vildomec, 1963). It follows, therefore, that damage to the right hemisphere is more likely to be associated with impairment of the second language, whereas damage to the left hemisphere is more likely to be associated with impairment of the first language. Attempts to validate this hypothesis using clinical case studies of individual bilingual aphasics are problematic. Most important, it is difficult to know how representative individual aphasic cases are of bilinguals in general. Case studies of individual bilingual aphasics are often published in the literature precisely because they are unusual and, therefore, interesting. Moreover, aphasic bilinguals may have different patterns of language localization than normal bilinguals because they have abnormal brains, thereby making it difficult to generalize to neurologically healthy bilinguals. It is for these reasons that carefully controlled experimental studies carried out on "normal" bilinguals with intact brains are so important in addressing this issue.

Current Conceptualizations about Hemispheric Specialization

Early researchers interested in language organization in bilinguals tended to ask rather categorically whether bilinguals' languages are localized differently and, in particular, whether the second language is located in the right hemisphere while, as in the case of most monolinguals, the first language is located in the left hemisphere. This question, however, is simplistic and does not fit with current thinking about hemispheric specialization of function in general. Since a neuropsychological model of language organization in bilinguals must ultimately be compatible with a neuropsychological model of language in general, it is important that we understand current thinking about hemispheric specialization of function in general. Early conceptualizations about the left and right hemispheres tended to emphasize differences in the types of stimuli that could be processed in each hemisphere. More specifically, it was generally thought that verbal or language stimuli (e.g., words) were processed in the left hemisphere, whereas nonlanguage stimuli (e.g., melodies) were processed in the right hemisphere. More current thinking, in contrast, emphasizes differences in processing modes of the two hemispheres. According to this view, the hemispheres differ not so much in the types of stimuli that they process but, rather, in their *manner* of processing particular stimuli given certain task requirements. Thus, what are lateralized are not stimuli, but different modes of processing. For example, it is thought that the left hemisphere is specialized to process information analytically and serially, whereas the right hemisphere is specialized to process information in a holistic, parallel manner. To the extent that a given stimulus can be processed more effectively using one of these strategies than the other, the hemisphere specialized for that process will be involved in performing the task. It is currently thought that the specialized processes of the left hemisphere, whatever they might be, are not specific to language, nor are the specialized processes of the right hemisphere specific to nonlanguage functions. Rather, the specialized competencies of each hemisphere are general processing modes.

A second important feature of current thinking about the two hemispheres concerns their degree of specialization. It is now thought that although each hemisphere may be specialized to process information in certain ways, it is not limited to that processing mode. More specifically, the left hemisphere appears to be able to engage in some holistic/parallel processing, and the right hemisphere seems to be able to engage in some analytic/serial processing. Thus, according to this perspective, the two hemispheres are not completely dissimilar with respect to the tasks they can perform.

Third, in contrast to earlier views of hemispheric specialization that regarded language as undifferentiated and processed only by the left hemisphere, the current view holds that language consists of different cognitive and perceptual components, some of which can be processed by the left hemisphere and others by the right hemisphere. This means that both hemispheres can contribute to language processing to some extent.

In light of these current views of hemispheric specialization, researchers interested in brain–language relations in bilinguals have been asking whether, to what extent, and why factors associated with second language acquisition influence the pattern of hemispheric involvement in language processing in bilinguals. Three factors have been investigated and will be reviewed here: (1) age of second language acquisition, (2) level of second language proficiency, and (3) manner of second language acquisition.

Age of Language Acquisition

If a bilingual learns his or her two languages successively rather than simultaneously, then one might expect different patterns of hemispheric involvement in first and second language processing, because the maturational state of the brain will differ during the periods of first and second language acquisition. On a cognitive level, as well, it is reasonable to postulate that if two languages are learned successively, there will be differences in cognitive organization during first and second language acquisition reflecting changes in cognitive development. The importance of age-related differences in cognitive organization for bilinguals is exemplified in the distinction between compound and coordinate bilingualism, first proposed by Weinreich (1953). This distinction has recently come to be defined in terms of age of second language acquisition relative to first (see Genesee et al., 1978, for example). *Compound bilingualism*, defined in terms of a common cognitive representational system underlying the bilingual's languages, is thought to characterize the individual who learns both languages simultaneously or nearly simultaneously—therefore, early in life. In contrast, *coordinate bilingualism*, defined in terms of different cognitive representational systems for the two languages, is thought to characterize the individual who acquires his or her second language after the first one and, therefore, later in life.

The effect of these two factors, the neurological and the cognitive, gives rise to the following hypothesis: *There will be more right-hemispheric involvement in second language processing the later the second language is learned relative to the first, or, conversely, there will be greater left-hemispheric involvement in second language processing the earlier the second language is learned relative to the first.* An alternative formulation of this is that the pattern of hemispheric involvement during language processing in bilinguals will more closely resemble that of monolinguals the earlier second language learning takes place, and will be more likely to differ from that of monolinguals the later the second language is learned.

There are at least 12 studies that are relevant to the age hypothesis. They have employed a variety of research techniques and have examined hemispheric involvement in processing a variety of different languages. (The interested reader is advised to consult the original reports for details of their methods.) Genesee et al. (1978), for example, measured average evoked responses from the left and right hemispheres of French-English balanced bilinguals while they were engaged in a language identification task. The subjects were presented with French and English words, one at a time, to either the left ear or the right ear separately. The subjects were required to identify whether each word was a French word or an English word. Electrical activity of the temporal areas of the left and right hemispheres was recorded during the task. Latency measures were then made of how long it took for certain critical electrical responses to occur in the left hemisphere and in the right hemisphere. Two groups of bilinguals were tested—early and late. The early bilinguals had acquired their second language in infancy or childhood (i.e., prior to age 12), and the late bilinguals had acquired their second language after age 12. Genesee et al. found that the latency of the neural responses of their early bilinguals was shorter in the left hemisphere than in the right, whereas the latency of the neural responses of their late bilinguals was shorter in the right hemisphere than in the left. They interpreted these results to reflect the tendency of early bilinguals to use the left hemisphere and late bilinguals to use the right hemisphere for this task. Using techniques similar to those of Genesee et al., Kotik (1980) also reported faster neural responding from the right than from the left hemisphere of Polish-Russian late bilinguals.

Vaid has used auditory and visual versions of the Stroop task to examine language processing in early and late French-English bilinguals (Vaid, 1979; Vaid & Lambert, 1979). In the auditory version of this task, subjects were asked to identify either the pitch level or the meaning of stimulus words (Vaid & Lambert, 1979). In some cases the pitch level of the word was congruent with the meaning of the word (e.g., the word *high* said in a high-pitched voice) and in other cases the pitch level of the word was incongruent with its meaning (e.g., the word *low* said in a high-pitched voice). It was found that the early bilingual subjects responded in the same manner as their monolingual controls, whereas late bilingual subjects reacted differently. In particular, the monolingual and early bilingual subjects exhibited significant left-hemispheric involvement in the task, whereas the late bilingual subjects exhibited significant right-hemispheric involvement.

Three studies have used a measure of finger tapping to examine the extent of hemispheric involvement in second language processing. With this procedure, subjects are required to perform a number of verbal tasks while simultaneously tapping as quickly as possible the index finger of their left or right hand. It is argued that if verbalization and finger tapping involve the same hemisphere, then verbalization will result in a deficit in tapping in the hand contralateral to the active hemisphere. For example, a greater deficit in left- than in right-handed tapping would signify more right- than left-hemispheric involvement in verbalization. Sussman, Franklin, and Simon (1982) found that late bilingual subjects were more likely than early bilingual subjects to demonstrate an equal decrement in *both* left- and right-handed tapping. These results can be interpreted in terms of bilateral hemispheric involvement. In contrast, their early bilingual subjects showed a greater decrement in right-handed finger tapping, indicating greater left-hemispheric involvement. Hynd, Teeter, and Stewart (1980) replicated these findings using the same procedures with a group of Navajo-English late bilinguals. Soares (1982), however, who also used a tapping task, failed to find evidence of bilateral hemispheric involvement in language processing by late bilinguals who spoke Portuguese and English.

Two studies have examined differential hemispheric involvement in young bilingual subjects. It will be recalled that according to the age hypothesis, bilinguals who learn both languages simultaneously or nearly simultaneously will have the same pattern of hemispheric involvement during language processing as monolinguals; the pattern to be expected in this case is greater left- than right-hemispheric involvement. Consistent with the age hypothesis, Bellisle (1975) found that 4-year-old French-English bilingual children, who had learned both languages simultaneously, showed the same pattern of left-hemispheric involvement during first and second language processing as did monolingual speakers of English and French. She used a dichotic listening procedure in which subjects listen to pairs of simple words presented simultaneously to their two ears; thus, a different word is heard in each ear at the same time. The subjects are asked to report what they hear. Most individuals can report more accurately the words presented to their right ear than those presented to their left ear. This is usually explained by the fact that the neural connections between the right ear and the left hemisphere, which is specialized for processing language, are stronger and faster than those between the left ear and the left hemisphere. Starck, Genesee, Lambert, and Seitz (1977) also found significant left-hemispheric involvement during dichotic listening in 5- and 6-year-old English monolinguals and English-French-Hebrew trilinguals.

Inconsistent with the age hypothesis, Soares and Grosjean (1981) reported comparable patterns of hemispheric involvement in language processing among late bilinguals and monolingual controls. They studied Spanish-English bilinguals and used a dichotic listening procedure. Contrary to the hypothesis, Gordon (1980) and Kotik (1975) reported evidence of *greater* left-hemispheric involvement during second compared to first language processing among a group of late bilinguals. Early bilinguals in these two studies showed equivalent laterality effects in their two languages.

In summary, the research reviewed in this section generally supports the hypothesis of greater right-hemispheric involvement in late versus early bilinguals, although there are some nonconfirming studies. It is interesting to note that some of the studies found greater right-hemispheric involvement for *both* first and second language processing (Genesee et al., 1978; Gordon, 1980; Vaid & Lambert, 1979). This finding is important because it suggests that early and late bilinguals have the same specialized hemispheric processes, which in turn may be the same as those of monolinguals. What distinguishes late bilinguals from early bilinguals and monolinguals appears to be the extent to which late bilinguals tend to use right-hemisphere-based processes where early bilinguals and monolinguals would use left-hemisphere-based processes.

The main implication, then, of the research on age of second language acquisition is that right- and left-hemisphere-based processes may be used differently by those who acquire the second language late relative to the first language. It also appears that these strategy differences may characterize both first and second language processing.

Level of Second Language Proficiency

Whereas the studies just reviewed focused on fully proficient bilinguals, other studies have examined bilinguals at different levels of proficiency. Research carried out with monolinguals suggests that although the left hemisphere may normally be predominant in language processing, the right hemisphere is capable of some language processing, albeit generally of a lower level than that possible in the left hemisphere (Zaidel, 1978). Recent psycholinguistic research suggests that the language skills of the second language learner, as well as the second language acquisition strategies of the learner, may be compatible with the linguistic capabilities that have been demonstrated for the right hemisphere. In particular, it has been shown that the speech of beginning second language learners consists of highly formulaic utterances (Wong Fillmore, 1979) and that their speech comprehension relies more on content than on function words, more on prosodic than on phonetic features, and more on pragmatic than on syntactic information (McLaughlin, 1978). These components of language are believed to be within the competence of the right hemisphere (Searleman, 1977; Zaidel, 1978). The apparent compatibility between right-hemispheric processing of language and the performance of beginning second language learners has led to the following hypothesis: *right-hemispheric involvement in second language processing will be more evident among nonproficient bilinguals than among proficient bilinguals* (Krashen & Galloway, 1978; Obler, 1977). This is often referred to as the *stage* hypothesis. It is interesting to note that this hypothesis is consistent with developmental studies of hemispheric specialization of function in monolinguals. This research suggests that the right hemisphere is more involved in the language functions of children than of adults (Witelson, 1977).

An ideal test of the stage hypothesis would involve assessing the relative participation of the two hemispheres of the *same* learners at different levels of second language proficiency. This has never been undertaken, in fact, because of the obvious difficulty of carrying out such a long-term study. The stage hypothesis has usually been tested by comparing patterns of hemispheric involvement during first and second language processing in subgroups of bilinguals who differ in second language proficiency. If the stage hypothesis is correct, then one would expect greater right-hemispheric involvement in less proficient groups in their less proficient languages.

A number of studies have obtained results in support of the stage hypothesis, but their findings could not be replicated in follow-up studies, or they are subject to alternative interpretations (see also Vaid, 1983, for a review of this research). For example, Maître (1974) reported that native English-speaking subjects who were learning Spanish as a second language through college courses showed less left-hemispheric involvement in second language processing than in first language processing during a dichotic listening task. A study by Galloway and Scarcella (1982) that used procedures similar to those of Maître nevertheless did not replicate Maître's finding. Obler, Albert, and Gordon (1975) found that nonproficient English-Hebrew bilinguals showed more left-hemispheric involvement in processing their first language relative to their second language. This finding, however, was not replicated in a follow-up study by Albert and Obler (1978).

Also in apparent support of the stage hypothesis, Schneiderman and Wesche (1980) found that nonproficient English-French bilinguals exhibited significant left-hemispheric involvement on a dichotic listening task in their first language (English), but no significant difference between the hemispheres when processing their second language (French). Since the investigators did not include unilingual French controls, however, it is not possible to rule out the possibility that their French stimulus materials were insensitive to processing differences between the hemispheres. Silverberg, Bentin, Gaziel, Obler, and Albert (1979) found a right-to-left hemisphere shift in processing English among groups of Hebrew speakers who had been studying English as a second language in school for two, four, or six years. However, since these children were exposed to English primarily in school, which emphasizes reading, it is possible that the evidence for right-hemispheric involvement that they noted among the second- and fourth-year groups reflected the effects of learning to read rather than a general second language effect. Indeed, Silverberg, Gordon, Pollack, and Bentin (1980) found right-hemispheric involvement for processing Hebrew among native Hebrew speakers who were learning to read.

Other studies pertinent to this hypothesis failed to find evidence in support of it (see Gordon, 1980; Kershner & Jeng, 1972; Piazza & Zatorre, 1981). Furthermore, contrary to the hypothesis, four additional studies have found evidence of *greater* right-hemispheric involvement in second language processing among fully proficient bilinguals, suggesting that in some cases right-hemispheric involvement may persist even when the individual achieves advanced levels of proficiency (Genesee et al., 1978; Gordon, 1980; Kotik, 1975; Vaid & Lambert, 1979). In its present form, the stage hypothesis cannot accommodate this possibility.

Overall, then, the stage hypothesis has received little reliable empirical support to date.

Manner of Second Language Acquisition

Finally, a small number of studies have reported results that suggest that *there may be greater right-hemispheric involvement in processing languages that are learned informally or, conversely, greater left-hemispheric involvement in processing languages that are learned formally.* This hypothesis is compatible with evidence from clinical studies of brain-damaged monolingual children which suggests that there is a greater likelihood of a language deficit following right-sided brain damage in children (30 percent) than in adults (10 percent) (Zangwill, 1967). The right hemisphere seems to be more involved in language processing in childhood, a period during which language is typically acquired informally. Stable left-hemispheric dominance in language processing does not appear to emerge until around 5 years of age (Krashen, 1974) or later, when language and cognitive processes become increasingly formal in nature (Rosansky, 1975). At the same time, a number of hemispheric specialization studies with infants indicate that the neurological basis for left-hemispheric dominance in language processing is present at birth (Molfese & Molfese, 1979). Witelson (1977) has postulated that what develops with age is cognition and not left-hemispheric specialization for language processing per se, which appears present at birth. According to this perspective, then, as cognitive functions develop that require the type of formal, analytic processing for which the left hemisphere is specialized, then these functions and any tasks dependent on such functions will be performed more by the left than by the right hemisphere. It follows, then, that language learning that is formal in nature may rely more on the left than on the right hemisphere, whereas language learning that is relatively informal will rely more on the right hemisphere.

In the second language literature, Krashen (1977) has proposed a distinction between language learning and language acquisition that may correspond in some ways to these two types of language processing. According to Krashen, language *learning* is characterized by contexts in which there is a conscious emphasis on the structure of language through, for example, grammar translation or drill practice as one might find in traditional second language programs. Such an approach to learning is thought to engender in the learner an awareness of language as an abstract, rule-governed system. On the other hand, language *acquisition* is thought to be characterized by a relatively unconscious internalization of linguistic rules through a process of creative construction. It is this process that typically occurs when languages are acquired in natural or naturalistic contexts where real, meaningful communication takes place.

The language processing strategies involved in language *learning* seem to correspond in some ways to the specialized analytic processes associated with the left hemisphere. The language processing strategies involved in language *acquisition* seem to correspond in some ways to the specialized processes of the right hemisphere. This line of reasoning is consistent with the manner hypothesis articulated earlier, namely, that there will be relatively more right-hemispheric involvement if second language acquisition is informal and greater left-hemispheric involvement if second language learning is formal. It is important to point out that even though the right hemisphere may be more involved in language processing in infancy and possibly during informal language learning, the left hemisphere always remains predominant for language processing. There are five studies relevant to this issue, and all support the hypothesis. Hartnett (1974) found evidence of greater left-hemispheric involvement in second language processing among English students who were learning Spanish in courses using deductive methods. In contrast, students learning Spanish as a second language in courses using inductive methods demonstrated greater right-hemispheric involvement in second language processing. Hartnett used a lateral eye movement technique in which the extent of leftward or rightward gazing during reflective activity is interpreted to indicate the amount of right-hemispheric and left-hemispheric participation, respectively, in the activity.

Kotik (1975) reported that Russian-Estonian bilinguals who had probably learned Estonian, their second language, informally in day-to-day contexts showed no difference in amount of left- and right-hemispheric processing, suggesting relatively more right-hemispheric involvement than usual. In contrast, a group of Estonian-Russian bilinguals who had learned Russian, their second language, formally in school showed typical left-hemispheric dominance. Similarly, F. Carroll (1980), studying English-Spanish bilinguals, and Gordon (1980), studying Hebrew-English bilinguals, found evidence of more left-hemispheric involvement using a dichotic listening procedure when their subjects were processing their second languages than when they were processing their first languages. Both groups of subjects had learned their second languages in formal school contexts.

A general weakness of these studies, and of the manner hypothesis as well, is the lack of clear definitions of formal and informal learning. Moreover, all of the studies have tended to define manner of learning in terms of the formality versus informality of the instructional method or context to which the learners were exposed. Clearly, however, manner of learning is not necessarily synonymous with context of learning. Taking these caveats into account, the available evidence generally supports the manner hypothesis that right-hemispheric involvement in second language processing will increase to the extent that the manner of learning and/or the context of learning is informal.

Discussion and Implications for Second Language Teaching

The available evidence suggests that right-hemispheric involvement in second language processing will be more likely the later the second language is learned relative to the first, and the more informal the learner's exposure to the language. Left-hemispheric involvement is more likely the earlier the second language is learned relative to the first, and the more formal the learner's exposure. There is little evidence that left- or right-hemispheric involvement depends on the level of second language proficiency (see also Vaid & Genesee, 1980).

A principle that emerges from this model is that bilinguals are more likely to show comparable patterns of hemispheric involvement in processing their two languages the more similar the conditions of first and second language learning, all other factors being equal. Conversely, the less similar the conditions of first and second language acquisition, the greater the likelihood that the pattern of hemispheric involvement will differ for the two languages. The direction of this difference will depend on a complex interaction of the effects of age, level of proficiency, and manner of acquisition.

So far, the effects of age, level of proficiency, and manner have been examined as if they operate in isolation. Clearly, however, they need not, and most, in fact, do not. Some interaction effects are discernible from a consideration of the existing research. Right-hemispheric involvement appears to be more likely among nonproficient, younger learners, as found by Silverberg et al. (1979), and less likely in the case of older learners (Galloway, 1979), because adults are more likely than children to use a formal mode of processing language, reflecting their more advanced stage of cognitive development. There is evidence suggesting that the pattern of hemispheric involvement in both children and adults at advanced levels of proficiency corresponds to differences in how proficiency in the second language is achieved. Thus, F. Carroll (1980) and Kotik (1975) found that the more formally the second language was learned, the greater the likelihood of left-hemispheric involvement, whereas Genesee et al. (1978), Gordon (1980), and Vaid and Lambert (1979) found that the more informally the second language was acquired, the greater the likelihood of right-hemispheric involvement.

It is important to emphasize here that these studies have examined language *processing*, not language *learning* per se. Although it is reasonable to suspect that the same neuropsychological substrates underlie both language learning and processing, this is not necessarily the case. What is being suggested here is that the neuropsychological processes involved in language learning may not be the same as those involved in using a second language for normal communicative or intellectual purposes. Whether or not they are the same is an empirical question. At present there appears to be no way to examine the neuropsychological bases of language learning themselves; at best, researchers can investigate language processing.

The evidence regarding second language processing that has just been reviewed is limited by the fact that it pertains to a very restricted set of language structures and skills. Most studies have used single lexical items as stimuli, and most have not examined different levels of language processing, such as semantic versus syntactic. There is a big difference between the language tasks required of subjects in these experiments and the task facing a language learner. Thus, the direct relevance of these findings to language teaching is seriously limited (see also Scovel, 1982).

EXPERIMENTAL STUDIES OF LANGUAGE-SPECIFIC EFFECTS AND SECOND LANGUAGE PROCESSING

Not all languages have the same characteristics. For example, many languages differ in their written forms. There is a fairly systematic relationship between the written symbols of English and the way they are pronounced. In contrast, there is relatively little relationship between the way Chinese words are written and how they are pronounced. Reading Chinese is thought to involve more visual processing, whereas reading English is thought to involve relatively more phonological processing. It follows, then, that Chinese and English may involve different processing subsystems of the brain.

Evidence that different languages may indeed involve different processing systems was first reported in early clinical studies of bilingual aphasics. In particular, a number of investigators reported that damage to the temporal cortex (see Figure 3.1) was associated with impairment of reading and/or writing scripts that are phonetically based, such as English, but not scripts that are nonphonetic (Hinshelwood, 1902). In comparison, lesions in the posterior occipitoparietal area of the left hemisphere were associated with impaired reading and writing of scripts, such as Chinese, that are ideographic (Lyman, Kwan, & Chao, 1938). These types of effects will be referred to as *language-specific effects*.

These effects are not unique to bilinguals; they presumably should also be evident in monolingual aphasics who know such languages. Neuropsychological studies of language-specific effects in bilinguals are of interest to the extent that bilinguals who know languages with these different processing requirements have different neurophysiological substrates for their two languages. That is to say, each language will involve different processing subsystems of the brain (e.g., visual versus phonological). Three characteristics have been examined experimentally for language-specific effects in bilinguals and will be reviewed here. They are related to (1) type of script (phonetic versus ideographic), (2) direction of script (left versus right), and (3) language mode (appositional versus propositional).

Type of Script

As noted earlier, lesions in the temporal cortex of the left hemisphere have been associated with greater impairment of reading and/or writing of scripts that are phonetically based, whereas lesions in the posterior occipitoparietal cortical areas of the left hemisphere have been associated with impairment in reading/writing of scripts with an ideographic or irregular phonetic basis (e.g., Chinese). Experimental investigations of different types of scripts have examined the hypothesis that phonetically based scripts will depend on the specialized analytic-sequential processing capacities of the left hemisphere, whereas ideographic scripts will depend on the specialized gestalt-holistic processes of the right hemisphere (see Vaid, 1983, for a complete review of this issue). Experimental researchers have not examined the possibility that processing these two types of scripts will involve different parts of the same hemisphere because most testing procedures do not permit an examination of intrahemisphere differences in processing. Clearly, however, this is possible.

In support of the hypothesis, a number of studies with neurologically intact Japanese subjects have found evidence of left-hemispheric involvement during the processing of *kana* (the phonetic Japanese script) but right-hemispheric involvement during the processing of *kanji* (the ideographic script used in Japanese) (Endo, Shimizu, & Hori, 1978; Hatta, 1977, 1981; Hink, Kaga, & Suzuki, 1980; Hirata & Osaka, 1967). These findings have been corroborated by case studies of Japanese patients who have undergone commissurotomy, that is, disconnection of the two hemispheres by severing the neural fibers that connect them. Sugishita and his colleagues report on one such patient they examined who had difficulty reading *kana* script presented to the right hemisphere but was unimpaired in reading *kanji* script under the same conditions (Sugishita, Iwata, Toyokura, Yoshida, & Yamada, 1978). Similarly, they describe a right-handed patient with disconnection of the two hemispheres who had difficulty writing *kana* but not *kanji* when using his left hand, which is under the control of the right hemisphere (Sugishita, Toyokura, Yoshioka, & Yamada, 1980). Thus, there is some evidence that different types of scripts may engage the two hemispheres differentially.

At the same time, other experimental research indicates that these findings may depend on task variables such as presentation conditions—whether single or double characters are presented (Hatta, 1978). Thus, the true extent of differential hemispheric involvement in processing languages with different script types remains to be established through more extensive experimentation (see Hung & Tzeng, 1981, for a review of research on orthographic variation and visual information processing).

Direction of Script

A number of studies have found that languages such as English that are written in a left-to-right direction are processed better when they are presented to the right of visual fixation for very brief durations than when they are presented to the left of fixation. In contrast, languages such as Hebrew that are written in a right-to-left direction are processed better when presented in the left visual field. According to one explanation, visual field effects of this sort are due to reading habits. Thus, words written left to right are normally scanned and read from left to right. When such words are presented to the right of fixation, reading can begin immediately because the beginning of the word is at fixation. If such words are presented to the left of fixation, then the person must first move his or her eyes leftward to the beginning of the word before reading can occur. Conversely, right-to-left words will be read more quickly in the left visual field because the beginning of the word is at fixation. When such words are presented in the right visual field, the reader must move his or her gaze right to the beginning of the word before reading can occur. The extra requirement of having to move to the beginning of the word reduces reading speed and, therefore, efficiency.

Of relevance to the present discussion is whether the left and right visual field preferences just noted involve different patterns of hemispheric involvement; that is, do left-to-right scripts, with their associated right visual field effects, engage the left hemisphere more than they do the right? Stimuli presented to the right of fixation for brief durations are projected onto the left half of each eye, and neural signals from the left half of each eye are then transmitted to the visual area of the left hemisphere. Neural signals are then transmitted from the left hemisphere to the right hemisphere via neural pathways that connect the two hemispheres. The opposite occurs when stimuli are presented to the left of fixation. Because of this pattern of transmission of visual information, it is possible to interpret visual field effects in terms of left/right hemisphere differences in information processing. In other words, a right visual field effect when reading English could mean that the left hemisphere is better than the right at processing left-to-right scripts. Conversely, a left visual field effect when reading Hebrew could mean that the right hemisphere is better at processing right-to-left scripts.

The question, then, is whether visual field effects are due to reading habits, as described previously, or to hemispheric differences in information processing. If the former is the case, then it is simply a question of peripheral scanning habits. If the latter is the case, then central neurocortical (hemisphere) mechanisms are involved. One way to disentangle peripheral scanning effects from central-hemispheric effects is to present the language stimuli vertically on either side of fixation, rather than horizontally. This procedure minimizes the effects of reading habits that occur with horizontal presentations. When this procedure is used with bilingual or monolingual subjects who know languages with scripts with different directionality, the pattern of results for each language is the same; namely, there is a right visual field preference for both languages. This, in turn, implies left-hemispheric processing of both languages (Barton, Goodglass, & Shai, 1965; Gaziel, Obler, & Albert, 1978; Orbach, 1967). These results are consistent with the conventional finding of left-hemispheric dominance for language processing and indicate that visual field preferences in reading languages with different directionality of script are probably due to peripheral visual scanning habits and not hemispheric differences.

Language Modes

It has been suggested that language shapes the user's thought processes and, in particular, the nature of his or her perception of or involvement with the physical and social world (Whorf, 1956). In this regard, a distinction has been made between appositional and propositional modes of thought. It has been suggested that Navajo and Hopi involve *appositional* modes—that is, holistic, integrated modes of thought that are based largely on the speakers' perceptions of and involvement with the physical environment (Rogers, TenHouten, Kaplan, & Gardiner, 1977). English, in contrast, has been said to involve *propositional* modes—that is, analytic, abstract modes of thought that orient the user away from the immediate physical context. Rogers et al. (1977) have speculated further that the modes of thought characteristic of English engage the specialized processing strategies of the left hemisphere, whereas the modes of thought associated with Navajo, Hopi, and similar languages engage the specialized processing strategies of the right hemisphere. Indeed, the left hemisphere has been characterized as an analytic processor and the right hemisphere as a holistic processor.

Consistent with this speculation, studies by Rogers et al. (1977), using electrical recording from the two hemispheres, and by Scott, Hynd, Hunt, and Weed (1979), using dichotic listening techniques, have found evidence of greater right-hemispheric involvement when processing Hopi and Navajo than English. Interpretation of the Rogers et al. findings is equivocal, however, since they did not equate the content of the verbal stimuli presented in English and Navajo, raising the possibility that the Navajo stimuli were more perceptually loaded than the English stimuli. Two additional studies using these languages failed to replicate their findings (F. Carroll, 1980; Hynd, Teeter, & Stewart, 1980). Furthermore, the distinction between propositional and appositional modes of thought is not clearly defined, thereby making the argument vague and circular.

Summary

In summary, experimental evidence suggests that languages that activate different modes of thought or that have different types of script (e.g., phonetic versus ideographic) may engage the left and right hemispheres differentially. In particular, propositional languages and phonetically based scripts appear to be associated with the traditional pattern of left-hemispheric language processing, whereas so-called appositional languages and ideographic scripts appear to be associated with right-hemispheric processing. There is a little evidence to support the hypothesis that scripts that differ in directionality involve the two hemispheres differentially. Taken together, these findings suggest that bilinguals who know languages that embody the appositional/propositional or phonetic/ideographic distinction have different neuropsychological substrates for each of their languages. The true nature and extent of the effects that have been found, however, are not clear, due to a lack of precise definitions of what the underlying distinctions really are and a lack of reliable evidence regarding the generalizability of the putative effects.

THE CRITICAL PERIOD HYPOTHESIS

In the preceding sections, we examined the possible effects of factors related to second language acquisition on hemispheric involvement in second language learning and processing. In this section, we will examine the possibility that there are changes during the development of the nervous system that influence second language acquisition in important ways. More specifically, we will examine the hypothesis that there is a neurophysiologically determined critical period during which second language acquisition occurs easily. After the critical period, second language learning becomes impossible or at best difficult.

The notion of critical period came initially from biology. It was proposed by embryologists as a result of their work on cell differentiation and specialization. The notion was popularized by ethologists in their studies of "imprinting" in geese, chicks, fish, and other animals. It was Penfield and Roberts (1959) who brought the concept into prominence in the field of language learning. They suggested that there is a critical period that terminates around 9 to 12 years of age, or at puberty, after which complete or nativelike mastery of languages, first or second, is difficult and unlikely. They argued that this critical period coincides with a period of neural plasticity—that is, a period during which different areas of the brain are able to assume a variety of functions, including language. After neural plasticity is lost, the functions of the different parts of the brain cannot be rearranged. Penfield thought that "the human brain becomes progressively stiff and rigid after the age of nine" (p. 236), making language learning difficult and usually incomplete.

Penfield and Roberts's claims regarding a critical period for language learning were based on their observations of language recovery following brain damage or disease in hospitalized patients. They noted that complete recovery of language function following brain damage was possible if the injury occurred before 9 to 12 years of age but was seldom achieved if injury occurred after this age. The recovery they observed prior to 12 years of age was thought to occur due to the presence of neural plasticity, and the lack of recovery after 12 was thought to be due to an absence of plasticity.

The *critical period hypothesis* (CPH) was developed further by Lenneberg (1967) in his classic book *Biological Foundations of Language*. According to Lenneberg, the critical period for language learning extends from 2 years of age until puberty. He thought that cognitive processes reach a state of "language-readiness" around 2 years of age and that this state declines in the "early teens." Most important, Lenneberg maintained that language learning was difficult after puberty because lateralization of language functions in the left hemisphere was thought to be completed by this age. Lenneberg based his argument on evidence that damage to the left hemisphere of children under 12 years of age often resulted in the transfer of language functions to the right hemisphere, but such transfer was not often found in individuals who suffered brain damage after 12 years of age. Lenneberg also cited a variety of neurological indices that exhibited developmental changes that coincided with his postulated critical period (e.g., changes in the size and structure of neurons, in the myelinization of neurons, and in the neurochemistry of the brain).

Thus, the CPH proposed by Penfield put an emphasis on general neurological plasticity, and Lenneberg's refinement of the hypothesis put an emphasis on hemispheric specialization of function. Both proposals have come under heavy criticism on both conceptual and empirical fronts (see also Krashen, 1974; Lamendella, 1977; and Neufeld, 1979, for discussion of the issue). We will now examine the hypothesis on both conceptual and empirical grounds.

Conceptual Issues

The CPH has a number of conceptual weaknesses. First, the evidence that Penfield and Lenneberg cite pertains to first language competence and, therefore, strictly speaking, does not necessarily apply to second languages. Second, their evidence pertains to relearning first language skills that had already been acquired. In the case of second language acquisition, what is in question is the ability to learn a new set of language skills for the first time. Third, their evidence pertains to adults with impaired first language skills as a result of brain damage or pathology. It does not necessarily follow that healthy adults with intact neurological systems will have difficulty learning a second language.

Lenneberg's assertion that the critical period for language learning terminates when complete lateralization of language functions in the left hemisphere is achieved has not found empirical support. There is now evidence that left-hemispheric specialization for language is present by 5 years of age (Krashen, 1974) and, in fact, may be present at birth (Molfese & Molfese, 1979). Thus, completion of lateralization cannot be used as the basis for explaining the termination of the critical period. Lenneberg's CPH concerns itself only with interhemispheric localization of function, but it is also quite likely that there is progressive localization of function within each hemisphere. For example, the localization of speech production in Broca's area and of comprehension in Wernicke's area, as mentioned before, takes place in one hemisphere. Lenneberg does not consider the possibility of *intra*hemispheric changes in localization with development.

Moreover, there is no reason to assume that localization occurs suddenly or at the same rate for all subsystems of the brain, as the CPH implies. It seems more likely that the neural plasticity on which the CPH is presumed to depend changes progressively with age and in some cases may extend beyond puberty. Several reviewers have suggested that it is more appropriate to talk about a *sensitive* rather than a critical period for second language learning (Lamendella, 1977; Seliger, 1978). According to this notion, certain language skills are acquired more easily at particular times in development than at other times, and some language skills can be learned even after the critical period, although less easily. This form of the CPH, referred to as the weak version, says in essence that there is not one critical period, but many. In fact, both Lenneberg and Penfield acknowledged that second languages could be learned beyond the critical period, but with difficulty. More will be said about the sensitive period hypothesis later.

Walsh and Diller (1981) have recently discussed an alternative basis for neural plasticity. They contend that changes in language learning ability with age can be understood in terms of maturational rates of different types of neurons in the brain. They distinguish between local-circuit neurons and macroneurons. Macroneurons are said to be fully mature and functional early in development. It is these neurons that provide a basis for the acquisition of "lower order language processes" like those found in early language development (e.g., basic analysis of speech). Local-circuit neurons, in contrast, develop much more slowly and, in fact, perhaps continue to develop even into adulthood. It is the slow development of these neurons that underlies neural plasticity and the development of "higher order language processes" that occur beyond childhood (e.g., semantic processing). On the one hand, Walsh and Diller's proposals have the advantages that they are consistent with the notion of a sensitive rather than a critical period for second language learning, and they allow for intra- as well as interhemispherically based language learning processes. On the other hand, their distinction between lower and higher order language processes lacks clear definition and substantiation. Furthermore, the distinction appears to dichotomize language in a somewhat artificial manner, despite current conceptions of language as a continuously developing, fully integrated multicomponential skill. Finally, a direct link between the neuro-developmental differences proposed by Walsh and Diller and changes in second language learning ability needs to be demonstrated for their proposals to evolve beyond the state of interesting conjecture.

The Empirical Evidence

Empirical evidence regarding the CPH for second language learning can be garnered from studies that have compared adult–child and adolescent–child differences in second language achievement (see Krashen, Scarcella, & Long, 1982, for a useful compendium and an excellent review of much of this research). In apparent support of the critics of the CPH, and contrary to Penfield and Lenneberg's expectation that second language learning is difficult for older learners, a number of studies have assessed the short-term achievement of older versus younger learners and have generally found that older learners achieve higher levels of second language proficiency than younger learners do. This has been found despite the fact that in some cases the younger learners had had more second language instruction and/or exposure than the older ones. Genesee (1981), for example, found that English students in Montreal who had attended two-year late immersion programs in grades 7 and 8 had achieved the same level of proficiency as comparable students who had attended an early total immersion program beginning in kindergarten. Both groups of students were the same ages at the time of the evaluations, which were conducted at the end of grades 8 to 11 (Adiv, 1980; Genesee, 1981). The early immersion students had had considerably more exposure to the second language in school than the late immersion students at the time of testing. At the end of grade 8, for example, the early immersion students had had approximately 5,000 hours and the two-year late immersion students 1,400 hours of exposure. Similar advantages have been reported for older students in more conventional second language programs (e.g., Burstall, 1974), as well as students in natural settings (see Snow & Hoefnagel-Höhle, 1977).

These findings attest to the learning efficiency of older learners relative to young learners, at least during the initial stages of learning. They indicate further that this is true both in naturalistic settings where learning is untutored (as in the case of Genesee's immersion students and Snow and Hoefnagel-Höhle's English-speaking immigrants in Holland) and in school settings where learning is formalized and directed (see, for example, Burstall, 1974, and Olson & Samuels, 1973). Penfield and Lenneberg felt that young children's facility at second language learning was particularly evident in natural language learning contexts. It is also evident from Genesee's and Snow and Hoefnagel-Höhle's studies, which included a variety of language assessment instruments including comprehension, grammar, pronunciation, and writing tests, that older learners are initially able to achieve higher levels of proficiency than are younger learners in most aspects of a second language.

Although these findings do not support the CPH, neither does it follow that they constitute sufficient evidence to reject it. The CPH identifies two constraints on second language learning: (1) that second language learning is more difficult and "labored" as one gets older, and (2) that nativelike proficiency, especially in phonology, is rarely achieved by older learners. Thus, the first constraint pertains to the process of second language learning and the second constraint to ultimate level of proficiency achieved. The research just reviewed is incompatible with the first constraint insofar as it found that older learners learn second languages faster than younger learners do. One would expect learning to be slower if it is more difficult. It is the second constraint, however, that is essential to the hypothesis (see also Snow & Hoefnagel-Höhle, 1978). Strictly speaking, these studies do not provide a valid test of this part of the CPH because they did not examine long-term achievement. Nor did they examine in some cases or establish conclusively in others whether the proficiency achieved by the older learners was in fact nativelike.

A number of other studies that have assessed long-term achievement among pre- and postpubertal learners permit examination of these issues. It will be recalled that it has traditionally been thought that puberty marks the end of the critical period. Five such studies are reproduced in the Krashen, Scarcella, and Long collection (1982). Most of the second language learners examined in these studies were American immigrants who were learning English as a second language in natural settings (cf. Seliger, Krashen, & Ladefoged, 1975). Three of the studies examined only accent (Asher & Garcia, 1969; Oyama, 1976; Seliger, Krashen, & Ladefoged, 1975). It is questionable whether acquisition of accent-free speech in a second language is simply a matter of peripheral neuromuscular control. One of the three studies examined only listening comprehension (Oyama, 1978). The assessment instrument used by Oyama in this study did not actually assess comprehension but, rather, tested verbatim repetition of sentences presented under different levels of interference. It may well be that this procedure tested some other skill or skills besides comprehension (such as mimicry). Only one of the studies contained in the Krashen et al. compendium examined syntactic competence (Patkowski, 1980). The evaluation of syntactic competence in this study was based on written transcripts of oral interviews, thereby eliminating phonological, prosodic, and intonational information.

All five studies found that, on average, second language proficiency was greater and tended toward nativelike levels the younger the learner at the time of immigration. Although these findings are in apparent support of the CPH, their interpretation must be qualified in accordance with the methodological limitations just noted. Moreover, in order to examine the CPH, it is not sufficient to establish that the prepubertal learners acquired higher levels of competence than the postpubertal learners did, nor even that more of the former than of the latter attained nativelike proficiency. More important, one must determine to what extent postpubertal learners failed to attain nativelike competence or, conversely, to what extent they actually attained nativelike second language proficiency. Evidence of nativelike proficiency among postpubertal learners would raise serious doubts about the validity of the CPH. Examination of the research findings with this focus reveals the following. In the Seliger, Krashen, and Ladefoged study, 5 to 7 percent of the 173 respondents included in their survey who had immigrated to the United States or Israel after 16 years of age rated their own second language speech as accentless. Asher and Garcia (1969) found the same percentage using a much smaller sample of 15 postpubertal bilinguals. In the Patkowski study, 4 of his 34 postpubertal learners were given a syntactic rating of 4 out of 5, and 1 was given a rating of 5 out of 5, representing nativelike proficiency. It is not possible to reexamine Oyama's data in this way because she reported average ratings.

Additional evidence that nativelike proficiency in a second language is possible after puberty is offered by Neufeld and Schneiderman (1980). In a systematic test of the CPH for the acquisition of phonology, they provided 18 hours of intensive instruction in Japanese, Chinese, or Eskimo phonology to 20 adult English-speaking learners. The learners were subsequently evaluated by native speakers of the languages, and 50 percent of them were judged to have nativelike accents. One can also find ample anecdotal evidence of individuals who have achieved nativelike second language proficiency after puberty. For example, the research by Genesee et al. (1978), discussed earlier, is relevant here. In their investigation of differential hemispheric involvement during language processing, Genesee and his colleagues identified and tested groups of "early" and "late" bilinguals; the latter were defined as individuals who possessed nativelike competence in French and English and who had acquired their second language after the age of 12. Selection was accomplished by having potential subjects judged by native speakers of French and English. Only bilinguals who were able to "pass" as unilingual speakers of each language were selected as subjects.

These diverse sources attest to the occurrence of nativelike proficiency among late second language learners. That the number or percentage of completely proficient postpubertal bilinguals appears small is difficult to interpret unequivocally, but it is possible that the research strategies used by the investigators are partly responsible. To be more specific, with the exception of the Neufeld study, which sought to produce proficient late learners, the other studies used random selection of second language learners. Furthermore, their sample sizes are quite small. This may have served to suppress artificially the number of proficient second language learners in the experimental samples by overlooking or failing to identify them. A more convincing demonstration of a low incidence of full proficiency among older learners would involve an active search for fully proficient bilinguals who have acquired their second language later in life. What is being suggested here is that the existing studies of this issue may have failed to find a high incidence of full bilingualism because they were not actively seeking it. That the incidence of fully proficient postpubertal second language learners is small is difficult to interpret for theoretical reasons as well. There is no theoretical basis on which to decide the smallest number of fully proficient bilinguals among postpubertal learners that would be acceptable to maintain the CPH. Attempts to reconcile the occurrence of full proficiency among postpubertal learners by resorting to the sensitive period hypothesis are largely unsuccessful and inappropriate. The sensitive period hypothesis is not a simple, actuarial prediction about the number of postpubertal learners who will be able to become fully proficient in a second language with advancing age. Rather, it is a complex, differentiated hypothesis according to which it becomes difficult to master certain language subsystems at different periods during the life span. The precise nature of these subsystems or skills that become progressively and differentially difficult to master has not been well defined, making it difficult to know precisely how one would actually test the hypothesis. Notwithstanding this problem, it is nevertheless clear that simply examining the incidence of full proficiency among learners of different ages, with no regard to their specific language skills, is not an adequate test of the sensitive period hypothesis.

At the same time, the apparently low incidence of nativelike second language proficiency among older learners could be explained in part at least by social and/or experiential factors. For example, the possibility of acquiring bilingual competence by virtue of being raised in a mixed language family probably contributes substantially to the incidence of early bilingualism but insignificantly to the incidence of late bilingualism. Other commentators on the CPH have also suggested that the different rates of full bilingualism that one finds at different ages may be due to other, nonneurophysiological factors, including cognitive, affective, and social ones (see, for example, Krashen, 1982, and Neufeld, 1979).

Summary

The hypothesis that there is a critical period for second language learning that is based on developmental neurophysiological changes has been examined from conceptual and empirical points of view. From a conceptual point of view, it does not follow that because adults or adolescents with neurological impairment experience difficulty in relearning, and in some cases an inability to relearn, a first language, neurologically intact adults will also have undue difficulty in or be incapable of learning a second language. It has been argued that direct evidence linking second language learning difficulties beyond the putative critical period with neurophysiological changes in the brain is needed to validate the hypothesis. Attempts to salvage the CPH in terms of the sensitive period hypothesis are inappropriate at this time given the lack of precise definitions essential to the hypothesis and the lack of suitable research to test the hypothesis.

The existing evidence indicates that (1) all aspects of second language learning appear to be learned more efficiently and, therefore, possibly more easily, at least in the initial stages, the older the learner; and (2) nativelike levels of proficiency in the phonological, syntactic, and comprehension aspects of the second language can be attained by postpubertal learners. The finding that more prepubertal learners than postpubertal learners achieve higher and more nativelike levels of second language proficiency does not constitute unequivocal support for the CPH because there is no rational way to determine the rate of full bilingualism among postpubertal learners that is unacceptable to the CPH. Moreover, there may be methodological or other nonneurophysiological explanations of the low incidence among postpubertal learners.

Thus, there is insufficient conceptual and empirical reason to justify making educational decisions on the basis of the CPH. This is not to say that there are not other kinds of factors associated with age that are relevant to second language educators. The existence of such factors can be inferred from some of the research results that have already been discussed. That researchers have found older learners to attain higher levels of proficiency in the short term than younger learners do suggests that there is an advantage to providing second language instruction relatively late in students' schooling. Older students' more mature cognitive system, with the capacity to abstract, classify, generalize, and consciously attend to language qua language, may be well suited for the task of learning a second language in school, where language is often used and taught in an abstract, decontextualized manner. The younger learner, who is thought to use unconscious, automatic kinds of learning strategies, may be at a relative disadvantage in such a context. There is some support for this argument in the general observation that older students tend to learn faster than younger students in most cognitive domains. Rosansky (1975) has made the contrasting argument—namely, that second language learning is "blocked" in the case of older learners by cognitive factors and, in particular, by the development of formal operations as defined by Piaget. As already noted, however, the evidence does not indicate that older learners are in fact "blocked."

The suggestion that older learners can make rapid progress because of their cognitive maturity is not to suggest that formalized, cognitively focused approaches to second language teaching be used with such learners in order to capitalize on their cognitive maturity. As already noted, it has been found that the apparent learning efficiency of the older learner is evident in both natural and school contexts. Moreover, the results of evaluations of late immersion programs in Montreal indicate the effectiveness of naturalistic approaches at all age levels (Genesee, 1983).

Notwithstanding the cognitive advantages of the older learner, there may be an advantage to second language instruction that begins relatively early; this advantage is associated with time. A number of studies indicate that duration of instruction can be an important correlate of second language achievement. J. B. Carroll (1975), in an international study on the teaching of French as a foreign language in eight countries, found that, among a number of different predictors of second language achievement, length of instruction was the most important one. Similarly, evaluations of Canadian immersion programs have found higher levels of achievement in immersion options that provide more exposure to French, for example, total versus partial early immersion (see Genesee, 1983, for a review).

Although the advantages associated with time are not linked directly with the age factor, the two factors are related to the extent that programs that begin second language instruction when the child is young have more potential time available for teaching than programs that begin instruction when the learner is older. A corollary advantage of extended instructional time in school is the opportunity it affords the learner to practice and learn the language outside school. Although this opportunity is available to both older and younger students, it is reduced in the former case because of the reduction in duration of the school program. The possibility of extracurricular use of the second language can be a major variable in educational decisions in bilingual communities where real opportunities to use the language exist. Thus, there is an advantage to early second language instruction, as in the case of any complex skill, insofar as it affords the learner more opportunity, discussed here in terms of time, to learn. Second language learning that begins when the learner is young can benefit not only from the advantages associated with the possibility of extended time to learn but also from the advantages associated with cognitive maturity as the learner continues his or her education. Taken together, then, the cognitive factor and the time factor should favor an early start to second language learning (Genesee, 1978).

No discussion of the optimal age for teaching second languages in school would be complete, however, without a consideration of pedagogical practices. Whether or not younger and older learners will actually benefit from the particular advantage(s) they bring to the task of second language learning will depend in no small way on the learning environment. This point can be illustrated by the following example. In conjunction with the evaluation of a regular one-year late immersion program, Stevens (1976) evaluated the effectiveness of an innovative activity-centered late immersion program. Both the regular immersion and activity-centered immersion programs under investigation were at the grade 7 level, and both were preceded by core French instruction from kindergarten. The programs differed substantially in their approaches. In the regular immersion program, teaching tended to be teacher-centered and group-oriented so that all students worked on the same material, at the same time, for the same length of time. In contrast, in the activity-centered program, the students worked individually or in small groups, at their own pace, on projects that they selected (see Stevens, 1983, for a complete description of this program). This program was based on Piagetian principles and was designed to capitalize on the learner's capacity to acquire language for self-motivated reasons. Another difference between the programs was that whereas the activity-centered program occupied 40 percent of the school day, usually the afternoon, the teacher-centered program occupied 80 percent of the day. Thus, the time factor favored the regular program. Despite this, a systematic comparison of carefully selected, matched groups of students from each program indicated that the students in the activity-centered program had achieved the same levels of proficiency as had the teacher-centered program students in interpersonal communication skills (i.e., speaking and listening) and almost the same levels of proficiency in literacy skills (i.e., reading and writing). These findings indicate clearly that it is not sufficient simply to provide more instructional time to produce higher levels of achievement—time must be translated into learning.

In summary, there are advantages related to time and cognitive maturity that are differentially associated with early and late second language learning. Late instruction confers an advantage to learning by virtue of the learner's cognitive maturity, whereas early instruction confers an advantage by virtue of the extended opportunities it provides for language learning and practice in and outside of school. The combined advantages of time and cognitive maturity favor an early start to second language learning with a continuation into the higher grades. Whether or not such advantages will be realized will depend to a significant extent on the nature and quality of the second language program.

CONCLUSION

Basic research on brain–language relations in bilinguals has grown in recent years in diverse and interesting ways, some of which have been illustrated in this chapter. Innovative and more powerful research techniques will continue to be developed and used as researchers seek to better describe and understand the neuropsychological basis of language learning, language representation, and language processing. Neuropsychological investigations of bilinguals can be doubly fascinating because not only are they interesting in their own right, but they may also reveal some important general truths about all brains, monolingual and bilingual alike.

The application of basic research findings to professional practice is always a risky business. This is no less true in the case of language education. As was indicated in the discussion of differential hemispheric involvement in second language processing, research findings are often too incomplete and limited to indicate substantial and unqualified practicial implications. To base educational practice on existing neuropsychological knowledge is at present not advisable. Seliger (1982) recounts an anecdote that illustrates the dangers of applying theoretical research findings to classroom practice in simplistic ways: A student at the Queens College English Language Institute reported receiving ESL instruction in which students were required to write English with their nonpreferred hand, which was the left hand in most cases. Apparently this approach was used in order to activate the right hemisphere, which is otherwise inactive, and in order to avoid interference from the left hemisphere, where the first language is stored. The course instructor justified this practice on the basis of current research findings.

Even if more complete or conclusive empirical evidence were available concerning language learning and the brain, it would not necessarily lend itself easily to developing new educational progams or approaches. There are no clear educational prescriptions associated with research findings regarding basic neuropsychological processes. And, as Scovel (1982) cogently states, "it is not necessary to employ . . . neurolinguistic research to justify good pedagogy or to condemn inadequate classroom practices; rather the contribution of neuropsychology . . . should be indirect and insightful" (p. 324). At the same time, a well-informed knowledge of research findings can lead to educationally pertinent and stimulating possibilities. As was illustrated in the review and critique of the CPH, research findings can challenge our sometimes complacent and poorly substantiated beliefs about the way learning occurs. These challenges can promote innovative and improved educational approaches.

REFERENCES

Adiv, E. A comparative evaluation of three immersion programs: Grades 10 and 11. Unpublished manuscript, Protestant School Board of Greater Montreal, 1980.

Albert, M., & Obler, L. *The bilingual brain*. New York: Academic Press, 1978.

Asher, J., & Garcia, R. The optimal age to learn a foreign language. *Modern Language Journal*, 1969, *8*, 334–341.

Barton, M., Goodglass, H., & Shai, A. Differential recognition of tachistoscopically presented English and Hebrew words in right and left visual fields. *Perceptual and Motor Skills*, 1965, *21*, 431–437.

Bellisle, F. Early bilingualism and cerebral dominance. Unpublished manuscript, Psychology Department, McGill University, May 1975.

Burstall, C. *Primary French in the balance*. Windsor, England: NFER Publishing Company, 1974.

Carroll, F. Neurolinguistic processing of a second language: Experimental evidence. In R. Scarcella & S. Krashen (Eds.), *Research in second language acquisition*. Rowley, MA: Newbury House, 1980.

Carroll, J. B. *The teaching of French as a foreign language in eight countries*. New York: Wiley, 1975.

Endo, M., Shimizu, A., & Hori, T. Functional asymmetry of visual fields for Japanese words in kana (syllable-based) writing and Japanese shape-recognition in Japanese subjects. *Neuropsychologia*, 1978, *16*, 291–297.

Galloway, L. The cerebral organization of language in bilinguals and second language learners: Clinical and experimental evidence. Unpublished doctoral dissertation, University of California at Los Angeles, 1979.

Galloway, L., & Krashen, S. Cerebral organization in bilingualism and second language. In R. Scarcella & S. Krashen (Eds.), *Research on second language acquisition*. Rowley, MA: Newbury House, 1980.

Galloway, L., & Scarcella, R. Cerebral organization in adult second language acquisition: Is the right hemisphere more involved? *Brain and Language*, 1982, *16*, 56–60.

Gaziel, T., Obler, L., & Albert, M. A tachistoscopic study of Hebrew-English bilinguals. In M. Albert & L. Obler (Eds.), *The bilingual brain*. New York: Academic Press, 1978.

Genesee, F. Is there an optimal age for starting second language instruction? *McGill Journal of Education*, 1978, *13*, 145–154.

Genesee, F. A comparison of early and late second language learning. *Canadian Journal of Behavioral Sciences*, 1981, *13*, 115–127.

Genesee, F. Bilingual education of majority language children: The immersion experiments in review. *Applied Psycholinguistics*, 1983, *4*, 1–46.

Genesee, F., Hamers, J., Lambert, W. E., Mononen, L., Seitz, M., & Starck, R. Language processing strategies in bilinguals: A neurophysiological study. *Brain and Language*, 1978, *5*, 1–12.

Gordon, H. W. Cerebral organization in bilinguals: I. Lateralization. *Brain and Language*, 1980, *9*, 255–268.

Hartnett, D. The relation of cognitive style and hemispheric preference to deductive and inductive second language learning. Unpublished master's thesis, University of California at Los Angeles, 1974.

Hatta, T. Recognition of Japanese *kanji* in the left and right visual fields. *Neuropsychologia*, 1977, *15*, 685–688.

Hatta, T. Recognition of Japanese *kanji* and *hiragana* in the left and right visual fields. *Japanese Psychological Research*, 1978, *20*, 51–59.

Hatta, T. Differential processing of *kanji* and *kana* stimuli in Japanese people: Some implications from Stroop test results. *Neuropsychologia*, 1981, *19*, 87–93.

Hink, R., Kaga, K., & Suzuki, J. An evoked potential correlate of reading ideographic and phonetic Japanese scripts. *Neuropsychologia*, 1980, *18*, 455–464.

Hinshelwood, J. Four cases of word blindness. *Lancet*, 1902, *1*, 358–363.

Hirata, K., & Osaka, R. Tachistoscopic recognition of Japanese letter materials in left and right visual fields. *Psychologia*, 1967, *10*, 7–18.

Hung, D. L., & Tzeng, O. Orthographic variations and visual information processing. *Psychological Bulletin*, 1981, *90*, 377–414.

Hynd, G. W., Teeter, A., & Stewart, A. Acculturation and the lateralization of speech in the bilingual native American. *International Journal of Neuroscience*, 1980, *11*, 1–7.

Kershner, J., & Jeng, A. G.-R. Dual functional asymmetry in visual perception: Effects of ocular dominance and postexposural processes. *Neuropsychologia*, 1972, *10*, 437–445.

Kolb, B., & Whishaw, I. Q. *Fundamentals of human neuropsychology*. San Francisco: W. H. Freeman, 1980.

Kotik, B. Investigation of speech lateralization in multilinguals. Unpublished doctoral dissertation, Moscow State University, 1975.

Kotik, B. An evoked potential study of Polish-Russian bilinguals. Personal communication, 1980.

Krashen, S. D. The critical period for language acquisition and its possible bases. *Annals of the New York Academy of Sciences.* 1974, *263*, 211–224.

Krashen, S. D. The monitor model for adult second language performance. In M. Burt, H. Dulay, & M. Finocchiaro (Eds.), *Viewpoints on English as a second language.* New York: Regents, 1977.

Krashen, S. D. Accounting for child–adult differences in second language rate and attainment. In S. Krashen, R. C. Scarcella, & M. H. Long (Eds.), *Child–adult differences in second language acquisition.* Rowley, MA: Newbury House, 1982.

Krashen, S. D., & Galloway, L. The neurological correlates of language acquisition: Current research. *SPEAQ Journal,* 1978, *2,* 21–35.

Krashen, S. D., Scarcella, R. C., & Long, M. H. *Child–adult differences in second language acquisition.* Rowley, MA: Newbury House, 1982.

Lamendella, J. General principles of neuro-functional organization and their manifestation in primary and non-primary language acquisition. *Language Learning,* 1977, *27,* 155–196.

Lenneberg, E. *Biological foundations of language.* New York: Wiley, 1967.

Lyman, R., Kwan, S. T., & Chao, W. H. Left occipito-parietal brain tumor with observations on alexia and agraphia in Chinese and English. *Chinese Medical Journal,* 1938, *54,* 491–516.

Maître, S. On the representation of second language in the brain. Unpublished master's thesis, University of California at Los Angeles, 1974.

McLaughlin, B. *Second language acquisition in childhood.* Hillsdale, NJ: Lawrence Erlbaum Associates, 1978.

Molfese, D. L., & Molfese, V. J. Hemisphere and stimulus differences as reflected in the cortical responses of newborn infants to speech stimuli. *Developmental Psychology,* 1979, *15,* 505–511.

Neufeld, G. A test of the critical period hypothesis, strong version. Paper, Department of Linguistics, University of Ottawa, 1979.

Neufeld, G., & Schneiderman, E. Prosodic and articulatory features in adult language learning. In R. C. Scarcella & S. D. Krashen (Eds.), *Research in second language acquisition.* Rowley, MA: Newbury House, 1980.

Obler, L. Right hemisphere participation in second language acquisition. Paper presented at the Conference on Individual Differences and Universals in Language Learning Aptitude, Durham, New Hampshire, 1977.

Obler, L., Albert, M., & Gordon, H. W. Asymmetry of cerebral dominance in Hebrew-English bilinguals. Paper presented at the Thirteenth Annual Meeting of the Academy of Aphasia, Victoria, British Columbia, 1975.

Olson, L., & Samuels, S. The relationship between age and accuracy of foreign language pronunciation. *Journal of Educational Research,* 1973, *66,* 263–267.

Orbach, J. Differential recognition of Hebrew and English words in right and left visual fields as a function of cerebral dominance and reading habits. *Neuropsychologia,* 1967, *50,* 127–134.

Oyama, S. A sensitive period for the acquisition of a non-native phonological system. *Journal of Psycholinguistic Research*, 1976, *5*, 261–285.

Oyama, S. The sensitive period and comprehension of speech. *Working Papers on Bilingualism*, 1978, *16*, 1–17.

Paradis, M. Bilingualism and aphasia. In H. Whitaker & H. Whitaker (Eds.), *Studies in neurolinguistics*. New York: Academic Press, 1977.

Patkowski, M. The sensitive period for the acquisition of syntax in a second language. *Language Learning*, 1980, *30*, 449–472.

Penfield, W., & Roberts, L. *Speech and brain mechanisms*. New York: Atheneum, 1959.

Piazza, D., & Zatorre, R. Right ear advantage for dichotic listening in bilingual children. *Brain and Language*, 1981, *13*, 389–396.

Rogers, L., TenHouten, W., Kaplan, C., & Gardiner, M. Hemispheric specialization of language: An EEG study of bilingual Hopi children. *International Journal of Neuroscience*, 1977, *8*, 1–6.

Rosansky, E. The critical period for the acquisition of language: Some cognitive developmental considerations. *Working Papers on Bilingualism*, 1975, *6*, 92–102.

Schneiderman, E., & Wesche, M. The role of the right hemisphere in second language acquisition. In K. Bailey, M. Long, & S. Peck (Eds.), *Second language acquisition studies*. Rowley, MA: Newbury House, 1980.

Scott, S., Hynd, G., Hunt, L., & Weed, W. Cerebral speech lateralization in the native American Navajo. *Neuropsychologia*, 1979, *17*, 89–92.

Scovel, T. Questions concerning the application of neurolinguistic research to second language learning/teaching. *TESOL Quarterly*, 1982, *16*, 323–332.

Searleman, A. A review of right hemisphere linguistic capabilities. *Psychological Bulletin*, 1977, *84*, 503–528.

Seliger, H. W. Implications of a multiple critical periods hypothesis for second language learning. In W. C. Ritchie (Ed.), *Second language acquisition research*. New York: Academic Press, 1978.

Seliger, H. W. On the possible role of the right hemisphere in second language acquisition. *TESOL Quarterly*, 1982, *16*, 307–314.

Seliger, H. W., Krashen, S. D., & Ladefoged, P. Maturational constraints on the acquisition of second language accent. *Language Sciences*, 1975, *36*, 20–22.

Silverberg, R., Bentin, S., Gaziel, T., Obler, L., & Albert, M. Shift of visual field preference for English words in native Hebrew speakers. *Brain and Language*, 1979, *8*, 184–190.

Silverberg, R., Gordon, H. W., Pollack, S., & Bentin, S. Shift of visual field preference for Hebrew words in native speakers learning to read. *Brain and Language*, 1980, *11*, 99–105.

Snow, C., & Hoefnagel-Höhle, M. Age differences in second language acquisition. *Language and Speech*, 1977, *20*, 357–365.

Snow, C., & Hoefnagel-Höhle, M. The critical period for language acquisition: Evidence from second language learning. *Child Development*, 1978, *49*, 1114–1128.

Soares, C. Language processing in bilinguals: Neurolinguistic and psycholinguistic studies. Unpublished doctoral dissertation, Northeastern University, Boston, 1982.

Soares, C., & Grosjean, F. Left hemisphere language lateralization in bilinguals and monolinguals. *Perception and Psychophysics*, 1981, *29*, 599–604.

Starck, R., Genesee, F., Lambert, W. E., & Seitz, M. Multiple language experience and the development of cerebral dominance. In S. J. Segalowitz & F. A. Gruber (Eds.), *Language development and neurological theory*. New York: Academic Press, 1977.

Stevens, F. Second Language learning in an activity-centered program. Unpublished master's thesis, Concordia University, Montreal, 1976.

Stevens, F. Activities to promote learning and communication in the second language classroom. *TESOL Quarterly*, 1983, *17*, 259–272.

Sugishita, M., Iwata, M., Toyokura, Y., Yoshida, M., & Yamada, R. Reading of ideograms and phonograms in Japanese patients after partial commissurotomy. *Neuropsychologia*, 1978, *16*, 417–426.

Sugishita, M., Toyokura, Y., Yoshioka, M., & Yamada, R. Unilateral agraphia after section of the posterior half of the truncus of the corpus callosum. *Brain and Language*, 1980, *9*, 215–225.

Sussman, H., Franklin, P., & Simon, T. Bilingual speech: Bilateral control? *Brain and Language*, 1982, *15*, 125–142.

Vaid, J. Visual field asymmetries on a bilingual Stroop test. Unpublished manuscript, McGill University, 1979.

Vaid, J. Bilingualism and brain lateralization. In S. Segalowitz (Ed.), *Language functions and brain organization*. New York: Academic Press, 1983, 315–339.

Vaid, J., & Genesee, F. Neurological approaches to bilingualism: A critical review. *Canadian Journal of Psychology*, 1980, *34*, 417–445.

Vaid, J., & Lambert, W. E. Differential cerebral involvement in the cognitive functioning of bilinguals. *Brain and Language*, 1979, *8*, 92–110.

Vildomec, V. *Multilingualism*. Leyden: A. W. Sythoff Printing Division, 1963.

Walsh, T. M., & Diller, K. C. Neurolinguistic considerations on the optimum age for second language learning. In K. Diller (Ed.), *Individual differences and universals in language learning aptitude*. Rowley, MA: Newbury House, 1981.

Weinreich, U. *Languages in contact*. New York: Linguistic Circle of New York, 1953.

Whorf, B. *Language, thought, and reality*. Cambridge, MA: MIT Press, 1956.

Witelson, S. F. Early hemisphere specialization and interhemisphere plasticity: An empirical and theoretical review. In S. Segalowitz & F. A. Gruber (Eds.), *Language development and neurological theory*. New York: Academic Press, 1977.

Wong Fillmore, L. Individual differences in second language acquisition. In C. J. Fillmore, D. Kempler, & W. S.-Y. Wang (Eds.), *Individual differences in language ability and language behavior*. New York: Academic Press, 1979.

Zaidel, E. Auditory language comprehension in the right hemisphere following cerebral commissurotomy and hemispherectomy: A comparison with child language and aphasia. In A. Caramazza & E. B. Zurif (Eds.), *The acquisition and breakdown of language: Parallels and divergencies*. Baltimore: Johns Hopkins University Press, 1978.

Zangwill, O. L. Speech and the minor hemisphere. *Acta Neurologica et Psychiatrica Belgica*, 1967, *67*, 1013–1020.

SUGGESTED READINGS

Grosjean, F. The bilingual person: Chapter 5. *Life with two languages*. Cambridge, MA: Harvard University Press, 1982.

Hatch, E. Neurolinguistics and bilingualism: Chapter 11. *Psycholinguistics: A second language perspective*. Rowley, MA: Newbury House, 1983.

Scovel, T. Questions concerning the application of neurolinguistic research to second language learning/teaching. *TESOL Quarterly*, 1982, *16*, 323–331.

Seliger, H. On the possible role of the right hemisphere in second language acquisition. *TESOL Quarterly*, 1982, *16*, 307–314.

Whitaker, H. A. Bilingualism: A neurolinguistic perspective. In W. C. Ritchie (Ed.), *Second language acquisition research*. New York: Academic Press, 1978.

four

CLASSROOM
RESEARCH
PERSPECTIVE

Instructed Interlanguage Development

Michael H. Long, University of Hawaii at Manoa

EARLY RESEARCH ON THE EFFECT OF INSTRUCTION, AND SOME CLAIMED IMPLICATIONS

One of the many positive outcomes of modern second language acquisition (SLA) research has been the jolt it has given the language teaching establishment. In the 1960s and 1970s, many language teachers were lulled into a false sense of security by the confident pronouncements of methodologists concerning the efficacy of contrastive analysis, pattern drill, structural syllabuses, notional-functional syllabuses, grammar explanations, translation, error correction, communicative language teaching, any number of language teaching "methods," or whatever else the writers happened to believe in. Most teachers assumed that the people making the pronouncements had taken the trouble to test them, that we *knew* how people learned second languages in classrooms and how best to teach them. In fact, of course, this was, and still is, simply untrue.

As wave after wave of unsubstantiated prescriptions washed over them (sometimes conflicting prescriptions emanating from the same "experts"), teachers and applied linguists adopted different defense mechanisms. Some converted to the dogma of one or a particular group of gurus (see Maley, 1983, for an insightful analysis of this phenomenon). Others (see Clarke, 1982) opted for eclecticism, and still others for the so-called eclectic method, whatever that might be. An increasing number, however, decided that a more responsible solution was to investigate systematically classroom language teaching and classroom SLA—the process that, as teachers, they were employed to facilitate.

Perhaps as a reaction to the extreme interventionist era of contrastive analysis, neobehaviorist learning theory and audiolingualism, many researchers began by looking for, finding, and stressing some of the inescapable *similarities* between naturalistic and instructed SLA. Not infrequently, they went on to claim that, therefore, teaching could have little or no effect on the acquisition process—a logical possibility, given the findings, but not necessarily true, as will become apparent.

An example of this type of research and argumentation is the work of some North American investigators who, in the 1970s, produced evidence that the order in which accurate suppliance of certain grammatical morphemes in obligatory contexts attained criterion (80 or 90 percent) was *similar* across learners from different first language backgrounds (see Burt & Dulay, 1980, and Krashen, 1977, for review), and in naturalistic and instructed learner groups (see, for example, Krashen, Sferlazza, Feldman, & Fathman, 1976). The first finding was interpreted by Dulay and Burt (1977) as evidence of a common underlying acquisition process, *creative construction.* Because it seemed that this process would operate automatically in child second language (SL) learners if they were exposed to natural samples of the target language, Dulay and Burt (1973) concluded that children *should not be taught syntax.*

Krashen (1982 and elsewhere), too, claimed that the similarities reflected a common underlying process, which he calls *acquisition*, responsible for the bulk of SLA in any context, including the classroom. Krashen also claimed that unconscious, "acquired" knowledge of the target language (TL) was responsible for normal SL performance. Conscious knowledge of simple TL grammar rules, *learning*, is rarely accessible in natural communication, when the language user is focused on meaning, not form. Further, it could not later become *acquisition* (Krashen & Scarcella, 1978). Hence, the instruction that produced *learning* was also relatively unimportant. *Most of a SL cannot be taught*, Krashen claims; it must be acquired.

Some related claims were soon being made by European researchers. Felix and Simmet (1981) studied the acquisition of English pronouns by German high school students over an eleven-month period. The researchers showed that the children (ages 10–12) acquired ESL (English as a second language) pronominalization in a highly systematic manner, with the errors resulting from substitutions of one pronoun for another falling into only eight of a mathematically far larger number of potential error types. The children followed a process of gradually adding grammatical and semantic features ([person] vs. [possessive] > [number] > [personal] > [gender]) to their interim pronoun grammars.[1] Needless to say, this was not the way their instructors were attempting to teach them English pronouns. Rather, new pronouns were being presented and drilled as distinct morphemes, with clusters of features ready packed, as it were. The acquisition strategies observed paralleled those noted in naturalistic acquirers, leading Felix and Simmet (1981) to conclude that

> [T]he students' instruction-independent learning strategies demonstrate . . . that the learning process can only be manipulated within narrow limits and that the principles and regularities of natural language acquisition must also be considered in foreign language instruction. (p. 26)

In another publication from the same study, Felix (1981) reported finding structural parallels between the interlanguage (IL) negation, interrogation, pronouns, and sentence types of German high school EFL (English as a foreign language) students and naturalistic acquirers of ESL. Felix concluded:

> . . . foreign language learning under classroom conditions seems to partially follow the same set of natural processes that characterize other types of language acquisition . . . there seems to be a universal and common set of principles which are flexible enough and adaptable to the large number of conditions under which language learning may take place. *These observations furthermore suggest that the possibility of manipulating and controlling the students' verbal behavior in the classroom is in fact quite limited.* (Reprinted with permission of *Language Learning* from "The Effect of Formal Instruction on Second Language Acquisition" by S. W. Felix, *Language Learning, 31*, no. 1 (1981), p. 109; emphasis added.)

In a similar vein, Wode (1981) compared findings on the acquisition of English negation in different types of language learning: child language development, foreign language learning, naturalistic second language learning and relearning, pidginization and creolization. Although he recognized that differences did exist, the similarities he found in the developmental structures and developmental sequences across acquisitional types, Wode claimed, reflected universal processing abilities and (innate) language learning strategies (e.g., the initial preference for free over bound forms), and the availability of these abilities and strategies in any language learning context and at any period in a learner's life. The results further indicated, according to Wode, that teachers "should not devise their teaching materials and teaching procedures to go counter to natural learner abilities" (Wode 1981, p. 231). Wode did not elaborate on what kinds of teaching would constitute "going counter to" (or facilitating) the working of these natural abilities. Neither Wode's nor Felix's research, it should be noted, had *studied* alternatives in language teaching.

The European and North American research has certainly been useful in drawing attention to the unarguable similarities between naturalistic and instructed SLA. At the very least, it emphasizes the importance of the learner's contribution to language learning, and serves as a healthy reminder to teachers that they are partners, not masters, in a joint enterprise.

Unfortunately, however, many of the conclusions about the limitations or inefficacy of instruction are non sequiturs or, at best, *inferences* from studies that have looked not at the *effects* of instruction, but at similarities in the interlanguages of naturalistic and classroom learners. Yet it has been the inferences, not research, that have in turn formed a large part of the basis for prescriptions for language *teaching*.

Although some researchers (e.g., Felix and Wode) have been more circumspect, the prescriptions have occasionally been of the kind that equate teaching with nothing more than the provision of comprehensible input. Krashen, for example, writes:

> The research on the efficacy of instruction, the research on methods comparisons, and the Fundamental Pedagogical Principle ["Any instructional technique that helps second language acquisition does so by providing comprehensible input." (Krashen, 1981, p. 59)] all lead me to the conclusion that the second language class is a very good place to acquire a second language! It is a place where the beginning student, especially the older beginner, can obtain the input necessary for improvement, CI [comprehensible input] that the outside world is often unwilling or unable to give. (Reprinted with permission of *Studia Linguistica* from "The 'Fundamental Pedagogical Principle' in Second Language Teaching" by S. D. Krashen, *Studia Linguistica, 35* (1981), p. 59.)

This is what is known as a left-handed compliment.

Currently, the major methodological realization of these ideas is known as the *natural approach*. Krashen and Terrell (1983) advocate provision of comprehensible input in the form of the roughly tuned teacher and peer speech that arise naturally from *communication*, delivered in a positive affective classroom climate, as the essential ingredient of any successful language teaching program. *Pro*scribed are structural grading, a focus on form, grammar and vocabulary explanations, error correction, and other traditional language teaching activities, except where those activities could help with the learning of a few low-level target language rules, help satisfy learner expectations, or serve as an indirect way of providing more comprehensible input. The goal of the classroom, Krashen writes:

> is not to produce native speakers or even error-free second language performance. It is, rather, to develop "intermediate" second language competence, to bring the student to the point where he can begin to understand the language he hears and reads outside the class and thus improve on his own. (Reprinted with permission of *Studia Linguistica* from "The 'Fundamental Pedagogical Principle' in Second Language Teaching" by S. D. Krashen, *Studia Linguistica, 35* (1981), p. 61.)

Another possible implementation suggested elsewhere by Krashen (1981, pp. 66–67) is for foreign university students to receive ESL at the "beginning" level (with the main purpose of instruction being the provision of comprehensible input); to take "sheltered subject matter" courses at the "intermediate" level (e.g., Psychology 101 for foreign students, along the lines of Canadian immersion programs), but with *optional* ESL work as a supplement; and to be mainstreamed into regular subject matter courses at the "advanced" level, with *no* accompanying ESL at all at this level.[2] Such prescriptions may yet turn out to be justified, but until the evidence is in, for example from SL classroom research, they need to be treated with great caution, a point that, to his credit, Krashen (1981, p. 67) himself stresses.

Opinions about the natural approach, sheltered subject matter classes, and the like will obviously vary depending on one's training and field experience in applied linguistics and language teaching. An experienced SL program designer, for example, *might* be impressed by the natural approach's psycholinguistic credentials and/or by its methodological innovations, but would flinch at its disregard for learner needs identification or, indeed, for any kind of syllabus (content) at all (see Long, 1985, for discussion).

Just how strong, in fact, is the evidence for the *in*efficacy of conventional SL instruction (with a focus on form) that is assumed by Krashen and implied, as we have seen, by various other SLA theorists? The following review will attempt to show that (1) SLA research to date has barely *begun* to probe the effects of instruction on IL development, but that (2) studies conducted so far have already revealed some potentially very positive contributions instruction can make. If *either* of these statements is correct, it follows that prescriptions from theorists at this juncture are premature if they effectively involve the abandonment of instruction. The review of research is not exhaustive. Rather, it attempts to delineate four distinct, though related, areas for future work, and to illustrate each with selected studies and findings.

THE EFFECT OF INSTRUCTION ON IL DEVELOPMENT

The Effect of Instruction on Acquisition Processes

The SLA literature contains a dazzling array of putative acquisition *processes*. A partial list includes transfer; transfer of training; (over)generalization; restrictive, elaborative, and conformative simplification; nativization; pidginization; depidginization; creolization; decreolization; regularization; stabilization; destabilization; and, of course, the onset of linguistic rigor mortis, fossilization.

Some of these processes have been linked to various contextual factors, including characteristics of the linguistic environment. Thus, pidginization is believed to be at least partly due to the attempt by speakers in bi- or trilingual contact to develop a common SL in spite of restricted and often deviant input from the superstrate language (Bickerton, 1976). Destabilization (of potentially fossilizable forms) is claimed to occur through the reception of expected negative feedback on the cognitive dimension, and fossilization through reception of predominantly expected positive feedback on the cognitive dimension (Vigil & Oller, 1976).

Other processes are thought to be encouraged by certain types of performance tasks. Transfer and restrictive simplification, respectively, for example, have each been claimed to be more frequent when learners are obliged to outperform their current SL competence (Krashen, 1981) or when they opt for communicative efficiency over accuracy (Meisel, Clahsen, & Pienemann, 1981).

Now, although most of these claims concern naturalistic language learning, contextual variation may also be a useful way of thinking about acquisition in the classroom. I would claim that, beneath superficial differences among teaching methods, materials, and syllabuses, alternatives in SL instruction consist essentially of varied selections among options of two kinds. First, there are *options in the way linguistic input to learners is manipulated.* Choices here exist fundamentally in such matters as (1) the *sequence* in which learners will encounter linguistic units of various kinds, along with (2) the *frequency/intensity* and (3) the *saliency* of those encounters.

Second, there are *options in the types of production tasks classroom learners are set.* It is reasonable to expect that formal instruction may trigger such processes as transfer, transfer of training, and (over)generalization, depending on the choices teachers and materials writers make in this area. For example, are students allowed or encouraged to avoid error, or are they set tasks that lead them to take linguistic risks, for example, by using generalization in applying a new linguistic item in a context in which they have not yet encountered its use? Do the pedagogic tasks teachers set allow more or less attention to speech, with resulting higher or lower rates of targetlike use (Sato, 1985; Tarone, 1984)?

Further, if various characteristics of (1) the linguistic and/or conversational environment and (2) the performance tasks are what trigger some of the processes, it would seem reasonable to expect instructed and naturalistic acquirers to exhibit either partially different acquisition processes or, at least, different degrees of preference for the same processes. For example, one result of teachers and textbooks isolating grammatical forms such as third person singular *-s* and progressive *-ing* is the increased saliency of those forms in the input. The increased saliency may cause instructed learners to notice and use the forms earlier, resulting in differing and perhaps ultimately "healthier" error profiles. Increased awareness of and attempts to use what are often, after all, communicatively redundant grammatical elements may also lead to *faster rates of acquisition* and/or to *higher levels of ultimate SL attainment*.[3] In addition, instructed learners may ultimately become more nativelike in the sense of exhibiting *greater grammatical accuracy*.

Exploratory work on the effect of instruction on acquisition processes by Felix (1981), Felix and Simmet (1981), and Wode (1981) was outlined earlier. The researchers' focus, it was noted, was the *similarities* that exist in the acquisition processes of classroom and naturalistic acquirers. Despite the potential effects of context on acquisition processes, there has been very little work to date that looks for *differences* as well as similarities in this aspect of interlanguage development, with the major study being that by Pica (1983). As with so much of the research on the effect of instruction on IL development to date, however, Pica's findings are highly suggestive, and encouraging for teachers.

Pica distinguished *three* acquisition contexts in her work: naturalistic, instructed, and mixed, the last being a combination of classroom instruction plus natural exposure in the target language environment. After some initial screening interviews, 18 adult native speakers (NSs) of Spanish learning ESL were identified whose learning histories placed them uniquely in one context. There was a total of 6 subjects per context, with the subjects in each cell in the criterion group design representing a fairly wide range of SL proficiency, as defined by the stage each had reached in his or her acquisition of ESL negation (*no* + verb, *don't* + verb, auxiliary-negative, and analyzed *don't*). Each speaker was interviewed informally (the 6 instruction-only subjects in Mexico City), with each conversation covering the same range of topics. Approximately one hour of free speech was transcribed and analyzed in a variety of ways.

The first and simplest analysis Pica performed was a supplied in obligatory contexts (SOC) analysis of nine grammatical morphemes in the speech of learners from the three language learning contexts. This revealed morpheme orders that correlated highly with each other and with a "natural order" previously established by Krashen (1977), suggesting some basic similarities in SLA, regardless of context, and providing additional support for the claims to this effect made by previous researchers.

Although the SOC morpheme rank orders for all groups correlated strongly with one another, Pica noted that there were considerable differences among the groups in the case of certain morphemes in terms of both the ranks they occupied and the SOC percentage scores on which the ranks were based. For example, the instruction-only group scored 19 percentage points and one or two ranks higher on plural -*s* than did the mixed and naturalistic groups, respectively, and 38 percent and 41 percent higher than the naturalistic and mixed groups on third person singular -*s*. Pica notes that both these morphemes have transparent form–function relationships ("easy grammar," in Krashen's terms) and suggests that it may be precisely in this area that instruction has its greatest effect.

Aware of the many limitations of SOC analysis (see Long & Sato, 1984 for a recent review), Pica next conducted a targetlike use (TLU) analysis of the same morphemes. The way researchers perform TLU analysis varies somewhat (see Pica, 1984, for a detailed account) but always involves looking not just at accurate suppliance of elements in obligatory contexts, but also at targetlike and *non*targetlike suppliance of the elements in *non*obligatory contexts. TLU analysis, therefore, captures such important distinctions as that between the following two (hypothetical) learners. As measured by SOC analysis, both supply definite articles with over 90 percent accuracy. But whereas one scores that high by differentiating between contexts for definite and indefinite articles, the other uses definite articles in *all* contexts for articles of both types (thereby scoring well for definite but zero for indefinite) and has not really grasped the use of definite articles at all.[4]

Pica's rank orders for TLU of the same morphemes correlated well across the three groups and with the SOC orders. What the TLU analysis also revealed, however, was a number of fascinating differences between the three groups, with the greatest differences obtaining between the instruction-only group and the other two.

Controlling for proficiency level as measured by negation stage, Pica looked at the *kinds* of errors made by the learners in all three groups, and compared the acquisition strategies and processes revealed by those errors. Pica found that learners who had never received formal SL instruction tended to *omit* grammatical morphemes, such as *-ing* and plural *-s*, whereas classroom learners (and to a lesser degree and in later stages, mixed learners) showed a strong tendency to *overapply* morphological marking of this kind.

Overapplication errors consisted of two types: (1) a small number (2 percent of the total errors for classroom learners, and 1 percent for naturalistic learners) of *overgeneralization* errors, involving suppliance of regularized irregular morphemes in obligatory contexts (e.g., "He buy*ed* a car yesterday"), and (2) frequent errors of *overuse* of morphemes in *non*obligatory contexts (e.g., "He liv*ed* in London now," "I don't understand*ing* these people"). Although *both* naturalistic and instructed learners made errors of these kinds, the frequency of such errors in instructed over uninstructed learners was significantly higher at almost all proficiency levels. Mixed learners performed like naturalistic learners at lower proficiency levels, but became more like instructed learners at higher levels of proficiency. Further, whereas instruction-only subjects used the plural *-s* form significantly more often than did subjects in the other two groups, the naturalistic group tended to omit targetlike noun endings and to use a free-form quantifier instead (*two book, many town*), a production strategy observed in many of the world's pidgins and creoles.

On the basis of these results (presented here in summary form only), Pica draws the following conclusions:

1. Similarities (e.g., common morpheme difficulty orders) across the three learner types support the idea that a great deal of SLA depends on learner, not environmental or contextual, factors.

2. Instruction affects SL production/performance (a) by triggering over-suppliance of grammatical morphology and (b) by *inhibiting* (not preventing altogether) the use of ungrammatical, even if communicatively effective, constructions found in pidgins.

The last point (b) appears to hold for *any* learners receiving formal instruction, that is, for mixed as well as instruction-only learners. Mixed learners show a greater inclination to pidginize in the early stages but appear to shake off this tendency later. In sum, Pica notes that, as evidenced by the error profiles of her subjects, "differing conditions of L2 exposure appear to affect acquirers' hypotheses about the target language and their strategies for using it" (1983, p. 495).

Pica cautions that no conclusions can be drawn about rate of acquisition or level of ultimate SL attainment from her findings, only about SL production. It is noteworthy, however, that the tendencies to overapply grammatical morphology and to avoid pidginization strategies distinguished instructed from totally uninstructed learners at nearly all proficiency levels in her (cross-sectional) study. This *could* signal long-term, even permanent, differences between the two types of learners.

More likely, such differences mean differing *probabilities* of eventual targetlike attainment for the groups. One hypothesis would be that the instructed learners will eventually *relinquish* what appears to be something akin to "psycholinguistic hypercorrection." (In a longitudinal study of francophone children learning English at school in what was effectively an EFL setting in Quebec, Lightbown (1983) found that the learners oversupplied -*s* on clause-initial noun phrases (NPs), but that this tendency gradually decreased over time.) Naturalistic acquirers, on the other hand, may be less likely to *begin* supplying what are often, after all, communicatively redundant and probably still nonsalient forms, especially after prolonged periods of communicatively successful TL use of their grammatically reduced codes.

This, however, is to enter the realm of speculation. What is needed is some research on the *long-term effects* (if any) of these initial differences in preferred acquisition processes. To my knowledge, not one study has addressed this *basic* issue. It goes without saying that until such work is done, it is premature to recommend that teachers give up on conventional SL instruction. Such suggestions may or may not turn out to be justified. At present, we simply do not know.

The Effect of Instruction on Acquisition Sequences

A major study of the effect of instruction on acquisition sequences is that by Lightbown and her colleagues in Montreal (Lightbown, 1983; Lightbown & Barkman, 1978; Lightbown & Spada, 1978; Lightbown, Spada, & Wallace,

1980). Using a panel design, Lightbown et al. conducted both longitudinal and cross-sectional studies of francophone children, ages 11 to 17, learning ESL in Quebec, few of whom had much contact with English outside the classroom. There were 175 children in grades 6, 8, and 10 in the first year of the study, and 100 of the same children in grades 7, 9, and 11 in the second year. All had started English in grade 4 or 5.

Early studies, using a variety of speech elicitation devices (verbally cued picture descriptions, communication games, etc.), found differences from previously established orders in the accuracy with which the French speakers produced various *-s* morphemes (copula, auxiliary, third person singular, plural, and possessive) and *-ing*. Several of these differences appeared attributable to influences from French, which uses the periphrastic possessive, and in which final /s/ is silent. The children were also observed to make large numbers of what Pica calls *overuse* errors, for example, "The girl*s* want a cookie," when describing a picture of only one girl.

Additional motivations for the error patterns were sought in various aspects of the instruction the learners received. No direct relationship was found between the frequency of the items in teacher speech or in their textbooks and either the frequency or accuracy of students' use of those forms at the same point in time. However, Lightbown (1983, p. 239) reports a "delayed" frequency effect.

Intensive practice of *-ing* early in grade 6 appeared to be what led to that item remaining in grade 6 students' speech throughout the year, even though it was relatively *in*frequent in classroom language after its initial presentation. Students' suppliance of *-ing* during this period included both accurate suppliance in obligatory contexts and overuse. Later, however, after uninflected verbs such as simple present forms and imperatives had been taught, both students' overuse *and* accurate use of *-ing* declined in favor of uninflected verbs, the forms favored by naturalistic acquirers from the outset. Lightbown wonders whether the kind of intensive drill work used in the audiolingual method to produce "overlearning" may not create artificial barriers to natural interlanguage development, obstacles that learners later have to overcome before they can construct their own productive interlanguage systems.

As reported earlier, after intensive practice of various *-s* morphemes, there was a parallel tendency for students to overuse those items, especially by adding *-s* to clause-initial NPs, errors that then decreased over time. An important difference between what subsequently occurred with *-ing* and with certain *-s* morphemes, however, was that, unlike the *-ing* form, *appropriate* use of *-s* in obligatory contexts for copula and auxiliary did *not* decrease in tandem with the decrease in overuse errors with *-s* morphology. With some of the *-s* morphemes, that is, instruction appeared to accelerate attempts to use the forms, but with some negative side effects (overuse errors). The side effects wore off with time, however, leaving the benefits intact.

While providing more evidence of possibly beneficial effects of instruction on acquisition processes, Lightbown's findings suggest overall that formal SL instruction is successful in altering acquisition *sequences* only in a trivial manner. On the basis of the Quebec findings, the effects in this second area seem to be temporary and possibly even harmful. Although some studies to be reported later in this chapter might superficially appear to show an alteration of sequences, too, this is probably not the case, as will become clear. Acquisition sequences may well be immutable.

Further support for the idea that acquisition sequences are impervious to instruction is to be found in a study by Pienemann (1984) (see also Daniel, 1983; Westmoreland, 1983). Through analysis of the spontaneous speech of 100 Italian children acquiring German as a second language (GSL) naturalistically, Pienemann identified 10 who were at stage 2 (adverb-fronting) or stage 3 (particle shift) in the GSL word order sequence in main clauses previously established in longitudinal and cross-sectional studies of migrant workers by the ZISA group (see, for example, Meisel, Clahsen, & Pienemann, 1981; Nicholas & Meisel, 1983). The 10 children, ages 7–9, then received two weeks of classroom instruction (including both linguistically focused and communicative exercises) in the fourth GSL word order stage (subject–verb inversion). At the end of this period, the children's spontaneous speech was again recorded and analyzed to determine whether they had progressed to stage 4 in word order development.

The results were fascinating and quite clear. Children who had begun at stage 3 had progressed to stage 4, a process normally taking several months in untutored development. Children who had begun the study at stage 2, however, were still at stage 2. Pienemann's interpretation of these findings is that students can learn from instruction only when they are psycholinguistically "ready" for it—the *learnability hypothesis*. The learnability of a structure in turn constrains the effectivenesss of instruction—the *teachability hypothesis*. Instruction in something for which learners are not ready cannot make them skip a stage in an acquisition sequence. Instruction for which they are ready can, however, speed up the rate of progress through the sequence.

The learnability/teachability hypotheses provide the most likely explanation for the results of several other studies that have shown either no effect or no lasting effect for instruction in particular structures. Thus, Lightbown, Spada, and Wallace (1980) found that instruction in the copula in equational sentences, locative prepositions, and some -*s* morphology resulted in an average 11 percent improvement in accuracy on those items on a grammaticality judgment test, compared with a control group's average improvement of 3 percent. The gain was temporary, however, with the experimental group's scores declining to the norm on a readministration of the same test six months later. Schumann's efforts to raise the performance of ESL negation in his subject, Alberto, directly from stage 1, *no* + verb ("No like hamburger") to stage 4, analyzed *don't* ("He doesn't like hamburgers") through intensive practice in the target forms had no effect on Alberto's spontaneous speech, although brief improvements were obtained during the drills themselves (Schumann, 1978). Similarly, Ellis (1984a) found no improvement in the spontaneously produced WH questions of 13 children following three hours of instruction both in the meaning of WH pronouns (*what, where, when,* and *who*) and in inversion in WH questions. The children's spontaneous speech prior to this part of Ellis's study showed that they were beginning to use *un*inverted WH questions (of any kind) when the instruction was provided.

It should be noted, however, that although a lack of effect for instruction in studies like these is probably due to the researchers' choice of items that were developmentally beyond the reach of the learners involved—that is, to poor *timing* of instruction—alternative or additional explanations are also possible. First, the findings in some studies (e.g., Bruzzeze, 1977; Schumann, 1978) could be the result of the subjects having fossilized before receiving the instruction. Second, instruction can be expected to have differential effects according to whether the targeted structures are *developmental* or *variational* for the particular learners receiving the tuition (Pienemann, 1985). Variational features, such as copula, are considered to reflect a learner's (relatively) integrative or segregative *orientation* to the target language (Clahsen, Meisel, & Pienemann, 1983), as well as some effect for native language (Johnston, 1985), and omission/suppliance of such features to depend on such considerations as communicative effectiveness and communicative effort (Nicholas, 1984). Once having appeared in a learner's interlanguage, variational features appear to be teachable (with lasting effects) free of the kinds of (processing) constraints that affect the teachability of developmental features (Pienemann, 1985).

Further research in this area is clearly a high priority, but investigators will need to select subjects and targeted structures very carefully. In addition, if the aim is to establish a causal relationship between instruction and SL development/performance, more researchers than have done so to date must be prepared to adhere to such principles of experimental design as the inclusion of a control group in their studies and random assignment of subjects to groups.

The Effect of Instruction on Rate of Acquisition

As noted before, Pienemann's 1984 study suggests that it is impossible to alter acquisition sequences, but simultaneously provides evidence of instruction's facilitating effect on the rate of SL learning. It is in the latter area, in fact, that instruction is most clearly beneficial, with empirical support for the claim strong and diverse. A rate advantage is, of course, theoretically less interesting than the possibility of altering acquisition sequences, since it demonstrates *that* instruction has an effect, but does not explain *how*. Nonetheless, speeding up acquisition is extremely important for teachers and learners and so worthy of consideration.

In an earlier paper (Long, 1983), 11 studies were reviewed, including 6 that clearly showed faster development in children and adults receiving formal SL teaching; 2 (Fathman, 1976; Hale & Budar, 1970) whose findings, though ambiguous, were arguably in the same direction; and 3 that showed minor or no effects for instruction. Table 4.1 summarizes the results of those studies.

Two additional studies appearing since that review was undertaken support the conclusion that instruction speeds up learning. First, Weslander and Stephany (1983) report a large-scale evaluation of "pull-out" ESL for 577 limited English-speaking children (grades 2-10) in public schools in Des Moines, Iowa. Results showed that children receiving more ESL instruction outperformed those receiving less on the Bilingual Syntax Measure (BSM), with effects being strongest at lower levels (BSM levels 2.2–2.8) in the first year of schooling, and then diminishing in importance in the second and third years.

Second, Gass (1982) describes an experiment at Michigan showing the effectiveness of instruction in accelerating the learning of relative clause formation (in Krashen's terms, "hard grammar," and so supposedly unteachable). Gass taught one group of adult ESL students relativization on the object of a preposition for three days' classes. Object of a preposition is the fourth lowest in Keenan and Comrie's (1977) proposed universal accessibility hierarchy of relative clause formation. A control group received the same amount of instruction in relativization, but starting from the highest (subject and object) positions in the hierarchy. Subjects' knowledge of any kind of relativization was minimal at the outset, as shown by their performance on pretests consisting of both grammaticality judgment and sentence-combining measures.

Posttests using the same measures produced two main findings of interest here. First, overall scores (all relativization positions) of the experimental group had improved significantly on the grammaticality task. Second, on the sentence-combining task, both groups' posttest scores were significantly improved, the experimental group's scores being better not just on object of a preposition relatives, but also for relatives in all the higher positions in the accessibility hierarchy, that is, those on which they had *not* received instruction, but which would be *implied* as known by subjects who knew object of a preposition relativization. As in the Pienemann (1984) study, in other words, here is more evidence not only of the effect of instruction on the rate of acquisition of particular structures, but also of the generalizability of the effect to other constructions, at least where these are the implied terms in a markedness relationship. (Similar findings have since been obtained by Zobl [1985] as discussed in the next section.)

Commenting on the Long (1983) review, Krashen (1985, pp. 28–31) maintains that the findings in Table 4.1 do *not* show an advantage for formal instruction. In his view, the fact that instructed learners outperformed naturalistic acquirers in most studies simply reflects the utility of the classroom as a

Table 4.1 RELATIONSHIPS BETWEEN INSTRUCTION (I), EXPOSURE (E), AND SECOND LANGUAGE ACQUISITION

Study	SLA type	Subjects	Proficiency (B, I, or A)	Acquisition environment	Test type (DP or I)	Instruction helps?	Exposure helps?	I>E or E>I?
Studies showing that instruction helps								
1. Carroll (1967)	FLL in USA and SLA abroad	Adults	B I A	Mixed	I	Yes	Yes	E > I
2. Chihara & Oller (1978)	EFL (Japan)	Adults	B I A	Poor	DP	Yes	No	I > E
3. Brière (1978)	SpSL (Mexico)	Children	B	Mixed	DP	Yes	Yes	I > E
4. Krashen, Seliger, & Hartnett (1974)	ESL in USA	Adults	B I A	Rich	DP	Yes	No	I > E
5. Krashen & Seliger (1976)	ESL in USA	Adults	I A	Rich	I	Yes	No	I > E
6. Krashen, Jones, Zelinski, & Usprich (1978)	ESL in USA	Adults	B I A	Rich	DP	Yes	Yes	I > E
Ambiguous cases								
7. Hale & Budar (1970)	ESL in USA	Adolescents	B I A	Rich	DP	?	Yes	E > I?
8. Fathman (1976)	ESL in USA	Children	B I A	Rich	I	?	Yes	E > I?
Studies showing that instruction does not help								
9. Upshur (1968; Experiment 1)	ESL in USA	Adults	I A	Rich	DP	No	—	—
10. Mason (1971)	ESL in USA	Adults	I A	Rich	DP	No	—	—
11. Fathman (1975)	ESL in USA	Children	B I A	Rich	I	No	—	—
Additional study showing that exposure helps								
12. Martin (1980)	ESL in USA	Adults	I A	Mixed	DP	—	Yes	—

Source: Table reprinted by permission of TESOL from M. H. Long, "Does Second Language Instruction Make a Difference? A Review of Research," *TESOL Quarterly, 17,* no. 3 (1983), p. 375.

Note: B = beginning; I = intermediate; A = advanced; DP = discrete-point; I = integrative.

source of comprehensible input (CI) for "beginners," who find it difficult to engage native speakers in conversation outside classrooms.

As pointed out in the original review, however, this argument is problematic in light of the findings of beneficial effects of instruction for intermediate *and* advanced learners—learners whose higher second language proficiency means they no longer depend on the classroom as a source of comprehensible input (Brown, 1981, and several studies in Table 4.1). Krashen's response to this (1985, pp. 28–31) is that learners in some of those studies are wrongly classified as "intermediates" and "advanced" in the 1983 review (and in Table 4.1). Two studies, he says, involved only "beginners," nonnative speaking university students in the Queens College English Language Institute (Krashen & Seliger, 1976; Krashen, Seliger, & Hartnett, 1974), and another used students "at various levels" in extension courses at Queens College (Krashen, Jones, Zelinski, & Usprich, 1978), "with large numbers in the lower levels" (Krashen, 1985, p. 29). Krashen agrees that the study by Carroll (1967) did involve more advanced learners (U. S. college foreign language majors with an average proficiency of 2+ on the FSI scale), but notes that the benefits of instruction there, though statistically significant, were not large, and that, despite a year abroad in the target language environment, the classroom was still a major source of CI for those learners.

Since Krashen provides no proficiency scores for the learners in question, nor defines what he means as a beginner, it is difficult to evaluate his arguments. One notes that students who were classified as "at various levels" of proficiency in the original research reports are now classified as "beginners" or as in "the lower levels." Further, whereas instruction was originally claimed to be useful only for beginners (and then only indirectly, as a source of CI), Krashen (1985) claims that "language classes are useful *primarily* for the beginner, and [that the studies] are consistent with the interpretation that their value is in the comprehensible input they supply" (1985, p. 29, emphasis added).

This statement raises two questions. First, does "primarily" mean that Krashen now accepts that instruction also helps learners who are more advanced than beginners (still undefined)? If so, just how advanced must they be before language teachers are wasting their time? Second, the original claim was that classroom learning was useful only as a source of CI in an "acquisition-poor" environment, that is, one in which target language exposure was *not* available outside the classroom. If this is a valid description of New York City (the setting for the three Queens College studies), Krashen needs to document that, at least for the subjects in his studies. Or is this claim also now being modified to recognize instruction as useful in "acquisition-rich" settings as well?

In fact, the Long (1983) review raised four counterarguments to Krashen's interpretations of the same research. It seemed that instruction was beneficial (1) for children (who lack the cognitive maturity to develop metalin-

guistic awareness and, hence, a monitor) as well as for adults, (2) for intermediate and advanced learners, (3) on (supposedly unmonitorable) integrative as
well as discrete-point tests, and (4) in acquisition-rich as well as acquisition-
poor environments. None of these findings are predicted by monitor theory.
Krashen (1985), as reported earlier, mentions and attempts to respond to only
two of them (2 and 4).

Finally, it is interesting to note how Krashen et al. (1978) originally
interpreted the findings of their own research, a result that they then claimed
"replicates and extends previous findings [Krashen & Seliger, 1976; Krashen,
Seliger, & Hartnett, 1974—that is, the New York series]" (Krashen et al., 1978,
p. 260). In my opinion, theirs was and still is the correct interpretation: "What
may be inferred from these results is that formal instruction is a more efficient
way of learning English for adults than trying to learn it 'on the streets'"
(Krashen et al., 1978, p. 260).

The Effect of Instruction on the Level of Ultimate SL Attainment

Even less research has been conducted in this fourth area, the long-term effects
of instruction on SL proficiency, than in the three areas discussed so far. This
is clearly a sad reflection on the state of knowledge concerning language
teaching, but, equally clearly, a fact that should (but has failed to) preempt
hasty conclusions about the (in)efficacy of instruction by SLA researchers and
theorists.

The major study to date is that by Pavesi (1984), who compared relative
clause formation in instructed and naturalistic acquirers. The instructed
learners were 48 Italian high school students, ages 14–18, who had received
from 2 to 7 years (an average of 4 years) of grammar-based EFL teaching, and
who, with the exception of 3 who had spent 2 months or less in Britain, had
had no informal exposure to English. The naturalistic acquirers were 38 Italian
workers (mostly restaurant waiters), ages 19–50, in Edinburgh, who had received only minimal or (usually) no formal English instruction. They had been
in Britain for anywhere from 3 months to 25 years (an average of 6 years),
during which time they had been exposed to English in a variety of home,
work, and recreational settings.

This is, then, a nonequivalent control groups design, preempting the
testing of any causal relationships. In addition to the difference in age between
the two groups, Pavesi notes that the overall educational level of the naturalistic acquirers was generally quite low, and their socioeconomic background also
lower than that of the school students. The latter, she reports, had also been
exposed to a substantial amount of British literature and other written English.
On the other hand, although the exact amount of informal SL exposure for the
naturalistic group was difficult to determine, the balance was clearly in their
favor; that is, they had had many more hours of exposure than the students
had had of instruction. Hence, finding, as Pavesi did, that the school students

outperformed the naturalistic acquirers provides further evidence of the positive effect of instruction—or a factor associated with it—on rate of SL development, assuming one discounts the intergroup differences. Rate of development, however, was not the focus of Pavesi's study.

Relative clause constructions were elicited by asking subjects about the identity of characters in a set of pictures ("Number 7 is the girl who is running," etc.), with relativization off all NP positions in the Keenan and Comrie accessibility hierarchy being elicited. Using implicational scaling, the developmental sequences for each group were then plotted and each found to correlate statistically significantly with the order in the accessibility hierarchy, with a progression from least to most marked constructions.[5] The learning context, that is, had not influenced acquisitional sequence (another result consistent with those of the studies reviewed earlier). This, as we have seen, is the kind of finding that has led some researchers to conclude that instruction does not affect acquisition at all. As Pica (1983) had done, however, Pavesi looked further before discounting instruction and, like Pica, found that her subsequent analyses revealed interesting differences between the two groups.

The differences were of two kinds. First, more instructed learners reached 80 percent criterion on all of the five lowest NP categories in the accessibility hierarchy, with differences between the groups attaining statistical significance at the second lowest (genitive, *whose*) position, and falling just short ($p < .06$) at the lowest (object of comparative) level. More instructed learners, that is (and, in absolute terms, very few naturalistic acquirers), were able to relativize off NPs at the more marked end of the implicational hierarchy. In gross terms, instructed learners had gone further or reached higher levels of SL attainment.

A second difference to emerge between the groups concerned the kinds of errors each made with regard to resumptive nominal and pronominal copies. Naturalistic acquirers exhibited statistically significantly more frequent noun retention than did instructed learners ("Number 4 is the woman who the cat is looking at *the woman*"). Instructed learners, on the other hand, produced statistically significantly more resumptive pronoun copies than naturalistic acquirers ("Number 4 is the woman who the cat is looking at *her*"). (The fact that neither Italian nor English allows copies of either kind, coupled with the finding that the developmental sequence for all learners followed the accessibility hierarchy, is further evidence of the need to treat interlanguage syntax as an emergent autonomous system.)

Although Pavesi's results have been presented here in terms of the differences they suggest can result from formal SL instruction, Pavesi herself does not in fact interpret them this way. Instead, following Ellis (1984b), she suggests that the instructed group's superior performance derived not from formal SL instruction per se but from the instructed learners' exposure to the more elaborated, more complex input of language used as the *medium* of instruction, that is, from their exposure to what Ochs (1979) terms "planned discourse." Planned discourse has been documented as containing, among other things, a higher degree of grammaticalization (Givón, 1979), including a higher frequency of linguistically more marked constructions. If an explicit focus on form—that is, the object, not the medium of SL instruction—was producing the observed effects, Pavesi argues, how could one account for the failure of such instruction to alter acquisition *sequences* that, as has so often been shown, do not reflect teaching syllabuses?

My own view is that the well-attested failure of interlanguage developmental sequences to mirror instructional sequences (for which Pavesi's study provides further evidence), is due to the powerful influence of universals— themselves the product of internal learner contributions—and/or to the failure of instruction to respect principles of learnability/teachability like those outlined by Pienemann. Further, in Pavesi's study, it is presumably those same universal tendencies that account for both instructed *and* naturalistic groups' use of resumptive nominal/pronominal copies, since these are disallowed in English and in Italian and would not have been present (let alone salient) in either simple/unplanned or complex/planned discourse modes. Hence, if the (marked) copies are not being acquired through exposure to planned discourse, why should one believe that the (marked) relative clause constructions are being acquired this way, and not as a result of the SL instruction itself?

Though an interesting idea, the "discourse mode" explanation also seems unlikely for the simple reason that so many of the marked/language-specific features that the elaborated mode undoubtedly contains (and provides exposure to) will nevertheless not be *perceptually salient* to the learner. The focus on form that (some kinds of) second language instruction provides, on the other hand, *would* draw the learner's attention to such items.

Strong impressionistic evidence for this view can be found in a recent diary study, supplemented by subsequent analyses of recorded interlanguage speech samples, of the acquisition of Brazilian Portuguese by a trained linguist and SLA researcher (Schmidt & Frota, 1986). Schmidt kept detailed notes of his interlanguage development over a six-month period, including records of linguistic items (1) that he was taught in a formal Portuguese as an SL class in Rio de Janeiro, (2) that he noticed/failed to notice in the Portuguese to which he was exposed outside the classroom, and (3) that he produced (not necessarily accurately) or ignored or avoided in his own speech.

After much detailed discussion of these and other data sources and of relationships among them, Schmidt and Frota conclude (1986, p. 281):

> It seems, then, that if R was to learn and use a particular type of verbal form, it was not enough for it to have been taught and drilled in class. It was also not enough for the form to occur in input, but R had to notice the form in the input. . . . R subjectively felt as he was going through the learning process that conscious awareness of what was present in the input was causal. (Reprinted with permission of Newbury House from "Developing Basic Conversational Ability in a Second Language: A Case

Study of an Adult Learner in Portuguese" by R. W. Schmidt and S. N. Frota, in *Talking to Learn: Conversation in Second Language Acquisition*, edited by R. R. Day, Rowley, MA: Newbury House, 1986, p. 281.)

Schmidt and Frota also note that several items, such as reflexive *se*, though frequent in the input, had little or delayed effect on Schmidt's production because of their lack of saliency.

Finally, his retrospective analyses convinced Schmidt that he usually noticed forms in the out-of-class input *after they were taught*. One excerpt from the diary must suffice to illustrate the process here:

Journal entry, Week 6

This week we were introduced to and drilled on the imperfect. Very useful! The basic contrast seems straightforward enough: *ontem eu fui ao clube* ["yesterday I went to the club"] vs. *antigamente eu ia ao clube* ["formerly I used to go to the club"]. L [the teacher] gave us a third model: *ontem eu ia ao clube*, "yesterday I was going to the club . . . but I didn't," which L says is a common way of making excuses. The paradigm is also straightforward . . . though maybe not as easy as I first thought. . . . Wednesday night A came over to play cards, and the first thing he said was: *eu ia telefonar para voce* ["I was going to call you"], exactly the kind of excuse L had said we could expect. I noticed that his speech is full of the imperfect, which I never heard (or understood) before, and during the evening I managed to produce quite a few myself, without hesitating much. Very satisfying! (Reprinted with permission of Newbury House from "Developing Basic Conversational Ability in a Second Language: A Case Study of an Adult Learner in Portuguese" by R. W. Schmidt and S. N. Frota, in *Talking to Learn: Conversation in Second Language Acquisition*, edited by R. R. Day, Rowley, MA: Newbury House, 1986, p. 279.)

Rather than "voting" on the discourse mode/formal SL instruction issue, however, one way of resolving it empirically would be to compare advanced nonnative speakers who received SL instruction with a focus on form with the graduates of immersion or submersion programs. The latter receive massive exposure to elaborated/planned SL discourse through being educated *through* a second language, but (at least in theory) with no focus on form. An indication of the way such a comparison might result can perhaps be seen in the findings of a study of the product of French immersion programs in Canada by Swain (1985). Swain's study shows that the results of SL learning through immersion education are impressive, but also documents the failure of immersion students to have mastered even a wide range of *un*marked morphology and syntax after seven years.

Further evidence for this interpretation may lie in the findings of a series of three studies reported by Zobl (1985) on the teaching of English possessive adjectives to French-speaking university students in Canada. Zobl's first study of the difficulty orders of 162 French-speaking learners of English corroborated linguistic arguments concerning markedness in two domains. The study showed (1) that *his* is the *un*marked member of the *his/her* pair, and (2) that categorical control of the rule governing gender marking of possessed animate or human entities (*"his* mother," *"her* father," etc.) implies categorical control of the rule governing possessed *in*animate, or *non*human, entities (*"her* hand," *"his* car," etc.), but not vice versa, that is, that *nonhuman* is the *un*marked member of the *human/nonhuman* pair.

Zobl next ran a study in which two randomly formed groups of approximately 20 low-level adult speakers of French each received 15 minutes of instruction in the use of the possessive forms. One group was exposed only to examples with human-possessed entities; the other group exclusively experienced examples with *non*human-possessed entities. Controlling for input frequency, the instruction consisted of intensive oral question and answer practice, based on pictures, with no overt explanations or rules, but with corrections from the teacher where necessary through rephrasings of incorrect student responses, that is, some focus on form. Pre- and posttests consisted of responses to questions written as quickly and unreflectingly as possible. A year later, a third (replication) study was run on a new sample of students.

The findings of the two experimental studies were (1) that students who had experienced the input containing marked (human) examples improved in both the human *and* nonhuman domains (confirmed in both studies), whereas (2) students who had received exposure only to *un*marked (nonhuman) input deteriorated in that domain (first study) or improved in that domain, but *less* than the human data group in that domain (replication study), and showed no improvement in the marked (human) domain (both studies). In other words, students who had been exposed only to marked data improved more than did students who had been exposed only to unmarked data in *both* the marked domain *and* the unmarked (nonhuman) domain in which the *other* group, and only the other group, had received instruction.

Zobl employed various measures of the students' test performance. Among other features he noted were a tendency for the groups receiving *un*marked input to show a higher incidence of rule simplifications following the treatment (e.g., overuse of the *un*marked determiner, *his*). Conversely, the group receiving marked input supplied more gender-marked, third person forms in new contexts, including overgeneralizations of the marked form, *her*, showed less use of articles (which the first, descriptive study had revealed as a transitional form in acquiring the possessive adjectives) and also less avoidance (through use of immature forms like the gender-neutral *your* or determiner omission).

Zobl concludes by offering a very interesting explanation for the finding that exposure to unmarked data appeared to lead to rule simplification (overgeneralization of the unmarked *his*), whereas exposure to marked data produced rule complexification (overgeneralization of the marked *her*). He suggests that "once grammars reach a certain level of complexity such that their rules begin to predict to unmarked structures with some regularity, marked data become necessary if progress on unmarked structures is not to stagnate" (Zobl, 1985, p. 343). Further, he notes that both experiments showed that exposure to the marked (human) domain led to overgeneralization of the marked *her*, whereas exposure to the unmarked (nonhuman) domain produced overgeneralization of the unmarked *his*. That is, exposure to the unmarked *nonhuman* triggers the correlated markedness value, unmarked *his*; conversely, exposure to the marked *human* triggers the correlated markedness value, marked *her*. If this explanation is correct, and if it translates from the experimental to the naturalistic acquisition context, Zobl hypothesizes, it would mean that acquisition along one parameter entails acquisition along another related parameter, which would in turn mean a significant reduction in the amount of input a learner requires to reach the same level as a learner who experiences mostly or exclusively unmarked data.

To the extent that instruction focuses on marked elements in the SL, here, then, is a potential explanation for its positive effect on the *rate* of acquisition. Note, too, that Zobl's findings on the benefits of exposure to marked data are consistent with those of Pavesi in two respects. They help explain the rate advantage for the Italian high school students, and they potentially explain the higher level of ultimate attainment. It could be that the preponderance of unmarked data that naturalistic acquirers encounter not only slows them down, but also leads to simplifications in the grammars before full target competence is attained, i.e., to premature fossilization.

CONCLUSION

The review of research on the effect of instruction on SL development suggests the following conclusions. First, formal SL instruction has positive effects on SLA *processes*, on the *rate* at which learners acquire the language, and on their *ultimate level of attainment*. Findings in the last area even suggest that it may be impossible to reach full native speaker competence *without* instruction. Instruction does not, on the other hand, seem able to alter acquisition *sequences*, except temporarily, and in trivial ways, which may even hinder subsequent development.

Second, there has clearly been insufficient research to warrant firm conclusions in *any* area we have considered, and no research at all in other important ones, such as the kinds of sociolinguistic competence (e.g., collocational abilities) achievable with and without instruction.

Third, and following from the first two, the position taken by some theorists and methodologists that formal instruction in a second language is of limited use (e.g., that it is good for beginners only, or for "simple" grammar only), is obviously premature and almost certainly wrong.

Fourth, future research on this issue must be conducted with greater rigor than has typically been the case to date. Reference has already been made to the need to choose subjects carefully, to follow standard procedures in their (random) assignment to treatments, to employ control groups, and to select for teaching experiments those aspects of the SL that are "learnable" at the time instruction is provided.

It is also important, however, for investigators to record and report precisely what "instruction" consisted of in their studies. This would have two effects. First, it would disambiguate potential confounds between such factors as a focus on the SL itself and exposure to linguistic features *through* the SL. Second, should instruction prove to be beneficial, as currently seems likely, it *might* help preempt misuse of such a finding as a blanket justification for returning to some of the more neanderthal teaching practices that, as was noted at the outset, SLA research first helped to discredit.

One example may help clarify the last point. For reasons beyond the scope of this paper, my own view is that a focus on *form* is probably a key feature of SL instruction, because of the saliency it brings to targeted features in classroom input, and also in input outside the classroom, where this is available. I do not think, on the other hand, that there is any evidence that an instructional program built around a series (or even a sequence) of isolated *forms* is any more supportable now, either theoretically, empirically, or logically, than it was when Krashen and others attacked it several years ago. It is not hard to imagine, however, that a return to teaching discrete grammar points, plus or minus overt grammar explanations, is just what some methodologists will see vindicated by *any* finding that formal SL instruction is beneficial. Clearly, we want to avoid an unwarranted inference of that kind. Were researchers to specify just what kind of instruction was involved in their studies, along this and other parameters, it *might* help avoid another pendulum swing in the field, and would certainly save a lot of time on subsequent research on the *relative* effectiveness of different types of instruction—time that all too few language learners can afford.

NOTES

1. It is not clear to me why, in this and other papers, Felix and Simmet collapse the longitudinal data from this study, and then resort to implicational scaling of (ostensibly) cross-sectional findings to establish acquisition sequences.
2. "Beginning," "intermediate," and "advanced" appear in quotes here since Krashen defines them vaguely and variably, although their meaning is often crucial for him in interpreting the outcome of studies (see, for example, Krashen, 1985, pp. 28–31) and could presumably be crucial for the success of his proposals for language teaching described earlier.
3. Pienemann (1984) has shown that instruction can also *slow down* development in certain areas, however, as when suppliance of copula inhibits learners' attempts to apply a new syntactic movement rule *over* copula in German as a second language word order development.

4. See Andersen (1985) for a real example of this sort.

5. Linguistic notions of *markedness* are usually defined in terms of complexity, rarity, or departure from something that is more basic, typical, or canonical in a language. Thus, one argument for treating masculine members of pairs like *waiter/waitress* and *man/woman* as the *un*marked (read "simpler" or "base") forms is the fact that English *adds* forms to produce the morphologically more complex feminine members. Similarly, morphemes are added to distinguish past from present, plural from singular, and so on, suggesting that present and singular are unmarked, past and plural are marked.

Markedness can also be ascertained typologically when cross-linguistic comparisons of languages show that the presence of some linguistic feature implies the presence of another feature. Languages that have voiced stops, for example, also have voiceless stops, whereas some languages that have voiceless stops do not have voiced ones, suggesting that voiced (which involves additional complexity in the form of an additional phonological feature) is marked, voiceless is unmarked.

In the case of relative clauses, surveys show that a language that allows relativization off direct object NPs will also allow relativization off subject NPs. One that allows relativization off indirect object NPs will also allow relativization off subject and direct object NPs, and so on. Conversely, if a language *only* allows relativization off one position, it will be subject position—not, say, indirect object position, and so on. Facts like these led Keenan and Comrie (1977) to posit a hierarchy of noun phrases, from least to most marked, for relativization.

This is an inevitably brief and superficial explanation of markedness. For further details and alternative notions of markedness, see, for example, Eckman (1985), Kellerman (1979), Rutherford (1982) and Zobl (1983).

REFERENCES

Andersen, R. W. What's gender good for, anyway? In R. W. Andersen (Ed.), *Second languages*. Rowley, MA: Newbury House, 1985.

Bickerton, D. Pidgin and creole studies. *Annual Review of Anthropology*, 1976, 5, 169–193.

Brown, J. Newly placed students versus continuing students: Comparing proficiency. In J. C. Fisher, M. A. Clarke, & J. Schachter (Eds.), *On TESOL '80*. Washington, D.C.: TESOL, 1981.

Bruzzese, G. English/Italian secondary hybridization: A case study in the pidginization of a second language learner's speech. In C. Henning (Ed.), *Proceedings of the Los Angeles second language research forum*. Los Angeles, CA: TESL Section, UCLA, 1977.

Burt, M., & Dulay, H. On acquisition orders. In S. W. Felix (Ed.), *Second language development*. Tübingen: Gunter Narr Verlag, 1980.

Carroll, J. B. Foreign language proficiency levels attained by language majors near graduation from college. *Foreign Language Annals*, 1967, 1, 131–151.

Clahsen, H., Meisel, J., & Pienemann, M. *Deutsch als Zweitsprache. Der Spracherwerb ausländischer Arbeiter*. Tübingen: Gunter Narr Verlag, 1983.

Clarke, M. On bandwagons, tyranny, and common sense. *TESOL Quarterly*, 1982, 16(4), 437–448.

Daniel, I. On first-year German foreign language learning: A comparison of language behavior in response to two instructional methods. Unpublished Ph.D. dissertation, University of Southern California, 1983.

Dulay, H., & Burt, M. Should we teach children syntax? *Language Learning*, 1973, *24*, 245–258.

Dulay, H., & Burt, M. Remarks on creativity in second language acquisition. In M. Burt, H. Dulay, & M. Finocchiaro (Eds.), *Viewpoints on English as a second language*. New York: Regents, 1977.

Eckman, F. R. The markedness differential hypothesis: Theory and applications. In B. Wheatley, A. Hastings, F. R. Eckman, L. Bell, G. Krukar, & R. Rutkowski (Eds.), *Current approaches to second language acquisition: Proceedings of the 1984 University of Wisconsin–Milwaukee Linguistics Symposium*. Bloomington: Indiana University Linguistics Club, 1985.

Ellis, R. Can syntax be taught? A study of the effects of formal instruction on the acquisition of WH questions in children. *Applied Linguistics,* 1984a, *5*(2), 138–155.

Ellis R. The role of instruction in second language acquisition. Paper presented at the IRAAL-BAAL Seminar on the Formal and Informal Contexts of Language Learning, Dublin, September 11–13, 1984b.

Fathman, A. Variables affecting the successful learning of English as a second language. *TESOL Quarterly*, 1976, *10*(4), 433–441.

Felix, S. W. The effect of formal instruction on second language acquisition. *Language Learning,* 1981, *31*(1), 87–112.

Felix, S. W., & Simmet, A. Natural processes in classroom L2 learning. Revised version of a paper presented at the IIIème Colloque Groupe de Recherche sûr l'Acquisition des Langues, Paris, May 15–17, 1981.

Gass, S. From theory to practice. In M. Hines & W. Rutherford (Eds.), *On TESOL '81*. Washington, DC: TESOL, 1982.

Givón, T. *On understanding grammar*. New York: Academic Press, 1979.

Hale, T., & Budar, E. Are TESOL classes the only answer? *Modern Language Journal,* 1970, *54*, 487–492.

Johnston, M. *Syntactic and morphological progressions in learner English*. Canberra, Australia: Commonwealth Department of Immigration and Ethnic Affairs, 1985.

Keenan, E., & Comrie, B. Noun phrase accessability and universal grammar. *Linguistic Inquiry*, 1977, *8*, 63–100.

Kellerman, E. The problem with difficulty. *Interlanguage Studies Bulletin,* 1979, *4*, 27–48.

Krashen, S. D. Some issues relating to the monitor model. In H. D. Brown, C. A. Yorio, & R. L. Crymes (Eds.), *On TESOL '77*. Washington, DC: TESOL, 1977.

Krashen, S. D. The "fundamental pedagogical principle" in second language teaching. *Studia Linguistica,* 1981, *35*(1–2) 50–70.

Krashen, S. D. *Principles and practice in second language acquisition*. New York: Pergamon Press, 1982.

Krashen, S. D. *The input hypothesis*. New York: Longman, 1985.

Krashen, S. D., Jones, C., Zelinski, S., & Usprich, C. How important is instruction? *English Language Teaching Journal,* 1978, *32*(4), 257–261.

Krashen, S. D., & Scarcella, R. C. On routines and patterns in language acquisition and performance. *Language Learning,* 1978, *28,* 283–300.

Krashen, S. D., & Seliger, H. W. The role of formal and informal linguistic environments in adult second language learning. *International Journal of Psycholinguistics,* 1976, *3,* 15–21.

Krashen, S. D., Seliger, H. W., & Hartnett, D. Two studies in second language learning. *Kritikon Litterarum,* 1974, *3,* 220–228.

Krashen, S. D., Sferlazza, V., Feldman, L., & Fathman, A. Adult performance on the SLOPE test: More evidence for a natural sequence in adult second language acquisition. *Language Learning,* 1976, *26,* 145–151.

Krashen, S. D., & Terrell, T. *The natural approach.* New York: Pergamon Press, 1983.

Lightbown, P. M. Exploring relationships between developmental and instructional sequences. In H. W. Seliger & M. H. Long (Eds.), *Classroom-oriented research on second language acquisition.* Rowley, MA: Newbury House, 1983.

Lightbown, P. M., & Barkman, B. Interactions among ESL learners, teachers, texts, and methods. Report to the Department of the Secretary of State of Canada, ED 166 981, 1978.

Lightbown, P. M., & Spada, N. Performance on an oral communication task by francophone ESL learners. *SPEAQ Journal,* 1978, *2*(4), 34–54.

Lightbown, P. M., Spada, N., & Wallace, R. Some effects of instruction on child and adolescent ESL learners. In R. C. Scarcella & S. D. Krashen (Eds.), *Research in second language acquisition.* Rowley, MA: Newbury House, 1980.

Long, M. H. Does second language instruction make a difference? A review of research. *TESOL Quarterly,* 1983, *17*(3), 359–382.

Long, M. H. A role for instruction in second language acquistion: Task-based language teaching. In K. Hyltenstam & M. Pienemann (Eds.), *Modelling and assessing second language development.* Clevedon, Avon: Multilingual Matters, 1985.

Long, M. H., & Sato, C. J. Methodological issues in interlanguage studies: An interactionist perspective. In A. Davies, C. Criper, & A. P. R. Howatt (Eds.), *Interlanguage.* Edinburgh: Edinburgh University Press, 1984.

Maley, A. "I got religion!" Evangelism in TEFL. In M. Clarke & J. Handscombe (Eds.), *On TESOL '82.* Washington, DC: TESOL, 1983.

Meisel, J., Clahsen, H., & Pienemann, M. On determining developmental stages in second language acquisition. *Studies in Second Language Acquisition,* 1981, *3*(2) 109–135.

Nicholas, H. Individual differences in interlanguage use. Paper presented at the Ninth Annual Conference of the Applied Linguistics Association of Australia, Alice Springs, 1984.

Nicholas, H., & Meisel, J. Second language acquisition: The state of the art. In S. W. Felix and H. Wode (Eds.), *Language development at the crossroads.* Tübingen: Gunter Narr Verlag, 1983.

Ochs, E. Planned and unplanned discourse. In T. Givón (Ed.), *Syntax and semantics*: Vol. 12. *Discourse and semantics.* New York: Academic Press, 1979.

Pavesi, M. Linguistic markedness, discoursal modes, and relative clause formation in a formal and an informal context. Paper presented at the IRAAL-BAAL Seminar on the Formal and Informal Contexts of Language Learning. Dublin, September 11–13, 1984.

Pica, T. Adult acquisition of English as a second language under different conditions of exposure. *Language Learning*, 1983, *33*(4), 465–497.

Pica, T. Procedures for morpheme data analysis in second language acquisition research: Reviewing the current debate and raising new issues. Paper presented at the Eighteenth Annual TESOL Conference, Houston, Texas, March 6–11, 1984.

Pienemann, M. Psychological constraints on the teachability of languages. *Studies in Second Language Acquisition*, 1984, *6*(2), 186–214.

Pienemann, M. Psycholinguistic principles of second language teaching. Manuscript. University of Sydney, Department of German, 1985.

Rutherford, W. Markedness in second language acquisition. *Language Learning*, 1982, *32*(1), 85–108.

Sato, C. J. Task variation in interlanguage phonology. In S. Gass & C. Madden (Eds.), *Input and second language acquisition*. Rowley, MA: Newbury House, 1985.

Schmidt, R. W., & Frota, S. N. Developing basic conversational ability in a second language: A case study of an adult learner of Portuguese. In R. R. Day (Ed.), *Talking to learn: Conversation in second language acquisition*. Rowley, MA: Newbury House, 1986.

Schumann, J. H. *The pidginization process: A model for second language acquisition*. Rowley, MA: Newbury House, 1978.

Swain, M. Communicative competence: Some roles of comprehensible input and comprehensible output in its development. In S. Gass & C. Madden (Eds.), *Input and second language acquisition*. Rowley, MA: Newbury House, 1985.

Tarone, E. Variability in interlanguage use: A study of style-shifting in morphology and syntax. Paper presented at the Eighteenth Annual TESOL Conference, Houston, Texas, March 6–11, 1984.

Vigil, N. & Oller, J. W., Jr. Rule fossilization: A tentative model. *Language Learning*, 1976, *26*(2), 281–295.

Weslander, D. & Stephany, G. V. Evaluation of an English as a second language program for Southeast Asian students. *TESOL Quarterly* 1983, *17*(3), 473–480.

Westmoreland, R. L2 German acquisition by instructed adults. Unpublished manuscript, University of Hawaii at Manoa, 1983.

Wode, H. Language-acquisitional universals: A unified view of language acquisition. In H. Winitz (Ed.), *Native language and foreign language acquisition. Annals of the New York Academy of Sciences*, 1981, *379*, 218–234.

Zobl, H. Markedness and the projection problem. *Language Learning*, 1983, *33*(3), 293–313.

Zobl, H. Grammars in search of input and intake. In S. Gass & C. Madden (Eds.), *Input and second language acquisition*. Rowley, MA: Newbury House, 1985.

SUGGESTED READINGS

Krashen, S. D. *Principles and practice in second language acquisition*. New York: Pergamon Press, 1982.

Lightbown, P. M. Exploring relationships between developmental and instructional sequences. In H. W. Seliger & M. H. Long (Eds.), *Classroom oriented research on second language acquisition*. Rowley, MA: Newbury House, 1983.

Long, M. H. Does second language instruction make a difference? A review of research. *TESOL Quarterly*, 1983, *17*(3), 359–382.

Pica, T. Adult acquisition of English as a second language under different conditions of exposure. *Language Learning*, 1983, *33*(4), 465–497.

Pienemann, M. Psychological constraints on the teachability of language. *Studies in Second Language Acquisition*, 1984, *6*(2), 186–214.

Wode, H. Language-acquisitional universals: A unified view of language acquisition. In H. Winitz (Ed.), *Native language and foreign language acquisition. Annals of the New York Academy of Sciences*, 1981, *379*, 218–234.

Zobl, H. Grammars in search of input and intake. In S. Gass & C. Madden (Eds.), *Input and second language acquisition*. Rowley, MA: Newbury House, 1985.

five

**BILINGUAL
EDUCATION
PERSPECTIVE**

Second Language Acquisition Within Bilingual Education Programs

Jim Cummins, Ontario Institute for Studies in Education

In the United States a large majority of students in bilingual education programs are from minority or subordinate (i.e., non-English) language backgrounds. By contrast, in Canada, students from English home backgrounds are the major group attending bilingual or "French immersion" programs. The Canadian research findings from immersion programs are relatively clear-cut. Students initially (e.g., K–grade 2) instructed exclusively through French (the minority language) make good academic and conversational progress in French at no long-term cost to their proficiency in English (e.g., Swain & Lapkin, 1982). In the United States, on the other hand, the research findings on the effectiveness of bilingual education appear anything but clear to most policymakers (e.g., Baker & de Kanter, 1981), and the issue is extremely controversial. Many commentators (e.g., Henry, 1983) argue that bilingualism is a disruptive force from both an individual and a societal perspective and regard the research as showing that "only total immersion in English clearly worked" (Henry, 1983, p. 31).

Despite the confusion that bubbles through the media accounts of bilingual programs in the United States, the research data are entirely consistent with the Canadian findings and, in fact, illustrate certain basic universal principles of second language acquisition. In this chapter, I shall attempt to reconcile apparent differences in the Canadian and U.S. bilingual education

145

data and show how each set of data supports certain principles of second language (L2) acquisition. The chapter will focus primarily on the more controversial U.S. context; thus, in the first section, the evolution of current policy issues will be briefly outlined. This will be followed by a discussion of the relationship between research, theory, and policy, after which some of the evaluation results from bilingual programs will be reviewed.

EVOLUTION OF THE BILINGUAL EDUCATION POLICY DEBATE

Early statements of the rationale for bilingual schooling (e.g., Gaarder, 1977) emphasized the potential benefits of initial L1 instruction in facilitating home-school relationships and in promoting a healthy self-concept among minority children as well as ensuring that children did not fall behind in academic content while they were learning English. But subsequent to the 1974 *Lau* v. *Nichols* decision and the widespread imposition of bilingual education on local school districts, attention increasingly focused on the linguistic mismatch between home language and school language as *the* cause of minority students' low achievement. This was due not only to the intuitive appeal of the argument that students could not learn in a language they didn't understand, but also to the assumption that constructs such as "language proficiency" and "dominance" were measurable and could therefore be used as indices to assess when and for how long bilingual programs were "needed." Thus, students who were "non- or limited-English-speaking" (NES and LES) were eligible for bilingual instruction until they had become "full-English speaking" (FES).

The first serious educational challenges to the rationale for bilingual education came in 1977 with the publication of Noel Epstein's monograph *Language, Ethnicity and the Schools* and the American Institute for Research (AIR) study on the impact of Title VII Spanish-English bilingual programs (Danoff, Coles, McLaughlin, & Reynolds, 1978). Epstein (1977) pointed out that research evidence in support of bilingual education was meager and also that the rationale for bilingual education was by no means as clear-cut as advocates suggested. The success of French immersion programs in Canada, he argued, showed that "the language factor itself can neither account for nor solve the educational difficulties of these minority students" (p. 59). This was by no means a new insight. Paulston (1976) had previously argued convincingly that language was an intervening variable and that the fundamental causal factors for minority students' low achievement were social in nature (see also Cummins, 1982; Ogbu, 1978). The impact of Epstein's analysis was considerable, however, insofar as it undermined the assumptions on which policy had been based—namely, that students can't learn in a language they don't understand—and reinforced the growing suspicions of many educators and policy-makers about the "real" aims of bilingual programs (i.e., increased Hispanic political power).

These suspicions received a further boost when the AIR study reported that according to teacher judgments, less than one-third of the students enrolled in bilingual classrooms were there because of their need for English instruction (although both Title VII and non–Title VII Hispanic students were functioning at approximately the twentieth percentile on measures of English academic functioning). The results of comparative analyses showed that students in Title VII programs were doing no better academically than were non-English background students in regular programs.

At around the same time that the Epstein monograph and the AIR study were beginning to undermine the pedagogical rationale for bilingual education, Rudolph Troike, then director of the Center for Applied Linguistics, compiled the results of 12 bilingual program evaluations that met criteria of methodological adequacy and whose results supported bilingual education. Though widely circulated to practitioners and policymakers, Troike's (1978) report had considerably less impact than the AIR findings, for obvious reasons. The AIR study was a million-dollar nationwide evaluation, whereas the findings of the small-scale evaluations cited by Troike did not appear generalizable outside their specific contexts. Nevertheless, Troike's report did have some policy impact insofar as it suggested that a high-quality bilingual education program can be effective in meeting the goals of equal educational opportunity for minority language children and reinforced the possibility that the AIR findings could be attributed to implementation difficulties in bilingual programs rather than to limitations in the concept of bilingual education itself.

Despite both severe methodological criticisms (e.g., O'Malley, 1978; Swain, 1979) and allegations of deliberate bias (Cervantes, 1979), the AIR findings were widely interpreted as evidence that bilingual programs were aiming for native language maintenance, and were frequently cited as evidence that the educational rationale for bilingual education lacked credibility. For example, Bethell (1979), after suggesting that the program represented "a surreptitious death wish on the part of the federal government," went on to cite the AIR findings as showing that the program was not working. He also approvingly quoted Congressman John Ashbrook's statement that "the program is actually preventing children from learning English. Some day somebody is going to have to teach those young people to speak English or else they are going to become public charges" (p. 32).

The most recent assault on the rationale for bilingual education comes from the literature review carried out by Baker and de Kanter (1981) of the Office of Planning, Budget and Evaluation in the U.S. Department of Education. Baker and de Kanter set up criteria for methodological adequacy that resulted in the exclusion of several studies hitherto regarded as strong evidence for the effectiveness of bilingual education (e.g., Egan & Goldsmith, 1981; Modiano, 1968; Rosier & Holm, 1980). They concluded on the basis of the evidence they regarded as acceptable that "there is no firm empirical evidence that TBE (transitional bilingual education) is uniquely effective in raising language-minority students' performance in English or in nonlanguage subject areas" (p. 16), and thus exclusive reliance should not be placed on transitional bilingual education in federal policy decisions. They suggested on the basis of both the Canadian findings and an evaluation at the kindergarten level in Texas (Peña-Hughes & Solis, 1980) that "structured English-only immersion" is a promising alternative to transitional bilingual programs in which children's first language (L1) is used on a temporary basis to facilitate acquisition of academic skills.

As with the AIR study, the Baker and de Kanter report was sharply criticized by proponents of bilingual education on methodological grounds (e.g., criteria for inclusion/exclusion of studies) as well as for misleading and unwarranted conclusions (e.g., Willig, 1981–1982). Nevertheless, its negative impact was considerable, as can be seen from the *New York Times* editorial of October 10, 1981:

> The Department of Education is analyzing new evidence that expensive bilingual education programs don't work. . . . Teaching non-English speaking children in their native language during much of their school day constructs a roadblock on their journey into English. A language is best learned through immersion in it, particularly by children. . . . Neither society nor its children will be well served if bilingualism continues to be used to keep thousands of children from quickly learning the one language needed to succeed in America. (From "In Plain English" (editorial), *New York Times*, October 10, 1981, p. 24. Copyright © 1981 by the New York Times Company. Reprinted by permission.)

Thus, the initial acceptance of bilingual education as a "pedagogically sound means" to help children learn English has come under increasing pressure during the past five years from the argument that if minority children are deficient in English, then they need instruction in English, not their L1. Bilingual education appears to imply a counterintuitive "less equals more" rationale in which *less* English instruction is assumed to lead to more English achievement. To skeptics of the bilingual education rationale, it appears more reasonable to assume a direct relationship between English achievement and exposure to English; hence, the more time devoted to L1 instruction, the poorer the language minority student's performance in English will be.

The validity of these claims for and against bilingual education can be assessed by examining the findings of bilingual program evaluations. A variety of programs for both majority students (e.g., English L1 speakers in North America) and minority students will be reviewed in order to clarify the patterns that exist in the research data.

BILINGUAL PROGRAM EVALUATIONS

Part of the confusion in the debate about the necessity and/or appropriateness of bilingual education for minority language students arises from the terminology used to refer to different types of programs. In particular, the term *immersion* has been used in a variety of ways. The term was originally used in the context of Canadian French immersion programs to refer to initial instruction primarily through the medium of French for English-background students. Thus, in these programs students are "immersed" in a second language classroom environment. The most common variant of immersion programs is *early immersion*, which begins at kindergarten level; however, *intermediate* and *late* immersion programs are also offered, beginning in grades 4 or 5 and 7 or 8, respectively. Currently, in Canada more than 100,000 students are enrolled in some form of French immersion program. English-medium instruction is gradually phased into immersion programs such that after about four years roughly half the time is spent in instruction through each language.

Three important characteristics of French immersion programs can be noted:

1. The teachers are bilingual; thus, they can understand what children say to them in English and can respond appropriately.
2. The input to the child in French is modified in various ways to make it comprehensible (e.g., through repetition, redundancy, use of context, gestures, etc.).
3. After the initial grades, a strong emphasis is placed on the development of English (L1) literacy skills.

Thus, immersion programs for majority students in the Canadian (and U.S.) contexts are actually *bilingual* programs designed to develop high levels of oral and literate proficiency in both L1 and L2. In the U.S. debate about the education of minority students, however, the term *immersion* is generally used to refer to a monolingual English-only program in which children are immersed in the L2 with no instructional support in the L1. The aim is proficiency in English (L2) rather than bilingual proficiency. In some cases the term *immersion* is used to refer to English-only programs that have *none* of the major characteristics of French immersion programs outlined here. The programs and teachers are monolingual, and no effort is made to modify the L2 input to make it comprehensible. Following Cohen and Swain (1976), such programs will be referred to as *submersion* rather than *immersion*. A minimal requirement for use of the term *immersion* in the following discussion with respect to English-only instruction for minority students is that some modification of the L2 input be made to facilitate comprehension.

In the U.S. context the term *immersion* has been used to refer to at least four very different types of programs for minority students. In discussing so-called immersion programs, then, it is necessary to distinguish

1. The language on which there is primary initial emphasis, that is, students' L1 or L2
2. Whether the program is bilingual or monolingual

3. Whether the program participants are from majority or minority
linguistic backgrounds

Thus, *L2 monolingual immersion programs for minority students* are programs that involve English-only instruction, but with some attempts made to modify the L2 input to facilitate comprehension. *L2 submersion programs for minority students* are similar monolingual programs, but with no attempt to modify the instructional input. *L1 bilingual immersion programs for minority students* are programs that "immerse" minority students in their L1 in the early grades in order to provide a conceptual foundation for the acquisition of English academic skills. These programs are bilingual in that both L1 and English are used as instructional languages at some point in children's schooling. *L2 bilingual immersion programs for minority students* place the primary instructional emphasis on English but also include some promotion of L1 skills. Examples of each of these program types will be considered in a later section.

The confusion in the U.S. debate can be seen from the fact that L2 monolingual immersion programs for minority students have been proposed as viable alternatives to transitional bilingual programs largely on the basis of the success of L2 bilingual immersion programs for majority students (i.e., French immersion programs) (e.g., Baker & de Kanter, 1981). Clearly there is a logical fallacy in arguing for monolingual programs on the basis of the success of bilingual programs. This issue is considered in more detail in a later section, after a review of the empirical and theoretical literature.

L2 Bilingual Immersion for Majority Students

Prior to the large-scale institutionalization of French immersion programs for English-background students in Canada, it was generally assumed that there was a direct relationship between the amount of instructional time devoted to a language (or any academic subject) and achievement in that language. Thus, initial fears with regard to French immersion were largely concerned with possible detrimental effects on the development of children's English academic skills. It seemed reasonable to assume that if English language arts were not introduced until grade 2, 3, or 4 (depending on the program variation), and if considerably less total time were spent through the medium of English, then English skills must inevitably suffer.

These initial fears, however, have not been borne out in practice. Evaluations from across Canada have consistently shown that although early immersion students tend to lag behind their monolingual peers in English language arts until formal English instruction is introduced (usually in grade 2), they quickly catch up and may even surpass their peers by grade 5 or 6. Also, the development of English academic skills appears to be relatively unaffected either by the grade level at which English language arts are introduced or by the amount of English instructional time (see Swain & Lapkin, 1982). Thus, although there is generally a significant relationship between amount of instructional time in the minority language (French) and achievement in that language, little relationship is observed between English achievement and instructional time through English.

In terms of French achievement, students by grade 6 perform close to native speakers in oral and written receptive skills. Their productive skills, however, are not nativelike, although they are fluent. Studies have shown that, as in regular programs, IQ is a good predictor of French and English academic proficiency but not of conversational proficiency (e.g., Genesee, 1976, 1984). A very similar pattern of results has been found in U.S. L2 immersion programs for majority students (see California State Department of Education, 1984).

L1 Bilingual Immersion for Minority Students

This type of program is relatively uncommon in the United States because a strong initial emphasis on minority students' L1 combined with maintenance of L1 instruction throughout elementary school appears to many educators and policymakers to place insufficient emphasis on the teaching of English. In Canada, however, such programs are common for minority francophone students, although they are seldom referred to by the term *immersion*. Examples from both the U.S. and Canadian contexts are considered here.

The San Diego Spanish-English Language Immersion Program. This demonstration project, implemented in 1975 in the San Diego City Schools, involved approximately 60 percent Spanish L1 and 40 percent English L1 students. Instruction was predominantly in Spanish from preschool through grade 3, after which half the time was spent through the medium of each language. Twenty minutes of English instruction was included at the preschool level, 30 minutes at grades K-1, and 60 minutes at grades 2-3. Originally implemented in just one school, the project has now spread to several others. The original project was located in a lower-middle-class area and, although participation was (and is) voluntary, the Spanish-background students appear typical of most limited-English-speaking students in regular bilingual programs.

The findings of the project evaluation parallel those of Canadian and U.S. L2 bilingual immersion for majority students. In the early grades, students were found to perform somewhat below grade norms in English academic skills, but by grade 6 they were performing above grade norms in both English and Spanish. Math achievement also tended to be above grade norms. The evaluation results for both groups of students are summarized as follows:

Native-English-speaking project students—because they do not receive instruction in English reading as early as do students in the district's regular elementary level programs—begin to develop English reading skills somewhat later than regular-program students. However, project students make rapid and sustained progress in English reading once it is introduced and, as has been noted, ultimately meet or exceed English language norms for their grade levels. Also, though native-Spanish-speaking project students are not exposed to English reading and writing as early as they would be in the regular English-only instructional program, they eventually acquire English language skills which are above the norm for students in regular, English-only instructional programs and, in addition, develop their native-language skills. (Reprinted with permission of the San Diego City Schools from *An Exemplary Approach to Bilingual Education: A Comprehensive Handbook for Implementing an Elementary-Level Spanish-English Language Immersion Program*, San Diego: San Diego City Schools, 1982, p. 183.)

Although these demonstration project results clearly must be treated with caution, confidence in their potential generalizability is increased by the fact that they are entirely consistent with date from similar programs involving minority francophones in the Canadian context.

Manitoba Francophone Study. A large-scale study carried out by Hébert et al. (1976), conducted among grades 3, 6, and 9 minority francophone students in Manitoba who were receiving varying amounts of instruction through the medium of French, found that the amount of French-medium instruction showed no relationship to children's achievement in English. In other words, francophone students receiving 80 percent instruction in French and 20 percent instruction in English did just as well in English as students receiving 80 percent instruction in English and 20 percent instruction in French. However, amount of instruction in French (L1) was positively related to achievement in French. In other words, students' French benefited at no cost to their progress in English (L2).

In conclusion, it is clear from the findings of these L1 bilingual immersion programs for minority students that there is no direct relationship between the amount of instruction students receive in the minority language (e.g., Spanish, French) and their academic achievement in the majority language (English). These results parallel those of L2 bilingual immersion programs for majority students and refute the common argument that minority students require maximum exposure to English in the school.

Bilingual Bicultural Preschool Programs

Between 1976 and 1979, Head Start funded the development of four distinct bilingual bicultural preschool models for use with Spanish-speaking children. The longitudinal evaluation of these models is extremely impressive in its thoroughness insofar as it involved stratified assignment of children on the basis of Spanish or English language preference, age, sex, and prior preschool experience to experimental ($N = 45$) and control ($N = 45$) groups in each of eight Head Start sites. On-site observation was also carried out to assess degree of implementation of each program (see Head Start Bureau, 1982; Sandoval-Martinez, 1982).

The results for the "Spanish-preferring" children are summarized by the Head Start Bureau (1982) as follows:

- On three out of four English language measures, children in the bilingual bicultural curricula, as a group performed significantly better than Head Start children not in the curricula. These three measures assessed: a child's ability to use English; a child's ability to think abstractly; a child's ability to coordinate eye and hand movements.
- On the fourth English language measure children in the bilingual bicultural curricula, as a group performed significantly better than Head Start children not in the curricula. The difference, however, was not statistically significant. This measure assessed a child's ability to understand English.
- On two of five Spanish language measures, children in the bilingual bicultural curricula, as a group performed significantly better than Head Start children not in the curricula. These measures assessed a child's ability to use Spanish and to think abstractly in Spanish.
- On the other three Spanish language measures children in the four bilingual bicultural curricula, as a group performed as well as Head Start children not in the curricula.
- Classroom observations supported these findings for Spanish-preferring children. On the whole, children in the bilingual bicultural curricula increased their English language use in the classroom by 21% from Fall to Spring. This increase was accompanied by the use of grammatical forms which they had not used regularly early in the year. (1982, pp. ii–iii)

In short, the Spanish-preferring children performed as well or better on all English-language and Spanish-language measures as did similar children in monolingual preschool curricula. In other words, bilingual preschool experiences had no detrimental effects on their English language skills, which, classroom observations confirmed, showed an improvement in quality over the course of the year. Both parents and teachers showed extremely positive attitudes toward the bilingual bicultural curricula.

Legaretta Study: Direct ESL–Bilingual Comparison

A study carried out by Legaretta (1979) in California compared the effectiveness of three types of bilingual treatments with two types of English-only treatments in facilitating the development of English communicative competence in Spanish-background kindergarten children. The three bilingual treatments were found to be significantly superior to the two English-only treatments in developing English language skills. The most effective program was one with balanced separated bilingual usage (50 percent English, 50 percent Spanish, morning/afternoon split).

The Milingimbi Aboriginal Program

Australian aboriginal students who had been educated bilingually (spending overall roughly half the time in L1-medium instruction, K–grade 6) were compared in grades 4–6 with the previous cohort of grade 4–6 students in the same school who had received monolingual English instruction. The results of this evaluation are summarized by Gale, McClay, Christie, and Harris (1981):

> Since the introduction of bilingual education at Milingimbi, the children are not only learning to read and write in their own language and furthering their knowledge and respect for their own culture, but they are also achieving better academic results in oral English, reading, English composition and mathematics than they were under the former English monolingual education system. (Reprinted with permission of TESOL from "Academic Achievement in the Milingimbi Bilingual Education Program" by K. Gale, D. McClay, M. Christie, and S. Harris, *TESOL Quarterly*, *15* (1981), p. 309.)

The advantage of the bilingually schooled students at the end of elementary school was greater in the more cognitively demanding higher level literacy (e.g., cloze and writing) and mathematics (multiplication and division) skills than in lower level skills that may depend more on rote learning (e.g., decoding, sight words, addition, subtraction). The authors point out, however, that despite their improved performance, the students were still considerably below national norms in achievement.

A variety of factors (in addition to bilingual instruction per se) may combine to produce such encouraging results. For present purposes, however, it is sufficient to note that transfer of academic knowledge and skills across languages has clearly occurred, and students have in no way suffered in English as a result of spending considerably less time in English-medium instruction.

Malherbe's Afrikaans–English Bilingual Education Study

E. G. Malherbe conducted a survey of almost 19,000 South African students from Afrikaans and English backgrounds in different types of school programs. The aim was to compare the effects of instructing children from each language background in bilingual as compared to monolingual schools. In the bilingual schools children generally received their instruction in the early grades through L1 and thereafter through both languages. Both intelligence level and home language were kept constant in comparisons of the effects of these two types of schools. At the time of the survey, 32 percent of the students spoke only English at home, 25 percent spoke only Afrikaans, and 43 percent were from homes that were bilingual in varying degrees. Fifty-one percent of the students received English-only instruction, 28 percent were taught only in Afrikaans, and 21 percent were in bilingual schools receiving instruction through both English and Afrikaans.

Some of the major findings of the study were as follows (see Malherbe, 1946, 1978):

1. South African students gained considerably in their L2 when it was used as a medium of instruction and not merely taught as a school subject.

2. The proficiency of students in their L1 was not adversely affected either by having the two languages represented in the same school or by using the L2 as a medium of instruction. In other words, as in French immersion programs, instructional time through the medium of L2 did not entail any loss in L1 academic skills.

3. Again as in French immersion programs, an initial lag in mastery of subjects taught through L2 was experienced by children from monolingual home backgrounds; however, this lag became progressively less and tended to disappear by the end of elementary school (grade 6).

4. In order to test the hypothesis that bilingual instruction might be appropriate for bright students but be too "challenging" for those who are less bright, Malherbe compared the performance of children at different IQ levels in bilingual and monolingual schools. He reported that the bilingual schools seemed to be especially appropriate for students of below-average IQ. This conclusion was based on the fact that the differences in L2 proficiency between below average IQ students in bilingual (L2 used as a medium of instruction) as compared to monolingual (L2 taught as a subject) programs was considerably larger than the difference in L2 proficiency between above-average IQ students in each type of program. An implication of this finding is that whereas brighter students can often profit from instruction that attempts to teach language outside of a meaningful communicative context, less bright students are severely handicapped under these conditions.

Many other examples of bilingual education both in the United States (see review by Baker & de Kanter, 1981) and elsewhere (see Cummins, 1983) illustrate essentially the same patterns of findings. What are the implications of these findings for educational policy?

Two arguments have dominated the public debate about the education of language minority students in the United States. Those in favor of bilingual programs have argued that academic retardation will almost inevitably result if minority students are required to learn exclusively through their weaker language (L2). This "linguistic mismatch" argument is refuted as a generalization by the success of majority students in L2 bilingual immersion programs where instruction in the early grades is exclusively through the medium of L2 (e.g., French, Spanish, etc.).

Opponents of bilingual education have argued that minority students need maximum exposure to English if they are to learn it adequately. This "maximum exposure" argument is similarly refuted by the research data in that students (both minority and majority) in bilingual programs who spend less time through English perform at least as well in English academic skills as do comparison students instructed exclusively through English.

In short, the research data show that much of the policy debate in the United States has been misdirected. The next section examines two theoretical generalizations that appear to be consistently supported by the research. The policy implications of such generalizations derive from the fact that generalizations permit policymakers to make reliable predictions about program outcomes in a variety of different contexts. If a prediction is not supported by the actual program outcomes, then the generalization on which the prediction is based is inadequate.

TOWARD THEORY AND PREDICTION IN BILINGUAL EDUCATION

The Common Underlying Proficiency Generalization

This generalization has been stated as follows:

> To the extent that instruction in Lx is effective in promoting proficiency in Lx, transfer of this proficiency to Ly will occur provided there is adequate exposure to Ly (either in school or environment) and adequate motivation to learn Ly. (Cummins, 1981, p. 29)

In other words, the fact that there is little relationship between amount of instructional time through the majority language and academic achievement in that language strongly suggests that L1 and L2 academic skills are interdependent, that is, manifestations of a common underlying proficiency.

In concrete terms what this hypothesis means is that in a Spanish-English program, Spanish instruction that develops L1 reading skills for Spanish-speaking students is not just developing *Spanish* skills, but is also developing a deeper conceptual and linguistic proficiency, which is strongly related to the development of *English* literacy and general academic skills. In other words, although the surface aspects (pronunciation, fluency, etc.) of, for example, Spanish and English or Chinese and English are clearly separate, there is an underlying cognitive/academic proficiency that is common across languages. This common underlying proficiency makes possible the transfer of cognitive/academic or literacy-related skills across languages.

Transfer is much more likely to occur from minority to majority language because the conditions of exposure and motivation are met, whereas this is usually not so in the opposite direction. This hypothesis has extremely strong empirical support in a wide variety of contexts (see Baker & de Kanter, 1981; Cummins, 1983). The major policy implication is that for language minority students, L1 academic skills can be strongly promoted at no cost to the development of English academic skills.

A second generalization that emerges from the data is that in order to acquire conversational and academic L2 skills, learners must be exposed to sufficient L2 comprehensible input.

The Sufficient Comprehensible Input Generalization

Most second language theorists (e.g., Krashen, 1982; Long, 1983; Schachter, 1983; Wong Fillmore, 1983a) currently endorse some form of the *input hypothesis*, which essentially states that acquisition of a second language depends not just on exposure to the language but also on access to L2 input that is modified in various ways to make it comprehensible. There is some disagreement on whether comprehensible input is a sufficient condition for L2 acquisition but virtually all theorists agree that it is a necessary condition (see Swain, 1983, for a discussion). Krashen (1982) posits four characteristics of optimal input for comprehension:

1. Optimal input is comprehensible; that is, the *message* is understandable by the learner regardless of his or her level of L2 proficiency.
2. Optimal input is interesting and/or relevant.
3. Optimal input is not grammatically sequenced.
4. Optimal input must be in sufficient quantity, although it is difficult to specify just how much is enough.

In addition, according to Krashen, acquisition is facilitated by a supportive affective environment. Wong Fillmore (1983a) has clearly described the ways in which L2 input must be modified to make it comprehensible:

the language used in instruction has to be shaped and selected with the learners' abilities in mind, and it must be embedded in a context of gestures, demonstrations and activities that lead and support the learners' guesses about what is going on. . . . Important adjustments also have to be made in instructional content when the language spoken by teachers serves both as linguistic input for learners and as the means of conveying academic subject matter to them. The learners' linguistic needs will necessarily limit what can be discussed and hence how much of the curriculum can be covered. (Reprinted with permission of TESOL from "The Language Learner as an Individual: Implications of Research on Individual Differences for the ESL Teacher" by L. Wong Fillmore, in *On TESOL '82: Pacific Perspectives on Language Learning and Teaching*, edited by M. A. Clarke & J. Handscombe, Washington, DC: TESOL, 1983, pp. 170–171.)

Other theorists have elaborated on the input requirements. Schachter (1983), for example, adds "negative input," that is, feedback regarding unsuccessful communication attempts, to the input requirements necessary for acquisition. Long (1983) suggests that among the most important ways of making input comprehensible are (1) "a 'here and now' orientation in conversation and the use of linguistic and extralinguistic (contextual) information and general knowledge" and (2) modification of the interactional structure of the conversation by means of devices such as self- and other-repetition, confirmation and comprehension checks, and clarification requests. Long concludes that "all the available evidence is consistent with the idea that a *beginning* learner, at least, must have comprehensible input if he or she is to acquire either a first or a second language" (1983, p. 210, emphasis in original).

The success of bilingual or immersion programs in teaching L2 skills in comparison to the mediocre results obtained in traditional second language programs provides strong support for the importance of sufficient comprehensible input. As is clear from Long's (1983) summary characterization of these two programs, their differential success can be attributed largely to differences in the extent to which each provides sufficient comprehensible input to students:

> . . . immersion may fairly be characterized . . . as focusing initially on the development of target language comprehension rather than production skills, content rather than form and as attempting to teach content through the SL [second language] in language the children can understand. Modern language teaching, on the other hand, generally focuses on formal accuracy, is structurally graded and sentence-bound and demands early (even immediate) production of nearly all material presented to the learner. (Reprinted with permission of TESOL from "Native Speaker/Non-native Speaker Conversation in the Second Language Classroom" by M. H. Long, in *On TESOL '82: Pacific Perspectives on Language Learning and Teaching*, edited by M. A. Clarke & J. Handscombe, Washington, DC: TESOL, 1983, p. 209.)

Wong Fillmore (1983a) expresses very clearly why teaching language as a subject works much less well for language acquisition than does using it as a medium of instruction:

> Wherever it is felt that points of language need to be imparted for their own sake, teachers are likely to make use of drills and exercises where these linguistic points are emphasized and repeated. And when this happens the language on which students have to base their learning of English is separated from its potential functions, namely those that allow language learners to make the appropriate connections between form and communicative functions. Without such connections language is simply not learnable. (Reprinted with permission of TESOL from "The Language

Learner as an Individual: Implications of Research on Individual Differences for the ESL Teacher" by L. Wong Fillmore, in *On TESOL '82: Pacific Perspectives on Language Learning and Teaching*, edited by M. A. Clarke & J. Handscombe, Washington, DC: TESOL, 1983, p. 170.)

One important link between the principles of sufficient comprehensible input and the common underlying proficiency generalization is that the knowledge (e.g., subject matter content, literacy skills, etc.) acquired in one language play a major role in making input in the other language comprehensible (Cummins, 1981; Krashen, 1981). For example, an immigrant student who already has the concept of "honesty" in his or her L1 will require relatively little input in L2 containing the term to acquire its meaning. Clearly, for an immigrant student who does not already have the concept in L1, a much longer developmental process is involved. In the context of bilingual programs such as the San Diego Spanish-English language immersion program, this same transfer process explains why considerably less input in English than minority students obtain in English-only programs is sufficient for good development of English conversational and academic skills.

CLASSROOM IMPLICATIONS

Two examples from studies that have involved detailed classroom observation (Moll, 1981; Wong Fillmore, 1983b) will illustrate the implications of these theoretical generalizations for bilingual instruction.

The study carried out by Moll and his colleagues (Moll, 1981) was a microethnographic investigation of reading instruction in Spanish and English in the context of a team-taught maintenance bilingual program. A considerable emphasis on higher level comprehension-oriented literacy activities (e.g., inferring meaning from the text, analyzing content, writing book reports, etc.) was observed among the high-ability reading group in the Spanish lesson. In the English classroom, on the other hand, students were

made to focus primarily on the mechanical tasks of practicing decoding skills, word sounds or lexical meaning. Practically absent are key activities that promote reading *comprehension* and help the students learn how to *communicate that knowledge* of content. (1981, p. 439, emphasis in original)

Moll suggests that a likely source of the problem is that the English teacher was confounding pronunciation and decoding problems.

The teacher seems to be assuming that decoding is a prerequisite to comprehension and that correct pronunciation is the best index of decoding. The implicit theory guiding instruction is that correct pronunciation (decoding) must precede comprehension (cf. Goodman, Goodman and Flores, 1979). Consequently, the teacher organizes the lessons to provide the children with the necessary time on the task to help them practice pronunciation, phonics, and other aspects of language learning such as lexical meaning. In so doing, higher order (comprehension) reading skills are structured out of the lessons' interactions. (Reprinted with permission of L. C. Moll from "The Microethnographic Study of Bilingual Schooling" by L. C. Moll, in *Ethnoperspectives in Bilingual Education Research*: Vol. III. *Bilingual Education Technology*, edited by R. V. Padilla, Ypsilanti, MI: Department of Foreign Languages and Bilingual Studies, 1981, p. 439; emphasis in original.)

These findings illustrate how bilingual instruction can develop academic skills that have the potential for transfer to L2. It is crucial, however, to know what minority children can do in their L1 so that appropriate opportunities for transfer can be provided. The study, in short, illustrates how important it is to take account of bilingual students' common underlying academic proficiency in providing comprehensible input that is appropriate for both their level of academic development and L2 (English) language skills.

Moll's (1981) study illustrates an example of L2 instruction that is inappropriate (too low level) for students' level of academic development. Wong Fillmore's data, on the other hand, show how certain kinds of bilingual instruction may communicate academic content but deprive students of language learning opportunities. In her study, as well as in Legaretta's (1979), it was observed that in classes where teachers frequently alternated languages in order to provide L1 input to both minority and majority students, students acquired very little of the second language. Videotape recordings showed students "turning off" as soon as the teacher used L2 and then paying attention again when the content was translated into L1. Wong Fillmore (1983b) points out that:

Language alternation can, to be sure, facilitate student comprehension of subject matter instruction and from the teacher's perspective may be the easiest and most immediately effective way to communicate information to students who lack sufficient control of the school language. But such practices clearly hinder the development of the English language skills the children need for effective participation in the life of the school classroom. In order for students to learn a second language efficiently, they must have access to language which is shaped to their needs and which at the same time makes specific kinds of cognitive demands on them. (Abstract, p. 1)

Wong Fillmore proposes that for the goals of both academic development and language acquisition to be achieved, there should be periods in which each language is in exclusive use for instructional purposes and the appropriate adjustments are being made.

IMMERSION AND BILINGUAL EDUCATION REVISITED

It was pointed out earlier that the linguistic mismatch hypothesis does not constitute a viable theoretical basis for bilingual education policy. But the popular arguments for English-only "immersion" rest on an even weaker theoretical assumption—namely, that there is a direct relationship between amount of exposure to English and academic learning in English. What emerges from the research data on bilingual education are two theoretical generalizations that are fully consistent both with each other and with virtually all the data on second (and first) language acquisition generally. To recapitulate, these generalizations are: (1) the *common underlying proficiency* generalization—that academic skills in L1 and L2 are transferable or manifestations of a common underlying proficiency; and (2) the *sufficient comprehensible input* generalization—that access to comprehensible input is a necessary condition for L2 acquisition.

These generalizations are clearly embodied in French immersion programs but less clearly so in many U.S. transitional bilingual programs for minority students. As noted earlier, there are three important characteristics of French immersion programs that contribute to making the L2 input comprehensible: (1) a bilingual teacher who can understand students' L1 questions and thereby respond appropriately in L2; (2) modified input, as discussed earlier; and (3) strong L1 literacy promotion, usually starting about grade 2, with L2 instruction reduced to about half the time by grade 5 or 6.

To what extent do the major program models that have been implemented or proposed for minority students in the U.S. context embody these aspects of comprehensible input? As noted earlier, it is possible to identify four program models to which the term *immersion* has been applied:

1. L2 submersion programs for minority students
2. L2 monolingual immersion programs for minority students
3. L2 bilingual immersion programs for minority students
4. L1 bilingual immersion programs for minority students

These are briefly described next, and the extent to which each is likely to promote comprehensible L2 input is outlined in Table 5.1. Transitional bilingual education is also included in this table for comparison purposes.

L2 submersion programs for minority students involve virtually no concessions to the child's language or culture and have well-documented negative effects for many children (e.g., Gaarder, 1977). L2 monolingual immersion programs for minority students take account of the need to provide minority students with modified L2 input but dispense with bilingual teachers and L1 literacy promotion. Little systematic observation has been made of the effects of monolingual immersion, but such a program might be appropriate under certain conditions. For example, in classes with a large number of languages

**Table 5.1   COMPREHENSIBLE INPUT IN MONOLINGUAL AND BILINGUAL
IMMERSION PROGRAMS**

Program	Comprehensible input		
	Bilingual teacher	L2 modified input	L1 literacy promotion
A. *Monolingual*			
1. L2 submersion for minority students	−	−	−
2. L2 monolingual immersion for minority students	−	+	−
B. *Bilingual*			
3. L2 bilingual immersion for minority students	+	+	+
4. L1 bilingual immersion for minority students	+	+	+
5. Transitional bilingual programs for minority students	+	?	?[a]

Notes: +: principle incorporated in program; −: principle not incorporated in program; ?: extent of incorporation will vary across programs.
[a]In transitional programs that are not of the quick-exit variety (e.g., some L1 instruction from kindergarten through the later elementary grades), L1 literacy skills are likely to be promoted.

represented, it might not be feasible to promote L1 literacy actively because of the lack of teachers or instructional aides fluent in the children's languages.

L2 bilingual immersion programs for minority students incorporate all three major characteristics outlined previously that contribute to making the L2 input comprehensible: bilingual teachers, modified L2 input, and L1 literacy promotion. The major emphasis in these programs is on L2 promotion, but L1 literacy is also developed. One such immersion program designed explicitly in accordance with the Canadian model has been introduced in McAllen, Texas, with encouraging results at the kindergarten level (see Baker & de Kanter, 1981; Peña-Hughes & Solis, 1980; Willig, 1981–1982). Mexican American students in this immersion variant of bilingual education who received about an hour a day of Spanish literacy-related instruction performed significantly better *in both English and Spanish* than did equivalent students in a transitional bilingual program.

The fourth program type that has been labeled "immersion" is the L1 bilingual immersion program for minority students discussed earlier with reference to the San Diego results. This type of program represents a considerably stronger commitment to promoting minority students' L1 proficiency than L2 bilingual immersion programs for minority students, although in both program types the support is more genuine and sustained than in most transitional bilingual programs.

Table 5.1 shows clearly why the L2 and L1 bilingual immersion programs for minority students appear to have more potential for success than the other three options. In each of these two programs, students are likely to be exposed to considerably more comprehensible input then in the other three; in addition they are likely to reap the personal and educational benefits of biliteracy (see Cummins, 1981).

CONCLUSION

We know considerably more about bilingual education and second language learning than one might suspect on the basis of the level of debate among U.S. policymakers, educators, and media commentators.

The opposing "linguistic mismatch" and "maximum exposure" arguments around which the policy debate has revolved are each refuted as generalizations by an enormous amount of research data. Although many issues remain unresolved, however, there *are* some strongly supported theoretical generalizations that provide a reasonable basis for predicting the outcomes of different program options implemented in a variety of contexts. Specifically, the common underlying proficiency generalization explains why students who have less instruction through the majority language perform at least as well in majority language academic skills. The sufficient comprehensible input generalization explains why more than just exposure to the L2 is required for L2 acquisition. In order to contribute to students' acquisition of L2 conversational and academic skills, the input must be comprehensible. In successful bilingual or immersion programs, provision of comprehensible input involves both the promotion of students' L1 conceptual skills and modification of the L2 conversational academic input by the teacher.

REFERENCES

Baker, K. A., & de Kanter, A. A. *Effectiveness of bilingual education: A review of the literature.* Washington, DC: Office of Planning and Budget, U.S. Department of Education, 1981.

Bethell, T. Against bilingual education. *Harper's,* February 1979.

California State Department of Education. *Studies on immersion education: A collection for United States educators.* Sacramento: California State Department of Education, 1984.

Cervantes, R. A. An exemplary consafic chingatropic assessment: The AIR report. *Bilingual Education Paper Series,* Vol. 2, No. 8, National Dissemination and Assessment Center, 1979.

Cohen, A. D., & Swain, M. Bilingual education: The immersion model in the North American context. In J. E. Alatis & K. Twaddell (Eds.), *English as a second language in bilingual education.* Washington, DC: TESOL, 1976.

Cummins, J. The role of primary language development in promoting educational success for language minority students. In California State Department of Education (Ed.), *Schooling and language minority students.* Los Angeles: Evaluation, Dissemination, and Assessement Center, 1981.

Cummins, J. *Interdependence and bicultural ambivalence: Regarding the pedagogical rationale for bilingual education.* Rosslyn, VA: National Clearinghouse for Bilingual Education, 1982.

Cummins, J. *Heritage language education: A literature review.* Toronto: Ontario Ministry of Education, 1983.

Danoff, M. N., Coles, G. J., McLaughlin, D. H., & Reynolds, D. J. *Evaluation of the impact of ESEA Title VII Spanish/English bilingual education program: Overview of study and findings.* Palo Alto, CA: American Institutes for Research, 1978.

Egan, L. A., & Goldsmith, R. Bilingual-bicultural education. The Colorado success story. *NABE News,* January 1981.

Epstein, N. *Language, ethnicity and the schools.* Washington, DC: Institute for Educational Leadership, 1977.

Gaarder, A. B. *Bilingual schooling and the survival of Spanish in the United States.* Rowley, MA: Newbury House, 1977.

Gale, K., McClay, D., Christie, M., & Harris, S. Academic achievement in the Milingimbi bilingual education program. *TESOL Quarterly,* 1981, *15,* 297–314.

Genesee, F. The suitability of immersion programs for all children. *Canadian Modern Language Review,* 1976, *32,* 494–515.

Genesee, F. Historical and theoretical foundations of immersion education. In California State Department of Education (Ed.), *Studies on immersion education: A collection for United States educators.* Sacramento: California State Department of Education, 1984.

Goodman, K., Goodman, Y., & Flores, B. *Reading in the bilingual classroom: Literacy and biliteracy.* Rosslyn, VA: National Clearinghouse for Bilingual Education, 1979.

Head Start Bureau. *An evaluation of the Head Start bilingual bicultural curriculum models.* Administration for Children, Youth, and Families, Washington, DC, 1982.

Hébert, R., et al. *Rendement académique et langue d'enseignement chez les élèves franco-manitobains.* Saint-Boniface, Manitoba: Centre de recherches du Collège Universitaire de Saint-Boniface, 1976.

Henry, W. A. Against a confusion of tongues. *Time,* June 13, 1983.

In plain English. *New York Times,* October 10, 1981, p. 24.

Krashen, S. D. Bilingual education and second language acquisition theory. In California State Department of Education (Ed.), *Schooling and language minority students: A theoretical framework.* Los Angeles: Evaluation, Dissemination and Assessment Center, 1981.

Krashen, S. D. *Principles and practice in second language acquisition.* Oxford: Pergamon Press, 1982.

Legaretta, D. The effects of program models on language acquisition by Spanish speaking children. *TESOL Quarterly,* 1979, *13,* 521–534.

Long, M. H. Native speaker/non-native speaker conversation in the second language classroom. In M. A. Clarke & J. Handscombe (Eds.), *On TESOL '82: Pacific perspectives on language learning and teaching.* Washington, DC: TESOL, 1983.

Malherbe, E. G. *The bilingual school*. Johannesburg, South Africa: Bilingual School Association, 1946.

Malherbe, E. G. Bilingual education in the Republic of South Africa. In B. Spolsky & R. L. Cooper (Eds.), *Case studies in bilingual education*. Rowley, MA: Newbury House, 1978.

Modiano, N. National or mother tongue language in beginning reading: A comparative study. *Research in the Teaching of English*, 1968, *2*, 32–43.

Moll, L. C. The microethnographic study of bilingual schooling. In R. V. Padilla (Ed.), *Ethnoperspectives in bilingual education research:* Vol. III. *Bilingual education technology*. Ypsilanti, MI: Department of Foreign Languages and Bilingual Studies, 1981.

Ogbu, J. *Minority education and caste*. New York: Academic Press, 1978.

O'Malley, J. M. A review of the evaluation of the impact of ESEA Title VII Spanish/ English Bilingual Education Program. *Bilingual Resources*, 1978, *2*, 6–10.

Paulston, C. B. Ethnic relations and bilingual education: Accounting for contradictory data. In J. E. Alatis & K. Twaddell (Eds.), *English as a second language in bilingual education*. Washington, DC: TESOL, 1976.

Peña-Hughes, E., & Solis, J. "abcs." McAllen, TX: McAllen Independent School District, 1980.

Rosier, P., & Holm, W. *The Rock Point experience: A longitudinal study of a Navajo school program*. Washington, DC: Center for Applied Linguistics, 1980.

San Diego City Schools. *An exemplary approach to bilingual education: A comprehensive handbook for implementing an elementary-level Spanish-English language immersion program*. San Diego: San Diego City Schools, 1982.

Sandoval-Martinez, S. Findings from the Head Start bilingual curriculum development and evaluation effort. *NABE Journal*, 1982, *7*, 1–12.

Schachter, J. Nutritional needs of language learners. In M. A. Clarke & J. Handscombe (Eds.), *On TESOL '82: Pacific perspectives on language learning and teaching*. Washington, DC: TESOL, 1983.

Swain, M. Bilingual education: Research and its implications. In C. A. Yorio, K. Perkins, & J. Schachter (Eds.), *On TESOL '79: The learner in focus*. Washington, DC: TESOL, 1979.

Swain, M. Communicative competence: Some roles of comprehensible input and comprehensible output in its development. Paper presented at the Tenth Annual University of Michigan Conference in Applied Linguistics, Ann Arbor, 1983.

Swain, M., & Lapkin, S. *Evaluating bilingual education: A Canadian example*. Clevedon, Avon: Multilingual Matters, 1982.

Troike, R. Research evidence for the effectiveness of bilingual education. *NABE Journal*, 1978, *3*, 13–24.

Willig, A. C. The effectiveness of bilingual education: Review of a report. *NABE Journal*, 1981–1982, *6*, 1–20.

Wong Fillmore, L. The language learner as an individual: Implications of research on individual differences for the ESL teacher. In M. A. Clarke & J. Handscombe (Eds.), *On TESOL '82: Pacific perspectives on language learning and teaching*. Washington, DC: TESOL, 1983a.

Wong Fillmore, L. Effective instruction for LEP students. Paper presented to the NABE Conference, Washington, DC, February 1983b.

SUGGESTED READINGS

California State Department of Education. *Beyond language: Social and cultural factors in schooling language minority students.* Los Angeles: Evaluation, Dissemination and Assessment Center, California State University, 1986.

Cummins, J. Empowering minority students: A framework for intervention. *Harvard Educational Review*, 1986, *56*, 18–36.

Hakuta, K. *Mirror of language: The debate on bilingualism.* New York: Basic Books, 1986.

McLaughlin, B. *Second-language acquisition in childhood:* Vol. 1. *Preschool children.* (2nd ed.). Hillsdale, NJ: Lawrence Erlbaum Associates, 1984.

McLaughlin, B. *Second-language acquisition in childhood:* Vol. 2. *School-age children.* (2nd ed.). Hillsdale, NJ: Lawrence Erlbaum Associates, 1985.

six

IMPLICATIONS OF SLA RESEARCH

Multiple Perspectives Make Singular Teaching

Thomas Scovel, San Francisco State University

The authors of the five preceding chapters have implicitly or explicitly suggested that their responsibility to summarize the various fields that pertain to language learning and teaching has been difficult to discharge, but I think all of them would acknowledge that the task I face in this concluding chapter is equally difficult. Not only is it hard to summarize what we have currently learned from fields like psycholinguistics, sociolinguistics, neurolinguistics, and the like, but it is also challenging to gather from these complex and disparate disciplines useful suggestions for teaching—specifically for teaching a second language. Because of the wide range of topics and issues that have been introduced, because of the difficulty of bridging research and theory to curricula and classrooms, and because of the wide diversity of conditions that language teachers face, I will choose only a few specific points introduced in each chapter and discuss their application to language teaching. Despite this selectivity, it is important for every reader to keep in perspective all of the issues that have been so ably summarized by the preceding authors. Human behavior is so complex, and learning and teaching are such complicated activities in and of themselves, that the only way we can begin to appreciate, let alone understand, language learning and teaching is constantly to keep in mind a broad perspective of the fields that are reviewed in this useful anthology. It is from this very diversity that we as language teachers can maintain an honest appreciation and perhaps even an understanding of the teaching process. And for this reason, I would claim in this summary chapter that multiple perspectives make for singular teaching. Not only do they help us maintain a unified eclecticism, they also can help us become more outstanding in our important profession.

Before I begin reviewing each chapter, I would like to step back for a moment and look at the relationship between theoretical concerns and practical applications in an area that at first seems completely unrelated to language teaching. I hope that through an analogy to athletics we can look at the disciplines reviewed in this anthology with a fresh appreciation of how theory indirectly influences practice. It is crucial for language teachers, both beginning and experienced, to realize this, because too many teachers ignore or reject theory as "irrelevant." Yet, as we can readily see from such a down-to-earth enterprise as high jumping, theoretical concerns can be extremely important because in this specific sport, for example, they have provided insights that have successively improved methods over the decades and have successfully raised the world record to the now unbelievable height of almost 8 feet.

The earliest documented method of high jumping is the so-called scissors method, where the jumper runs at the crossbar at about a 45 degree angle from the left and leaps over the bar with a scissoring motion of the legs, landing upright in the pit. Behind this simple procedure is an important principle from a relevant scientific discipline, the field of physics. This is the notion that the jumper must seek a delicate compromise between the speed of the approach run and the height of the spring. Too fast an approach will prevent the athlete from transforming horizontal kinetic energy into vertical lift; too slow an approach will not provide enough horizontal speed to cross the bar at all. What we see from this first example is that physics or "theory" does indeed have a relationship to good "practice," but that this relationship is indirect. Physics itself does not tell jumpers how to perform the scissors method, but insights from this theoretical discipline can help coaches and athletes make practical decisions that improve performance.

For many decades, the scissors method was employed as the only acceptable way to high jump. Gradually, however, coaches and jumpers began to experiment with other methods, and gradually the scissors was replaced with alternative ways of jumping, and records began to improve. At the end of World War II, a new and immediately successful method, the straddle style, began to supersede all predecessors. Here, the jumper approached from the right, not the left, and, instead of crossing the bar in a sitting position and landing upright, the jumper rolled over, straddling the bar face down, and then landing (still rolling) in a horizontal position in the landing pit.

It is of paramount importance to note, first of all, that straddle-style jumpers incorporated all the insights from physics that previous methods employed. For example, they too were keenly aware of approaching the bar at the right speed—neither too fast nor too slow—in order to ensure that they would have a maximum conversion of horizontal speed into vertical lift, but they also incorporated several additional insights from physics. One involved getting the jumper's center of gravity as close to the crossbar as possible. Since the center of gravity is in the middle of the torso, approximately where the navel is located, rolling over the bar on one's stomach saves several inches of clearance compared to crossing the bar in a sitting position. Another big advantage of the straddle style can be traced to one of Newton's laws of thermodynamics: For every action, there is a reaction, equal in strength but opposite in direction. If we consider the high jumper in mid-flight as a kind of floating dumbbell with hips and legs weighing down one side of the center of gravity, and arms and head balancing the other, then, in this new method, the athlete thrusts arms and head down over the bar, with hips and legs trailing behind. This downward action of the pectoral girdle causes a simultaneous reaction of the pelvic girdle, equal in strength but opposite in direction, raising the hips and legs upward over the crossbar. Needless to say, jumping records improved considerably after the adoption of the straddle style, and by the 1960s, jumpers were able to clear 7 feet for the first time in history.

Given the competitive and innovative nature of athletics, however, it was not long before this method was replaced by an alternative that was, quite literally, revolutionary. This new method was developed by a jumper from Oregon in the late 1960s, and he was so successful using it that it is named after him—the Fosbury flop. Rather than approach the bar from either the left or the right, he began from the middle of the jumping area and then ran in a semicircular loop, ultimately arriving at the bar from the lefthand side. Here is where the most dramatic difference from all previous methods occurs. Rather than cross the bar in a sitting or prone position, the jumper twists on takeoff, and crosses the bar on the back—head first—and lands on the shoulders and neck! Avant garde and revolutionary as this new method appears, it is instructive to emphasize that the Fosbury flop was highly principled—it attempted to incorporate, indeed, even to improve, all the principles of physics that previous methods employed. For example, by crossing the bar backwards, the jumper using the flop gets the center of gravity about an inch closer to the bar than do straddle stylers, who are crossing the bar on their stomach.

But the Fosbury flop also tried to incorporate a new insight for which no previous methods had accounted. This method added a third dimension to jumping, because the semicircular approach run generates centrifugal force, another important notion of physics, which pivots the body in rotation as soon as the feet leave the ground. There appear to be two advantages to this: All the energy at the takeoff can be expended directly into vertical lift, so that no precious spring is lost in placing the body in a horizontal trajectory; also, the centrifugal twist seems to add spring to the legs, almost like a turning screw. Needless to say, virtually every high jumper in the world employs the Fosbury flop today, and new records are constantly being set by athletes of all ages, sexes, and races using this most recent application of insights from physics to the progressive sport of high jumping.

Recognizing that there are many substantial differences between methods of high jumping and second language teaching methodology—not the least of which is that methods used in the former are quantifiable, whereas for the latter, it is almost impossible to substantiate the efficacy of a method—we can still learn several lessons from this brief analogy to sports. Clearly, one of the major lessons is that there can and should be specific theoretical insights—principles if you will—which should be consciously employed in the formation and execution of a method designed to teach a second language. All methods should be built on theoretical approaches, a fact long recognized by ESL/EFL experts (Anthony, 1963; Richards & Rodgers, 1982), but it is important for teachers to identify what specific theoretical insights are adopted in the method or methods they employ in their classrooms.

An equally valuable lesson from this analogy is the admirable manner in which each new method of high jumping carefully builds on the past. In contrast, many a baby has been thrown out with the bathwater in the evolution of second language pedagogy, and so it is illuminating to realize that in athletics at least, constructive innovation does not have to entail destructive elimination. Indeed, as we have already observed from the analogy, athletes who employ new methods of high jumping often do an even better job of utilizing a principle than their predecessors—those who actually chose that principle in the first place!

Other lessons come to mind. Note that improvement in materials invariably intertwined with innovation in jumping styles. Sometimes it is difficult to determine which comes first. Did the softer landing pits of the 1960s encourage more adventuresome techniques, or did the daring experiments of innovative jumpers like Fosbury encourage the manufacture of better pits? Analogously, was the rise of the audiolingual method of the 1950s dependent in part on the growing popularity of the tape recorder? Did language labs encourage the proliferation of this method, or was it actually the reverse?

One final observation from this analogy is that we should always remember that high jumpers don't waste their time in classrooms and libraries studying physics—they are out on the field jumping or in the weight room building up their muscular strength. It is their coaches who are keenly interested in physics, psychology, and other such esoteric disciplines because their task is not to become athletes themselves, but to train jumpers and to develop new methods of jumping. Similarly, second language learners should not spend their time studying psycholinguistics, sociolinguistics, and the like in order to pick up skills in the target language. It is about as useful to require that an ESL/EFL student devote an hour a day to studying transformational-generative grammar as it is to demand that a high jumper spend an hour of daily practice examining solid-state physics. Charles Fries (1945), the founder of ESL/EFL in the United States, put it succinctly and well: Language students should "learn the language," not learn "about the language." In distinct contrast, however, it is vital that ESL/EFL *teachers* devote a great deal of time and attention to theory and research in linguistics, sociology, psychology, etc.,

because they, like athletic coaches, must keep abreast of theoretical developments in order to do an effective job of teaching and in order to assess and
develop new methods and curricula. The theory and research summarized in
this book may not be of direct importance to language learners, but they are
certainly of crucial concern to all second language teachers, especially those
who are interested in reaching new heights of success.

PSYCHOLINGUISTIC PERSPECTIVE

Looking at the very first contribution to this anthology, the review of psycholinguistics, we can see Seliger is making the same point that I have illustrated in
my high jumping analogy when he begins by describing the significance of the
Chomskyan revolution in linguistics and psychology to the field of second
language acquisition. Here we can immediately apply an insight from theory to
pedagogical practice. Until the publication of Chomsky's second major book,
Aspects of the Theory of Syntax (1965), linguists and grammarians of the
preceding classical and structural traditions concentrated on what Chomsky
called "surface structure," almost to the exclusion of "deep structure" analysis.
Thus, to pursue a specific example, compare the analyses of the following two
sentences:

1. She asked me *to be* her friend.
2. She considered me *to be* her friend.

If an EFL/ESL grammar class that was based on a classical or structural
model were asked whether the two *to be*'s were similar or different, the teacher
would probably expect a response that they were identical. According to
transformational-generative (TG) grammar, however, at least following what
has now been called the "extended standard theory" of Chomsky, the teacher is
deluded by surface structure similarities. These verbs are merely homonyms
and actually have very different "deep structures," something that becomes
more conspicuous in the next four examples:

3. She asked me to become her friend.
4. *She considered me to become her friend.
5. She considered me her friend.
6. *She asked me her friend.

Now it is more obvious that we have two different verbs in the original
pair of sentences, and although they seem to be similar in sentences 1 and 2, we
realize that *to be* in sentence 1 is understood as having the same meaning as *to
become* in sentence 3. We cannot substitute *to become* for *to be* in sentence 4
because that sentence is a different structure entirely. Conversely, *to be* in
sentence 2 can be deleted as a complement in sentence 5, but *to be* in sen-

tence 1 cannot be deleted at all. Otherwise the sentence will be ungrammatical, as in sentence 6.

One of the major contributions of Chomsky's TG grammar to the field of linguistics, and, indirectly to second language teaching, was its insistence on the need to distinguish between surface structures and their underlying, abstract representation, or deep structure. I think that this insight into the structure of all languages, not just English, can be most easily understood if we talk about two types of sentences: utterances that differ in obvious ways in their surface structures but share a common, underlying deep structure, and sentences that are just the opposite: They have very similar surface structures but differ demonstrably in their meanings (sentences 1 and 2 are an example of the latter). Sentences 7–10 look quite different grammatically, but these dissimilarities are actually quite trivial, for all four sentences are identical in meaning.

7. Life is certain to be difficult.
8. Life will certainly be difficult.
9. It is certain that life will be difficult.
10. That life will be difficult is certain.

Let us pretend for a moment that we are back in the EFL/ESL grammar classroom. A teacher steeped in a classical or even a structural tradition of language will immediately devote a lot of time and attention to contrasting all the superficial ways in which these sentences differ. I can envision some teachers urging their students to make the following observations: Sentence 7 is a simple sentence, present tense; sentence 8 is a simple sentence, future tense; sentence 9 is a complex sentence, present tense; and sentence 10 is a complex sentence, future tense. This kind of classroom activity deflects the second language student's attention away from the central point. The essential lesson for students to learn with these four sentences is that they are four ways of saying the same thing: They are paraphrases of each other.

A different way of looking at this same TG insight is to take sentences that appear to be almost identical on the surface, and then demonstrate how they are really derived from quite different underlying structures. The best examples of this are ambiguous sentences, but we need not resort to ambiguity to illustrate this phenomenon. Note, for example, that in English adverbs can frequently be moved about the sentence with no change in meaning and virtually no stylistic aberrations either.

11. Sometimes, she can jump six feet.
12. She can sometimes jump six feet.

With the choice of another adverb, however, differences in placement result in entirely different underlying meanings. The different location of *even* in utterances 13 and 14 arises from two disparate claims by the speaker of these two sentences. In sentence 13, the speaker is saying that it is so easy to jump six feet that even an ordinary jumper like her can attain that height; in sentence 14, by way of contrast, the speaker is asserting that she is such a good jumper that she has even been able to reach the difficult height of six feet.

    13. Even she can jump six feet.
    14. She can even jump six feet.

I do not want to imply that TG grammar answers all pedagogical questions for second language teachers. One serious limitation of Chomsky's model of language—one that is shared, unfortunately, by all current linguistic theories—is the inability of linguists to deal satisfactorily with the pragmatic use of language. In my discussion of these fourteen sentences, I have confined our observations solely to questions of grammar and meaning but have ignored the important issue of communicative concerns. For the latter, we must look to other theoretical fields for insights—disciplines like discourse analysis and sociolinguistics. But I hope that this first example of a pedagogical implication from theory is well taken: Second language teachers cannot continue to base their grammatical insights on outdated models of linguistic analysis, and if teachers have not been introduced to TG grammar during their university studies, then it is important for them to try to get some training in TG analysis, especially in Chomsky's extended standard theory, which I believe to be more amenable to pedagogical practice than other competing generative models that are currently popular in linguistics.

A second "revolution" in psycholinguistics that Seliger mentions is the one initiated by Corder (1967) and others two decades ago. This was the idea that the systematic errors made by second language learners (not their random "mistakes" or slips of the tongue) can provide a window to the mind of the learner and help us see what learning processes are actually taking place (or, for that matter, whether any learning is transpiring at all). Here we should note that this "revolutionary" emphasis on the learner, rather than on the learning process or on the teacher, did not only take place in psycholinguistics and second language acquisition. It was also evident in the emergence of innovative, "humanistic" methods of foreign language teaching, which focused on what was happening to students, not on what teachers were doing. And, as Allwright (1983) shows in his classification of classroom research, researchers investigating classroom interaction were also shifting away from an initial interest in what *teachers* did to their present concern about what *learners* do in the classroom. Consequently, we see that this same change of perspective in psycholinguistics discussed by Seliger is simultaneously a "revolution" found in other fields related to second language teaching. What are the implications of this new student-centered approach toward errors in a second language class?

One that I believe to be immediately relevant to second language teaching is the treatment of errors in the classroom. Obviously, errors are not "misdemeanors" that our students have committed and for which they have earned punishment, but they are almost always intelligent attempts to master a new linguistic system. Sometimes they stem from an overenthusiastic application of a rule or pattern from the mother tongue (negative transfer or interference), and here the behavioral insights from psychologists like Skinner are useful for the teacher to consider. At other times, they come from the overenthusiastic use of a newly learned rule or pattern from the target language (overgeneralization), and here the cognitive insights of psychologists Ausubel (1968) are of use to classroom practitioners. Usually, however, they originate from some combination of both processes simultaneously; that is, most second language errors arise from students trying to apply something they have learned from the new language while, at the same time, they are being influenced by expectations they harbor about language that come from their mother tongue or from another language they have acquired.

Actually, when we apply current psycholinguistic insights to our understanding of second language learning errors, the situation is even more complicated than just described, because, along with transfer and overgeneralization, we must consider the implications of markedness (Eckman, 1977; Mazurkewich, 1984). Marked forms (e.g., plural forms) are found less frequently among the world's languages than unmarked structures (e.g., singular forms). Many languages, for example, do not have plural forms. Also, marked forms are usually learned only after unmarked ones in children's first language acquisition. We must take into account whether or not a structure is marked when we investigate second language learning errors, because along with transfer and overgeneralization, markedness seems to influence the speed and accuracy of acquisition.

Because student errors are influenced by at least three psycholinguistic factors—the mother tongue (transfer), the hypotheses that students make about the new patterns in the target language (overgeneralization), and the relative intrinsic difficulty of the structures learned (markedness)—I would strongly encourage all second language teachers to reject the pejorative comments one sometimes hears or reads about particular psycholinguistic viewpoints and their relevance to second language teaching. It is fairly common, to cite one example, to hear people say that "behaviorism" is out of fashion or is out of touch with modern methods, or that a certain writer has nothing useful to contribute to learning theory because he or she is a "behaviorist." Recall the exemplary equanimity with which high jumpers accepted the insights of previous jumping methods. One does not overhear high jump coaches denigrating the usefulness of a correct speed/spring ratio because it is associated with older methods like the scissors. No, coaches and jumpers have even gone so far as to improve on the speed/spring ratio of the scissors in the straddle style and the Fosbury flop. So it should be with second language teachers. I would like to see teachers be open-minded about recognizing how a behavioral perspective can, in fact, account for learner errors—not all of them, of course, but it is patently obvious from teachers' experiences and from abundant research over the past three decades that second language students are influenced by their first tongue. Yet it is equally obvious that this is neither the sole nor, perhaps, even the major source of errors. Often, this process of transfer plays a relatively insignificant role, and this is exactly why a hypothesis-testing perspective is useful and also why an understanding of markedness is of value.

The contributions from psycholinguistics, then, are clear: Errors are the result of intelligence, not stupidity. Most of them come from a conscious or unconscious attempt by students to use what they have learned to learn even more. For this, they should be rewarded, not chastised. Obviously, I am not suggesting that teachers should leap to praise students when they come out with, "*I yesterday visited my grandmother," or "*I goed to my grandmother's house yesterday." The former is most probably a transfer error, whereas the latter is more clearly a result of overgeneralization and markedness. Rather than criticizing the sin or the sinner, however, an astute teacher would paraphrase these sentences correctly so that both the errant student and the entire class would have an accurate target of what the student was originally aiming for. "I see, you visited your grandmother's house yesterday," or "You say you went to your grandmother's house yesterday." This kind of correction would then serve as continued dialogue with that particular student or with the class as a whole.

In our discussion of the contributions of error analysis to language teaching, we have so far looked only at what Seliger has wittingly termed "sins of commission." I would also like us to remember the "sins of omission" when we consider the application of this area of psycholinguistics to second language teaching. Here we are talking about "avoidance": the conscious or unconscious attempt by a second language learner not to use a certain structure in the target language, most commonly because that structure differs a great deal from related structures in the student's mother tongue, and possibly because that structure is marked as well. Schachter (1974), Kleinmann (1977), and more recently Dagut and Laufer (1985) are all brief but illuminating introductions to the topic. For a more detailed account, especially for a good description of experimental protocol, Kleinmann's doctoral dissertation is worth examining (Kleinmann, 1976).

The best examples of avoidance occur where a language has two different ways of saying essentially the same thing (two surface structures for one deep structure), and the second language student opts for the "simpler"—the one closer to the student's mother tongue—and avoids the other pattern almost completely. As Seliger has already reviewed for us, this is what Schachter found in her study of the compositions written by Japanese and Chinese EFL students. Because relative clauses in these languages are what linguists would classify as "left branching," in contrast to the "right branching" relative clauses in English, Schachter discovered that her Asian EFL students made few relative clause errors for a very simple reason—they wrote precious few relative clauses. Instead of using sentences like sentence 15, they frequently ended up with non-relativized paraphrases like sentence 16.

> **15.** My friend who is a teacher lives in Tokyo.
> **16.** My friend is a teacher, and she lives in Tokyo.

There are subtle stylistic and discourse differences between these two sentences, something that will cause trouble later on for students in advanced classes, especially when they try to develop their composition skills, and this is exactly why sins of omission are a problem: They encourage an early fossilization of certain grammatical and communicative skills, and they tend to inhibit the ultimate success of students in the second language. For this reason, I think that the psycholinguistic research on avoidance has an immediate practical implication. Classroom teachers should be just as concerned about the mistakes their students *don't* make as they are about the sins of commission.

It is hard to recognize avoidance. It is no accident that researchers themselves have only recently begun to examine the phenomenon; the mere fact that students do not use a particular structure in the target language does not necessarily mean that they are avoiding it. As the humorist Robert Benchley observed, one cannot prove a platypus does not lay eggs simply by taking a picture of it not laying eggs. But here is where a teacher's experience with and understanding of the target language can be extremely useful. Especially in advanced classes, students should be expected to produce a versatile range of structures, both grammatical and communicative. Again, I would like to stress the importance of paraphrase; this skill, used constantly by native speakers in both spoken and written discourse, is one that provides a language user with stylistic flexibility, sociolinguistic versatility, and communicative impact.

SOCIOLINGUISTIC PERSPECTIVE

I have devoted much attention to several pedagogical applications drawn from the initial chapter by Seliger largely because psycholinguistics is my own central field of interest. Although I will not expend quite as much attention on the second contribution of this anthology, the chapter on sociolinguistics by Beebe, I readily acknowledge that the field of sociolinguistics, even when confined for purposes of discussion to microsociolinguistic issues, is even more relevant for second language teaching and pertains even more directly to language pedagogy than does the discipline of psycholinguistics. And when we remember that issues in macrosociolinguistics have an enormous impact on all language pedagogy, it is clear to me that no single discipline is more relevant or more consequential to second language teaching than sociolinguistics. One simple but telling example of the import of macro issues on foreign language pedagogy is the government policy of the People's Republic of China: In the early 1950s Russian was decreed the most important foreign language, and thousands of former EFL teachers were retrained as teachers of Russian; now, thirty years later, the tables have been completely turned, and former Russian instructors have been retrained to teach English (J. Scovel, 1982). Clearly, the effects of these macro-level decisions on the teaching of EFL in China have been enormous.

Beebe's introductory review of five schools of sociolinguistic thought reminds us that within all of the ancillary disciplines to second language learning discussed in this book, there are always several schools and models; therefore, one important lesson for second language teachers to learn is that there is never only one approach that all psychologists, or linguists, or sociologists follow in their specialty. This diversity of approaches is even found in the relatively "hard" science of neuropsychology, where researchers sometimes differ quite sharply about which is the most appropriate model to adopt. I am not qualified to make comparative judgments about the five sociolinguistic schools reviewed, but I would point out that only the fifth, Lambert and Gardner's study of "achievement," grew directly out of an interest in and a study of second language acquisition; the other four approaches, as Beebe indicates, developed primarily out of a concern with how people communicate in their mother tongue.

The central concern of this chapter on sociolinguistics is interlanguage variation, and there are two useful lessons that we can draw from Beebe's discussion of the models and the research in this area of the field of sociolinguistics. First of all, we want to remember all the evidence cited to show that this variation is indeed systematic. Contrary to what some teachers might believe from their daily impressions of their students' oral and written performances in class, most errors are not sporadic and haphazard. Viewed carefully over time, they usually follow certain patterns—patterns that appear to be strongly influenced by several variables, many of them sociolinguistic in origin (Beebe, 1977; Dickerson & Dickerson, 1977). There is a certain irony here when we contrast the way teachers and researchers look at errors. Teachers usually are concentrating on a specific structural point, which usually changes from assignment to assignment and from day to day; because of this, they tend to believe that students' errors are unsystematic. Researchers, however, usually view errors longitudinally, ignoring the specific structural point that was taught and concentrating instead on sociolinguistic variables that are extraneous to the structural focus of a class. Using this perspective, sociolinguistic researchers often find a consistent pattern—like the phonetic variation in /r/ and /l/ that the Dickersons discovered in ESL students learning English or that Beebe encountered in Chinese-Thai bilinguals. The irony, then, is that second language learning errors appear to be unsystematic if viewed unsystematically; with the rigor and systematicity that a sociolinguist uses, however, these same errors appear to be systematically influenced by certain social variables. As second language teachers, then, the first lesson we can learn is that much of the variation that our students produce in class and on assignments (irrespective of whether this variation is an overt error or a slight deviation from the target language form), is regular and rule governed and is affected by who is speaking to whom, where the interaction is taking place, what topic is being discussed, and other such sociolinguistic variables. Since the style of all the oral and written discourse in our mother tongue is influenced by these variables, it is natural that these same factors influence the style of second language discourse in our students. As Beebe aptly observes, "This style shifting, being common to native and nonnative speakers alike, is something the teacher must accept, understand, and work with slowly, not impatiently try to stamp out, for it is a natural characteristic of human language" (see Chapter 2, page 49).

The second useful lesson we can glean from this chapter on sociolinguistics concerns the role of "attention to speech" in achieving fluency and accuracy in a second language. Until this decade, almost all teachers and researchers have matter-of-factly assumed that there was a direct correlation between a student's attention to speech performance and linguistic success: The more we devote our attention to the speaking task, the better we become in speaking, all other things being equal. As Beebe (1980) and Tarone (1985) have demonstrated, however, this assumption, previously supported by research in the Labovian tradition, does not necessarily hold true for second language acquisition. Following the speech accommodation theory, rather than the better known Labovian paradigm, Beebe provides support in her chapter for several reservations she has about the relevance of "attention to speech" for success in second language learning and teaching. They bear repetition here in this final chapter on pedagogical applications:

1. Attention to speech sometimes correlates inversely with standardness or correctness.
2. Many differences in style and speech shifts cannot be categorized as "correct" or "incorrect"; thus, style shifting, an extremely important aspect of all linguistic intercourse, cannot be easily linked to standardness or correctness.
3. Attention to speech may not be causally related to style shifting in either experimental or naturalistic conditions.

These reservations might appear frustrating to the second language teacher in that their pedagogical utility has only negative ramifications; that is, Beebe's review of the recent research seems to suggest that we should encourage our students *not* to pay attention to linguistic form, because attention apparently does not relate to accuracy or to facility in style shifting. But I think that it is more helpful to see how this research actually has a positive application, and again I think it is beneficial to reflect back to the high jumping analogy. When teaching physical skills in athletics or music, a great deal of the initial instruction involves much attention to specific details. Thus, a high jumper perfecting the Fosbury flop might concentrate exclusively on a particular aspect of the jump. Each part of the jump is broken down into components, and attention is paid to each detail of the overall jump, one at a time—for example, the precise placement of the takeoff foot. Success in the jump ultimately involves success in each individual component of performance, but during the jump itself, it is impossible to pay attention to each particular detail of the jump. In fact, such detailed attention will virtually guarantee an unsuccessful performance, because the athlete must be able to perform every aspect of the jump successfully in one unified and concerted effort.

I think there is a similar process going on in second language acquisition: Attention to form is important in the initial, focal learning situations of the second language classroom, but such attention to detail is not helpful when that form is finally incorporated within a total communicative task. Indeed, such particular attention is probably detrimental to linguistic correctness or communicative competence. Using terms introduced by Schneider and Shiffrin (1977) (see also McLaughlin, Rossman, & McLeod, 1983), attention to form is beneficial when it is used in focal and controlled situations, but is either useless or actually debilitating when it is applied to situations where the production of linguistic forms should be peripheral and automatic. Beebe's reservations about the role of attention to linguistic structures provide us with an important pedagogical insight: Attention to form is an important part of the initial learning process, but it actually decreases the likelihood of success if it *always* plays an important role in the learning process. I would go so far as to say that attention to form should be inversely related to a student's linguistic maturity in the target language: High attention is important when knowledge about form and function is low; attention should be low when knowledge about the form and function has become high.

NEUROLINGUISTIC PERSPECTIVE

Turning now to the contribution by Genesee on neuropsychological issues, I am impressed with his review of studies that pertain to second language learning and use, and I am in complete agreement with his overall perspective of this relatively new scientific discipline, but I do think his prudent caution at the end of his contribution about facile applications of brain research bears repeating. Whether they are teaching the mother tongue or a second language, language instructors, by and large, are trained in the humanities or education and not in the behavorial or physical sciences; therefore, they are easily daunted by references and excursions into the so-called hard sciences and are quick to pick up on any current scientific or technological fad. Brain research, as Genesee clearly documents, has developed rapidly over the past few years, and we now have techniques available, such as positron emission tomography (PET) scans that were unheard of a decade ago. This rapid proliferation of research tools has given the appearance to lay people outside the field of neuropsychology that we are not very far from resolving the ancient philosophical paradox—where does the body end and the mind begin? In this case, the "body" is the brain. Many educated lay people, including teachers, have been seduced into believing that we have now located language, memory, perception, cognition, personality, and so on in the brain and, further, that by pinpointing their location we have somehow solved the problem of accounting for how people learn to speak, learn to remember, and the like. Nothing could be further from the truth.

We know that the majority of language processing and production resides in the parasylvian region of the left temporal cortex for most humans. But that does not mean we know anything more about how people learn their first or second language. What we have learned about learning comes mostly from other fields, like psycholinguistics, but neuropsychology or neurolinguistics has not made a major contribution here. Most important, teachers should not resort to knowledge of the brain to justify techniques, methods, or materials. If singing songs in the target language helps certain students learn suprasegmental patterns more effectively, then experience and/or empirical classroom research will justify the inclusion of this technique in the second language syllabus. It is ludicrous to attempt to validate this technique by claiming that it helps students to use both the left and right cerebral hemispheres simultaneously in the classroom. This is exactly the kind of pseudoscience I have heard advocated several times at conferences and have read in print, and I hope that most teachers will have enough common sense to realize that good ideas are not made more valid by invalid substantiations. If the contention that two hemispheres are better than one is true, then we might as well encourage our students to write with both hands simultaneously so as to activate the motor cortex of both hemispheres. My advice for teachers about the implications neuropsychology might have for second language teaching is simple: Don't use the brain, use your brain. I hope that this summary accurately reflects the perspective adopted by Genesee in his informative review of brain research.

CLASSROOM RESEARCH PERSPECTIVE

It is a long jump from brain-centered research and neuropsychology to classroom-centered research and pedagogy, but this is exactly the transition we make when we turn to the next contribution in the anthology on instructed interlanguage development by Long. If direct applications of neuropsychology are difficult to find, pedagogical applications of classroom-centered research are correspondingly easy, and this chapter is a rich source of ideas and applications on second language teaching. Long begins the chapter with an informative review of second language acquisition research undertaken in both North America and Europe. Incidentally, Americans who do not realize the scope and significance of European research on second language learning and teaching since World War II may want to read the detailed and elucidating book by van Els, Bongaerts, Extra, van Os, and Janssen-van Dieten (1984).

More important, Long comments critically on one of the sentiments popular in some SLA circles nowadays—the notion that formal instruction is often inefficient and of limited value to second language success. The most prominent contemporary advocates of this point of view are Krashen and Terrell (1983), who argue for the value of a "natural" approach with a special focus on "comprehensible input." Krashen and Terrell's model offers only the minimally acceptable criteria for second language learning success, and it is important for all second language teachers to realize that in the eyes of many researchers, this "natural" approach is not an adequate model on which to base a language curriculum.

But is the only message that Long and other SLA researchers interested in classroom interactions have for teachers to be wary about methodological claims or possible applications of research to teaching? Not at all. Several recent studies that Long reviews can help give classroom teachers some guidance and direction—no firm and simplistic answers, for whenever we deal with human learning behavior, we are grappling with incredible diversity and complexity—but certainly there are insights worth gleaning from many of these studies. Pica (1983), for example, should be reintroduced here because she was specifically contrasting naturalistic, instructed, and mixed acquisition settings. As Long summarizes, one of Pica's findings was that the instruction-only group clearly outscored the other two groups in learning the plural and the third person singular -*s* morpheme. Here we see the direct value of formal instruction and of focus on form, because most experienced EFL/ESL teachers notice that these two morphemes are commonly absent in nonnative adult speakers who have acquired the language with very little instruction. It is interesting, however, that these same two morphemes are frequently deleted in the writing of EFL/ESL students, even those who have had intensive formal instruction. This only confirms the diversity and complexity of second language learning behavior. Learning to *write* a second language is, in some ways, similar to learning yet another linguistic code—a third language, so to speak; thus, errors arise in composition that have largely disappeared in spoken discourse. It is almost as if we have two interlanguages—a somewhat advanced form in speech, and a more reactionary form, which appears in composition.

Another insight from studies of classroom interactions that is applicable to teaching comes from Long's summary of the research by Lightbown (1983) and Pienemann (1984). This is the notion that there could be a gap between what second language students are psycholinguistically ready to learn (the *learnability* hypothesis) and the effectiveness of instruction (the *teachability* hypothesis). This is an exceedingly complicated area of inquiry, involving not only classroom research but also developmental psychology and developmental psycholinguistics, because we are dealing with contrasts in maturational age as well as contrasts in linguistic structures, instructional techniques, and teaching styles. In some ways, this area of investigation is reminiscent of Krashen's claim that language students perform best if they are given language always slightly above their current ability level—"$i + 1$" (Krashen, 1982). Experienced language teachers intuitively recognize the existence of this gap between what they teach and what is learned; as Long indicates, however, this is an important phenomenon to study and should be a high priority for research.

Here is an excellent example of how the tables can be turned and teachers can contribute to theory. I would encourage all second language teachers to try to isolate those structures and those conditions in everyday EFL/ESL teaching situations that seem either to enhance or to diminish this gap between teaching and learning. I would particularly encourage teachers of younger learners to focus on this problem. Significant progress in diminishing or even eliminating this discrepancy is possible if classroom teachers can carefully record their ideas and observations and share them with others. We need teaching experience as well as classroom experiments.

Although the next study was not mentioned in Long's chapter, I do want to introduce the article that he has recently written with Porter (Long & Porter, 1985) because it fits nicely into any discussion of classroom interactions, and because it provides a useful pedagogical insight. Long and Porter reviewed several classroom studies of the usefulness of student-to-student group work in second language oral communication classes and found consistent correlations between opportunities for group work and progress in students' oral communicative competence. Long and Porter's article is directly relevant to classroom practice because many second language teachers still devote too much of their time to teacher-to-student dialogue instead of allowing creative and constructive opportunities for their students to interact in the target language with each other. To counter a concern that some teachers might have, it does not appear from the classroom research reviewed by these two authors that students who interact in groups lose structural accuracy. Here, then, is yet another application of great value from classroom research.

Long reviews many other important studies. It would be repetitive to comment here on potential pedagogical applications for each one, and, in fact, we still have insufficient evidence to make firm conclusions from many of these studies—a major point that Long himself emphasizes at the conclusion of his chapter. Second language teachers can, at the very least, be reassured by this chapter, because Long provides fair but firm evidence that formal classroom instruction is almost certainly of great benefit to progress in second language acquisition.

BILINGUAL EDUCATION PERSPECTIVE

The final perspective to which we look for possible pedagogical implications is the chapter on bilingual education programs. Cummins's remarks are not only relevant for politicians and bilingual policymakers, but appear also to be germane for language teachers, who implement policy through their teaching. Consider, for example, the three reasons Cummins cites that research on bilingual programs has largely been ignored by policymakers—but in each instance substitute "second language teachers." First, Cummins claims that they ask preordained and unanswerable questions. As someone who has been interested in bridging theory and practice for many years, I have found an identical problem when training teachers: Questions are often rhetorical and not informative.

For example, many teachers ask some version of the following question: "Shouldn't adults learning a second language try to copy what children do when learning their first language?" This query really means: "Tell me the ways that adults learning a second language can copy what children do when they acquire their first language." I do not want to imply that there are absolutely no similarities between children and adults or between first and second language acquisition; in fact, similarities abound. But the first step is to recognize that there are differences as well as similarities between these two different populations.

Brown (1980) has illustrated this very effectively in his comprehensive chapter on child and adult language learning, where he describes how misleading it is to pair adult second language learners with child first language acquirers because we are not simply contrasting older and younger learners, but also simultaneously contrasting first and second language acquisition. A more revealing comparison would be between adult and child second language learners, because the intervening variable of first versus second language is eliminated. And an even more justifiable pairing would be to contrast adult second language learners with older child second language learners (e.g., young teenagers), since the latter have passed through the earlier Piagetian stages that create certain important cognitive differences between young and older learners. As Gass (1984) and Gass and Ard (1980) have demonstrated in their research, it is precisely these cognitive differences between young children and adults that seem to cause certain differences in the strategies older second language learners adopt. All this serves further to validate the work of Cummins and other bilingual researchers who have a large amount of data on how children of different ages and at different stages acquire a second language. These data, I believe, are much more applicable to adult second language acquisition than even the large body of material that has been collected on child first language acquisition.

A second criticism Cummins has of policymakers that I feel is appropriate for teachers to consider is that they may cling to conventional wisdoms and screen out or dismiss incompatible data. I do not want to single out second language teachers in the discussion of this point. It is a natural human tendency to retain a position until it is proved completely untenable. These so-called conventional wisdoms can be notions we have believed for many centuries or ideas that have only recently come into vogue. Let me cite an example of each.

One conventional wisdom that I have encountered among language teachers all over the world is a misunderstanding about the extent to which TG grammar has influenced linguistics and a concomitant reluctance to accept TG grammar as a viable alternative to classical or structural models of how language can be analyzed. Many teachers admit that they don't like or don't understand this "new" TG grammar; if asked about their sentiments concerning contrastive analysis and the transfer of mother tongue habits on second language learning, these same practitioners say that they no longer believe in an exclusive use of contrastive analysis because it is old-fashioned. A historical footnote is illuminating here: Chomsky's *Syntactic Structures*, which introduced TG grammar, was published the same year, 1957, as the definitive textbook introducing contrastive analysis, Lado's *Linguistics across Cultures*. Unfortunately, if language teachers persist in clinging to this "wisdom" that a classical, Latinate model of English will serve them well in the classroom, and that the "new-fangled" TG grammar is only a recent and passing fad, they will miss some important pedagogical insights. Second language teachers who are unwilling to consider new models and insights are akin to high jump coaches who are reluctant to accept the possible implications of centrifugal force for the field of high jumping. William James once enjoined teachers to be "tender-minded in considering new ideas."

But some conventional wisdoms are recent. Krashen's model of second language acquisition (Krashen, 1982) and the so-called *natural approach* that stems from it (Krashen & Terrell, 1983) divides the picking up of a second language into either "learning" or "acquisition" and has provided several conventional wisdoms for many second language teachers nowadays. One of these is that whereas acquisition can initiate utterances and lead to fluency, learning can do neither of these. This implies that learning does not facilitate acquisition (i.e., conscious instruction of a target pattern will never allow the learner to use that pattern automatically in discourse). Teachers who accept the natural approach also accept the conventional wisdoms that are part and parcel of it; if we scrutinize second language acquisition research carefully, however, we can find considerable evidence against the wisdom that learning cannot initiate utterances and lead to fluency.

First there is the problem with the learning–acquisition dichotomy. McLaughlin (1980; McLaughlin et al., 1983) has discussed many criticisms from his own perspective as a psychologist. Gregg (1984, 1986) has added a great deal to this critical review. Further limitations of Krashen's views are brought out in Schmidt's fascinating account of an adult second language "acquirer" and his detailed description of the strengths and weaknesses of untutored acquisition (Schmidt, 1984). But even more relevant are the questions and criticisms that researchers are currently raising about Krashen and Terrell's model (Takala, 1984; Taylor, 1984). I do not want to dwell here on the limitations of the model, because there are also some important contributions that Krashen's ideas have made to second language acquisition research and pedagogy, but I cite it as a new "wisdom" that many EFL/ESL teachers espouse, and I simply want to challenge these teachers to reconsider, just as

Cummins has challenged policymakers to reassess the beliefs they bring to bilingual education. Again, William James provides us with apt advice: "Be tender-minded in considering new ideas," he admonished, "but be tough-minded in accepting them."

The third and final suggestion that Cummins offered to policymakers and that I am extrapolating to language teachers as well is that data and "facts" be placed in a coherent theory; they do not have coherence in and of themselves, apart from a theoretical framework. I think this suggestion is relevant for second language teachers because I have frequently found that many classroom practitioners try to adopt a certain technique or embrace a particular method without looking at broader concerns. Here, again, the high jumping analogy is especially pertinent. Dick Fosbury did not run toward the bar in a semicircular loop simply to be different; he did not choose to flip over the bar backwards only because no one else had ever done it that way and he wanted to gain attention. All the techniques he chose to include in his method were *principled* and *systematic*; that is, they were all chosen because they either enhanced principles employed in previous methods that Fosbury believed to be useful, or they added new insights that other styles of high jumping had previously ignored. The backward flop was an even more efficient way of getting the center of gravity closer to the crossbar—an improvement on a principle to which older methods had adhered. And the semicircular run was adopted because it developed centrifugal momentum—a principle that was a unique contribution of Fosbury's new method.

When I review some of the techniques and some of the methods advocated in second language teaching circles today, I sometimes wonder if they are proposed simply because they are different or because they are indeed grounded in a principled and coherent theory of language acquisition. The almost exclusive use of tape-recorded material for an intensive week of study, the belief that playing Baroque music in a relaxing atmosphere will greatly enhance lexical learning, and the practice of having students exhaust a great deal of their time and energy physically responding to oral commands—these are examples of some of the techniques I am thinking about here. I am not decrying the use of these particular techniques in and of themselves, but just as Cummins has encouraged bilingual education policymakers to examine data within the context of a theoretical model, so I would encourage teachers to incorporate these techniques into an overall picture of what language learning and teaching is all about. Actually, techniques should evolve from a model, not the other way around. Teachers should seize on a particular classroom procedure because it is congruent with their ideas about second language acquisition, just as Fosbury came up with the technique of a semicircular run because it allowed him to use an additional insight from physics. In summary, Cummins has not only challenged people involved with bilingual education policy. I believe he has given all of us involved with second language teaching some equally thought-provoking ideas.

CONCLUSION

I hope you have not been unduly intimidated by the wide-ranging and far-reaching topics introduced in this book. If some of your ideas about what constitutes good second language teaching have been challenged, if you have been encouraged to take a broader multidisciplinary perspective, if you have been introduced to a wider range of variables affecting your students' success, then the authors of this anthology have capably discharged their task of interpreting these multiple perspectives to you. And if you have also been able to glean some specific pedagogical applications from the chapters you have read, so much the better.

Let me reemphasize the importance of contextualizing all that you have read and learned within a single framework. Bits and pieces of knowledge, even if they are very good and very current, are of no pedagogical application unless they are part of a structured approach to how your students learn and how you should teach. It does not matter whether you go so far as to claim that this approach is your "model" of second language acquisition, but it is important that you integrate this *experimental* information with your own *experiential* knowledge to form the framework for all your ideas about second language teaching. With this foundation, you can be assured that all of the multiple perspectives introduced in this book will contribute to your own singular perspective and will, in turn, make you a truly singular second language teacher.

REFERENCES

Allwright, R. Classroom-centered research on language teaching and learning. *TESOL Quarterly*, 1983, *17*, 191–204.

Anthony, E. Approach, method, and technique. *English Language Teaching*, 1963, *17*, 63–67.

Ausubel, D. *Educational psychology: A cognitive view*. New York: Holt, Rinehart and Winston, 1968.

Beebe, L. The influence of the listener on code-switching. *Language Learning*, 1977, *27*, 331–339.

Beebe, L. Sociolinguistic variation and style shifting in second language acquisition. *Language Learning*, 1980, *30*, 433–447.

Brown, H. D. *Principles of language learning and teaching*. Englewood Cliffs, NJ: Prentice-Hall, 1980.

Chomsky, N. *Syntactic structures*. The Hague: Mouton, 1957.

Chomsky, N. *Aspects of the theory of syntax*. Cambridge, MA: MIT Press, 1965.

Corder, S. P. The significance of learners' errors. *IRAL*, 1967, *5*, 161–170.

Dagut, M., & Laufer, B. Avoidance of phrasal verbs—A case for contrastive analysis. *Studies in Second Language Acquisition*, 1985, *7*, 73–80.

Dickerson, L., & Dickerson, W. Interlanguage phonology: Current research and future directions. In S. P. Corder & E. Roulet (Eds.), *The notions of simplification, interlanguages, and pidgins, and their relation to second language pedagogy.* Geneva: Faculté des Lettres Neuchâtel, 1977.

Eckman, F. Markedness and the contrastive analysis hypothesis. *Language Learning,* 1977, *27,* 315–330.

Fries, C. *Teaching and learning English as a foreign language.* Ann Arbor: University of Michigan Press, 1945.

Gass, S. A review of interlanguage syntax: Language transfer and language universals. *Language Learning,* 1984, *34,* 115–132.

Gass, S., & Ard, J. Second language data: Their relevance for language universals. *TESOL Quarterly,* 1980, *14,* 443–452.

Gregg, K. R. Krashen's monitor and Occam's razor. *Applied Linguistics,* 1984, *5*(2), 79–100.

Gregg, K. R. Review of *The input hypothesis: Issues and implications* by Stephen D. Krashen. *TESOL Quarterly,* 1986, *20*(1), 116–122.

Kleinmann, H. Avoidance behavior and its predictability in adult second language acquisition. Unpublished PhD dissertation, University of Pittsburgh, 1976.

Kleinmann, H. Avoidance behavior in adult second language acquisition. *Language Learning,* 1977, *27,* 93–107.

Krashen, S. *Principles and practice in second language acquistion.* Oxford: Pergamon Press, 1982.

Krashen, S., & Terrell, T. *The natural approach.* Oxford: Pergamon Press, 1983.

Lado, R. *Linguistics across cultures: Applied linguistics for language teachers.* Ann Arbor: University of Michigan Press, 1957.

Lightbown, P. Exploring relationships between developmental and instructional sequences. In H. Seliger & M. Long (Eds.), *Classroom oriented research on second language acquisition.* Rowley, MA: Newbury House, 1983.

Long, M., & Porter, P. Group work, interlanguage talk, and second language acquisition. *TESOL Quarterly,* 1985, *19,* 207–228.

McLaughlin, B. Theory and research in second language learning: An emerging paradigm. *Language Learning,* 1980, *30,* 331–350.

McLaughlin, B., Rossman, B., & MacLeod, B. Second language learning: An information-processing perspective. *Language Learning,* 1983, *33,* 135–158.

Mazurkewich, I. The acquisition of the dative: Alternation by second language learners and linguistic theory. *Language Learning,* 1984, *34,* 91–110.

Pica, T. Adult acquisition of English as a second language under different conditions of exposure. *Language Learning,* 1983, *33,* 465–497.

Pienemann, M. Psychological constraints on the teachability of languages. *Studies in Second Language Acquistion,* 1984, *6,* 186–214.

Richards, J., & Rodgers, T. Method: Approach, design, and procedure. *TESOL Quarterly,* 1982, *16,* 153–168.

Schachter, J. An error in error analysis. *Language Learning,* 1974, *24,* 205–214.

Schmidt, R. The strengths and limitations of acquisition: A case study of untutored language. *Language Learning and Communication,* 1984, *3,* 1–16.

Schneider, W., & Schiffrin, R. M. Controlled and automatic processing: I. Deletion, search, and attention. *Psychological Review,* 1977, *84,* 1–66.

Scovel, J. Curriculum stability and change: English foreign language programs in modern China. Unpublished PhD dissertation, University of Pittsburgh, 1982.

Takala, S. Review of Krashen. *Language Learning*, 1984, *34*(4), 157–174.
Tarone, E. Variability in interlanguage use: A study of style shifting in morphology and syntax. *Language Learning*, 1985, *35*, 373–403.
Taylor, G. Review of Krashen. *Language Learning*, 1984, *34*(3), 97–104.
van Els, T., Bongaerts, T., Extra, G., van Os, C., & Janssen-van Dieten, A.-M. *Applied linguistics and the learning and teaching of foreign languages*. London: Edward Arnold, 1984.

SUGGESTED READINGS

Brown, H. D. *Principles of language learning and teaching*. Englewood Cliffs, NJ: Prentice-Hall, 1980.
Clarke, M. On bandwagons, tyranny, and common sense. *TESOL Quarterly*, 1982, *16*, 437–448.
Kleinmann, H. Avoidance behavior in adult second language acquisition. *Language Learning*, 1977, *27*, 93–107.
McLaughlin, B., Rossman, B., & MacLeod, B. Second language learning: An information processing perspective. *Language Learning*, 1983, *33*, 135–158.
Richards, J. A non-contrastive approach to error analysis. *English Language Teaching*, 1971, *25*, 204–219.
Schmidt, R. The strengths and limitations of acquisition: A case study of untutored language. *Language Learning and Communication*, 1984, *3*, 1–16.
Scovel, T. The effect of affect on foreign language learning: A review of the anxiety research. *Language Learning*, 1978, *28*, 129–142.
Scovel, T. Questions concerning the application of neurolinguistic research to second language learning/teaching. *TESOL Quarterly*, 1982, *16*, 323–331.
Taylor, B. The use of overgeneralization and transfer learning strategies by elementary and intermediate students in ESL. *Language Learning*, 1975, *25*, 73–107.